Looking at Lines

Interesting Objects and Linear Functions

Authors

Dr. Arthur Wiebe
Jim Wilson
Sheldon Erickson
Michelle Youngs
Chris Brownell

Editor

Betty Cordel

Illustrator

Brenda Richmond

Desktop Publisher

Tracey Lieder

This book contains materials developed by the AIMS Education Foundation. **AIMS** (**A**ctivities **I**ntegrating **M**athematics and **S**cience) began in 1981 with a grant from the National Science Foundation. The non-profit AIMS Education Foundation publishes hands-on instructional materials (books and the monthly magazine) that integrate curricular disciplines such as mathematics, science, language arts, and social studies. The Foundation sponsors a national program of professional development through which educators may gain both an understanding of the AIMS philosophy and expertise in teaching by integrated, hands-on methods.

ISBN **1-881431-91-6**
Printed in the United States of America

I Hear and I Forget,

I See and I Remember,

I Do and I Understand.

—Chinese Proverb

Table of Contents

Looking at Lines:
Interesting Objects and Linear Functions

What do stacking cups, tying of knots, bouncing balls, expanding squares, costs of long-distance calls, and floating straws have in common?
All involve linear functions!

The uniqueness of AIMS is evidenced by the extensive use made of real-world situations as the context for building an understanding of linear function concepts. Drawn from science, business, geometry, and other real-world phenomena, the activities in *Looking at Lines* have students experience important algebraic concepts in their natural setting. Hands-on involvement heightens student interest and deepens understanding.

Real-world situations that can be modeled by linear functions occur more often than those modeled by any other type of function. They provide especially rich contexts for the integration of mathematics and science. Because of the AIMS approach, linear function concepts can be introduced as early as the fifth grade and continuously nurtured through middle school. Algebraic thinking involved in finding the rule for patterns, graphing on the coordinate plane, and distinguishing between proportional and non-proportional relationships, is within the grasp of students at these grade levels.

The investigations in *Looking at Lines* are framed by the schema in the *AIMS Model of Mathematics.* This model is readily translatable into the *AIMS Model of Functions* by substituting linear function terminology.

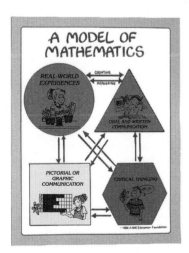

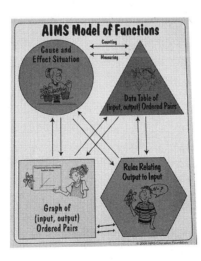

- Cause and effect arise from real-world situations.
- Input/output data tables are created with data abstracted from these situations.
- (Input, output) ordered pairs are graphed on the coordinate plane to provide an additional perspective for analysis. Both table and graph are searched for patterns.
- When a pattern is discovered, a rule is formulated to fit the data and tested against all available data. If the rule survives these tests, it can be used to predict the output for any input.

A function consists of three parts:
- a set of input numbers,
- a parallel set of output numbers, and,
- a rule that assigns a unique output number to each input number.

Students need to learn linear function language. The term *function*, in particular, needs careful attention. It is a synonym for *it depends*. A linear function involves an *it depends* relationship. The output *depends* on the input and the output *is a function of* the input carry the same meaning.

Slope refers to the steepness of the line pictured in the graph. It is the rise/run ratio of that line and represents a constant rate of change. In the linear function rule, the letter *m* is used to represent the slope.

The *y-intercept* is where the graphed line crosses the y-axis or f(x)-axis. In the rule, this point is represented by *b*.

The input is represented by *x* and the output by *f(x)*, read as "function of x."

A linear function is defined by this relationship:

$$\text{Output} = (\text{slope})(\text{input}) + \text{y-intercept, or}$$
$$f(x) = mx + b$$

m and *b* are constants that arise from the situation.

Three Sub-Groups of Linear Functions

Proportional Relationships

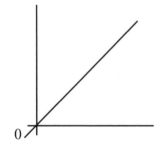

- A straight line graph through the origin is the only one that *involves proportional relationships*.
- When the line passes through the origin, the *output is proportional to the input*.
- Outputs increase as inputs increase so the slope and *m* in the rule are positive.
- Because the graph is a straight line, the rise/run ratio is a constant.
- The line passes through the origin so the y-intercept and *b* in the rule are zero.
- This linear function belongs to the division clan in which $c = \text{rise/run} = y/x$ where *c* is a constant.
- The rule simplifies to $f(x) = mx$ with *m* positive.

Non-Proportional Relationships with a Positive Slope

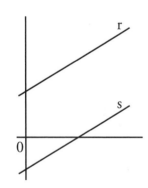

- These situations *do not involve proportional relationships* because neither line passes through the origin.
- *Outputs are not proportional to inputs.*
- Outputs increase as inputs increase so the slopes and *m* in the rule are positive.
- Because the graphs are straight lines, the rise/run ratios are constants. The lines do not pass through the origin so the y-intercepts and *b* in the rule have values other than zero.
- In *line r* the y-intercept and *b* in the rule are positive; in *line s* they are negative.
- Both belong to the clan given by the rule $c = (y-b)/x$ where *c* is a constant.
- The rule for both is $f(x) = mx + b$, with *m* positive for both and *b* positive for *line r* and negative for *line s*.

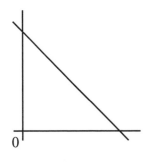

0

Non-Proportional Relationships with a Negative Slope

- This situation *does not involve proportional relationships* because the line does not pass through the origin.
- *Outputs are not proportional to inputs.*
- Outputs *decrease* as inputs *increase*.
- Because the graph is a straight line, the rise/run ratio is a constant.
- The line does not pass through the origin so the y-intercept and *b* in the rule have a value other than zero.
- The slope and *m* in the rule are negative.
- The y-intercept and *b* in the rule are positive.
- The graph belongs to the clan characterized by the rule $c = a + b$ where c is a constant.
- The rule is $f(x) = mx + b$ with m negative and b positive.

(AIMS has a poster set that displays the AIMS Model of Functions and the three basic types of linear function graphs. Each graph is accompanied by a series of statements defining characteristics of that particular linear function. Having these posters on display during investigations of linear function situations and relating elements in the investigation to statements on the posters adds powerful support to learning the concepts.)

In these activities students will learn to:
- derive data from real-world situations;
- graph data on the coordinate plane;
- write a rule for a set of (input/output) ordered pairs;
- write a rule for the graph of a line;
- relate each aspect of a rule to its real-world counterpart, the data table, and the graph of a line;
- use a rule to generate ordered pairs; and
- translate a rule into a graph using ordered pairs.

How to Use *Looking at Lines*

Looking at Lines provides an in-depth exposure to linear function concepts. A major goal in middle school mathematics is for students to acquire a deep understanding of these concepts.

Mastery includes facility with identifying and interpreting each element in the linear function rule in five ways: in the real-world situation, a data table, a graph, a written statement, and a rule; and the ability to translate from any of these forms into any other.

Looking at Lines is designed for maximum flexibility of use. *Which, in what order, and how many activities are used should be based on the progress of students.* The activities cover a broad range of situations, demonstrating the fact that linear functions can found in abundance in the real world. It is important, however, to begin by building a solid foundation. The activities in *Part One* are recommended for this purpose.

The grouping of activities is loosely by type rather than by difficulty. We advise that the collection be surveyed and selections made based on student ability and interest. Most of the activities involve hands-on investigations and students find them inherently interesting.

Part Two involves typical science investigations in which students also gain an understanding of important science concepts. *Part Three* provides practice in building data tables, graphs, and rules and reading graphs. *Parts Four* and *Five* involve investigations involving a variety of interesting everyday objects. *Part Six* deals with inequalities as well as equalities and these serve well as culminating activities.

Looking Back

A fundamental practice in problem solving is to "look back" at a solution and the situation to which it applies. *Looking Back* provides a generic set of questions that may be used with any of the activities in this publication. These are the key questions that students should be able to answer if they have mastered the concepts in context. Rather than include such questions with every activity, they are provided in this form so that the teacher can insert them at any time desired and at key intervals.

Looking Back

Now that you have finished the investigation, review the results and answer the following questions.

1. Identify and justify your answer:
   a. Independent or input variable:

   b. Dependent or output variable:

2. Describe the relationship between the dependent and independent variables.

3. Is the relationship between the dependent and independent variable proportional? Please describe.

4. What evidence is there for your conclusion in 3 above in the:
   a. table?

   b. graph?

   c. rule?

5. What is the slope? Please explain.

6. How can you identify the slope in the:
   a. table?

   b. graph?

   c. rule?

7. How can you identify the y-intercept in the:
   a. table?

   b. graph?

   c. rule?

I'm hooked on Algebra !

NCTM Standards 2000* Applied in *Looking at Lines*

Number and Operations
Understand numbers, ways of representing numbers, relationships among numbers, and number systems
- Understand and use ratios and proportions to represent quantitative relationships

Algebra
Understand patterns, relations, and functions
- Represent, analyze, and generalize a variety of patterns with tables, graphs, words, and, when possible, symbolic rules
- Relate and compare different forms of representation for a relationship
- Identify functions as linear or nonlinear and contrast their properties from tables, graphs, or equations
- Understand relations and functions and select, convert flexibly among, and use various representations for them
- Interpret representations of functions of two variables
- Describe, extend, and make generalizations about geometric and numeric patterns

Represent and analyze mathematical situations and structures using algebraic symbols
- Develop an initial conceptual understanding of different uses of variables
- Explore relationships between symbolic expressions and graphs of lines, paying particular attention to the meaning of intercept and slope
- Use symbolic algebra to represent situations and to solve problems, especially those that involve linear relationships

Use mathematical models to represent and understand quantitative relationships
- Model and solve contextualized problems using various representations such as graphs, tables, and equations

Analyze change in various contexts
- Use graphs to analyze the nature of changes in quantities in linear relationships
- Investigate how a change in one variable relates to a change in a second variable.

Geometry
Analyze characteristics and properties of two- and three-dimensional geometric shapes and develop mathematical arguments about geometric relationships
- Understand relationships among the angles, side lengths, perimeters, areas, and volumes of similar objects
- Create and critique inductive and deductive arguments concerning geometric ideas and relationships, such as congruence, similarity, and the Pythagorean relationship

Specify locations and describe spatial relationships using coordinate geometry and other representational systems
- Make and use coordinate systems to specify locations and to describe paths

Use visualization, spatial reasoning, and geometric modeling to solve problems
- Use geometric models to represent and explain numerical and algebraic relationship

Measurement
Understand measurable attributes of objects and the units, systems, and processes of measurement
- Understand both metric and customary systems of measurement
- Explore what happens to measurements of a two-dimensional shape such as its perimeter and area when the shape is changed in some way

Data Analysis and Probability
Formulate questions that can be addressed with data and collect, organize, and display relevant data to answer them
- Represent data using tables and graphs such as line plots, bar graphs, and line graphs

*   Reprinted with permission from *Principles and Standards for School Mathematics*, 2000 by the National Council of Teachers of Mathematics. All rights reserved.

The Technology Principle*

Technology is essential in teaching and learning mathematics; it influences the mathematics that is taught and enhances students' learning.

Students can use graphing calculator and computer representations to study, summarize, and review linear relationships, particularly the ideas of slope, y-intercept, and uniform change. In the first example, the effect of changing the slope of the line is explored. In the second example, the effect of changing the y-intercept is explored.

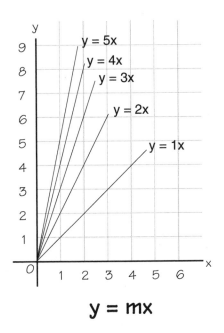

$$y = mx$$

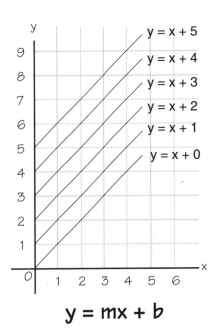

$$y = mx + b$$

As an extension to any *Looking at Lines* activity, the data table from the activity can be entered into a graphing calculator or spreadsheet program for analysis or display.

* Reprinted with permission from *Principles and Standards for School Mathematics*, 2000 by the National Council of Teachers of Mathematics. All rights reserved.

AAAS *Benchmarks for Science Literacy** Applied in *Looking at Lines*

These *Benchmarks* for grades 3-12 have heavily impacted the writing of the activities in *Looking at Lines*. Since it is impractical to list all of these with each activity, students would benefit from a periodic review of this list. Together, the *Benchmarks* build a solid foundation for understanding the mathematics derived from real-world situations.

- *Mathematics is the study of many kinds of patterns, including numbers and shapes and operations on them. Sometimes patterns are studied because they help to explain how the world works or how to solve practical problems, sometimes because they are interesting in themselves.*
- *Much of the work of mathematicians involves a modeling cycle, which consists of three steps: (1) using abstractions to represent things or ideas, (2) manipulating the abstractions according to some logical rules, (3) checking how well the results match the original things or ideas. If the match is not considered good enough, a new round of abstraction and manipulation may begin. The actual thinking need not go through these processes in logical order but may shift from one to another in any order.*
- *Mathematics provides a precise language for science and technology—to describe objects and events, to characterize relationships between variables, and to argue logically.*
- *Numbers and shape—and operations on them—help to describe and predict things about the world around us.*
- *Mathematical ideas can be represented concretely, graphically, and symbolically.*
- *Graphical display of numbers may make it possible to spot patterns that are not otherwise obvious, such as comparative sizes and trends.*
- *The graphical display of numbers may help to show patterns such as trends, varying rates of change, gaps, or clusters. Such patterns can sometimes be used to make predictions about the phenomena being graphed.*
- *Graphs can show a variety of possible relationships between two variables. As one variable increases uniformly, the other may do one of the following: always keep the same proportion to the first, increase or decrease steadily, increase or decrease faster and faster, get closer and closer to some limiting value, reach some intermediate maximum or minimum, alternately increase and decrease indefinitely, increase or decrease in steps, or do something different from any of these.*
- *Tables and graphs can show how values of one quantity are related to values of another.*
- *Tables, graphs, and symbols are alternative ways of representing data and relationships that can be translated from one to another.*
- *Any mathematical model, graphic or algebraic, is limited in how well it can represent how the world works. The usefulness of a mathematical model for predicting may be limited by uncertainties in measurement, neglect of some important influence, or by requiring too much computation.*
- *Measurements are always likely to give slightly different numbers, even if what is being measured stays the same.*
- *Sometimes changing one thing causes changes in something else. In some situations, changing the same thing in the same way has the same result.*
- *Mathematical statements can be used to describe how one quantity changes when another changes. Rates of change can be computed from magnitudes and vice versa.*

* American Association for the Advancement of Science. *Benchmarks for Science Literacy*. Oxford University Press. New York. 1993.

Part One:
Algebraic Thinking in the Context of Linear Functions

Linear functions provide particularly appropriate contexts in which students can learn about and exercise algebraic thinking. Algebra is frequently characterized as generalized arithmetic. Generalizing patterns is, therefore, an important aspect of algebraic thinking. Sample data involving two variables are often sufficient for arriving at a generalization that covers an infinite number of cases. Such is the power of algebraic thinking!

Algebraic thinking also requires knowledge about and the ability to use a variety of tools, such as determining ordered pairs in real-world situations, organizing data in tables, graphing the ordered pairs on the coordinate plane, constructing statements to describe phenomena, and deriving rules or generalizations. It is important for students to understand and master the use of these tools early on because they are used throughout the ensuing activities.

The activities selected for *Part One* are elementary but powerful. It is instructive to read the introductory article entitled *Helping Students Gain Understanding Through Investigations* for a perspective on what follows. The commentary is driven by actual classroom experiences where linear functions were introduced. The accompanying *Temperature Conversion* activity is elementary and straightforward enough to serve as a good introduction to important linear function concepts and processes. Through it students can be introduced to gathering ordered pair data, building data tables, graphing ordered pairs, arriving at a rule or generalization, and applying the rule to a new situation.

Algebraic Ups and Downs provides a good model for thinking about the elements in linear functions. It is well worth the effort necessary to construct and use the model because it illustrates important concepts. It was motivated by a question students new to algebra frequently have but rarely ask, "What is x?" While the question may seem trivial, it is not. From the beginning, students need to know that x is more than something they are asked to manipulate in the mysterious ways of algebra. It frequently has a physical presence in the real world of science, business, geometric figures, and events. The elevator model in this activity helps students build a firm mental image of linear function concepts.

On the Level I and *II* deal with using the language of algebra to describe data collected from an equal-arm balance. The balance models an equation. Students collect and analyze data to discover a linear relationship between a one or more weights added to the same position on the right side of the lever and a single weight added to the left side. They prepare data tables and graphs and write a rule for the relationship. By constructing a simple balance, students come to recognize the sensitivity of this device. This model exemplifies the sensitivity with which equations must be treated to maintain equality.

In the *Paper Clip Chains* activity, students measure objects with standard and jumbo paper clips. They build data tables and graph the results to develop their understanding of proportional reasoning and linear functions as they relate to rates and graphic displays. The proportional nature of rates is shown graphically as a line passing through the origin of a coordinate graph with each of the axes representing one system of measurement.

Drawn from the discipline of geometry, *Functions in Circles* has students measure the circumference and diameters of various objects to establish the fact that the circumference of a circle is a function of its diameter. By constructing the circumferences and diameters directly on a graph rather than from a data table, students see that the end points of the (diameter, circumference) ordered pairs lie in an approximate straight line passing through the origin, indicating a linear function. They find that the line has a slope equal to the value of pi.

Mixing Measures asks students to measure lengths of objects in inches and centimeters to determine a conversion rate. They construct a scatter plot of the data to reveal a linear function that contains a proportional relationship. The results will "scatter" or deviate from being points on a straight line due to errors in measurement and rounding. Students need to develop an understanding that measurement in the real world is always approximately, never exact, and that they need to be careful to minimize error as they make measurements.

2

HELPING STUDENTS GAIN UNDERSTANDING THROUGH INVESTIGATIONS

If you know how high a ball is when it is dropped, can you predict how high it will bounce? If you know how many times a nut is rotated on a bolt, can you predict how far it has moved? Can you predict how long a rubber band will be if you know how many pennies are suspended from it? All of the above examples are *Key Questions* from AIMS investigations. The answers to all these questions are based on direct correlations or functions. Students need to be provided with experiences in which they can connect real-world events with mathematical concepts.

Traditionally mathematics has approached functions with the use of symbols and coordinate graphing. This approach is very abstract for the middle-school student. As concrete thinkers the middle-school learners need to gather numbers that have meaning to them. Placing those numbers in organized lists or charts provides the opportunity to find patterns within those numbers. By working with meaningful numbers, students are able to verbalize the pattern between their sets of numbers and translate that pattern into a rule or function. When they see the pattern of those numbers applied to a coordinate graph, they discover the similarities of the number and visual patterns. Students realize that a chart, a graph, and a function all communicate the same information but in different ways. As students become familiar with these multiple representations, they find they can translate the information into the form that is most meaningful for them.

Integrating the multiple representations provides successful ways for all students to solve these problems. They are able to choose the representation that provides the most meaning for them as it allows them to work at the level of understanding for which they feel most comfortable.

AIMS investigations have students gather and record data in both chart and graphical form. They are asked to describe verbally and mathematically the patterns they find. From these experiences students develop an understanding of the concepts and the skills needed to solve the problems. Each student is not expected to develop this understanding independently.

3

While collaborating with peers, the student is guided by a teacher who questions, probes, and clarifies. Acting as a facilitator, the teacher does not tell students how to do the problems. Rather, at first, there are orchestrated discussions in which questions are posed that require the students to look carefully for patterns in their data, and then they are helped in clarifying and summarizing their discoveries.

Such a route of learning means that a map cannot be precisely drawn. Each student and class will have various side trips, detours, or shortcuts. Following is a probable route for a representative problem of a linear functional relationship. It is not written to be prescriptive but to provide a general outline of how students tend to approach these problems and how a teacher might facilitate.

Sample Problem

Students are provided with a thermometer with Celsius and Fahrenheit scales up to a 50 degree Celsius reading. The problem they are asked to solve is, "How can you change a Celsius temperature, like 70 degrees, to its Fahrenheit equivalent?"

Students at this point usually say, "See how Fahrenheit changes when Celsius changes." The teacher should now encourage the students to organize the numbers so that a pattern can be easily discovered. The teacher might ask how the numbers might be organized. The students need to recognize that the problem says, "You know Celsius and you want to know Fahrenheit." That means Celsius temperature is the independent variable, and Fahrenheit temperature is the dependent variable. Again the teacher should encourage students to consider the easy route. Since they are free to choose what Celsius numbers are used, they should be encouraged to choose numbers at regular intervals to clarify the pattern.

Below is a sample of a student's chart. The student chose consistent Celsius increments. Due to typical measurement error, the Fahrenheit measures are not accurate.

C	F
0	32
5	42
10	50
15	59
20	68
25	78
30	86
35	94
40	104
45	113
50	122

When students have completed a chart to this point, the teacher might ask them to identify what patterns they see and have them confer with other students if they are in agreement. Students quickly identify a consistent

4

difference of five degrees in the Celsius column. Most students at this point will not be able to identify a pattern in the Fahrenheit column except that the numbers get greater as you go down the column.

Now the teacher might suggest that students find the differences between each number in the Fahrenheit column. (The resulting chart is shown below.) Students are quick to say that the Fahrenheit column goes up about eight to ten degrees each time. The teacher might help the students clarify at this point that for every change of five degrees Celsius, there is an eight to ten degree Fahrenheit change.

```
                    C  |  F
              ┌──── 0  | 32 ────┐
         5 <──┤                 ├─> 10
              └──── 5  | 42 ────┘
         5 <──┤                 ├─> 8
              ──── 10  | 50 ────
         5 <──┤                 ├─> 9
              ──── 15  | 59 ────
         5 <──┤                 ├─> 9
              ──── 20  | 68 ────
         5 <──┤                 ├─> 10
              ──── 25  | 78 ────
         5 <──┤                 ├─> 8
              ──── 30  | 86 ────
         5 <──┤                 ├─> 8
              ──── 35  | 94 ────
         5 <──┤                 ├─> 10
              ──── 40  | 104 ───
         5 <──┤                 ├─> 9
              ──── 45  | 113 ───
         5 <──┤                 ├─> 9
              ──── 50  | 122 ───
             ────                 ────
              50                   90
```

The teacher should pose the question of how to get a more accurate answer than "about eight to ten." Students will suggest finding an average. A total change of 90 degrees for ten measurements gives the average of a nine degree change each time.

The teacher might challenge the students to find a quicker way to determine the total change than adding up the differences. If it is not suggested, focus students' attention on the first and last numbers in each column of the table. Suggest they try some operations with those numbers. Students will propose that you find the difference between the first and the last temperature. (The next chart shows these differences.) Students should be encouraged to make the observation that a change of 50 degrees Celsius is the same as a change of 90 degrees Fahrenheit.

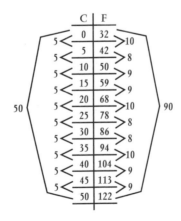

At this point, the teacher might return to the original question of finding the Fahrenheit equivalent of 70 degrees Celsius. Many students will suggest that five degrees be added to the Celsius column, and nine degrees to the Fahrenheit column until 70 degrees Celsius is reached. This will take four additions to each column. The Celsius temperature will be 70 and the Fahrenheit temperature 158. The teacher should ask the students to clarify how they came to this conclusion. They might say, "Five was added four times to a starting temperature of 50 to get to 70. So there will be four groups of nine degrees greater than 122, or 122 + 36 = 158."

When students understand this relationship, they can be challenged to determine what the Fahrenheit temperature would be for 71 degrees Celsius. Have the students recall that five degrees Celsius is equal to nine degrees Fahrenheit. Then they may be asked how to convert five degrees to one degree. They should note that five divided by five gives one. The teacher should then encourage the students to recognize that the nine Fahrenheit degrees can also be divided into five groups. Students should be encouraged to verbalize the meaning of the resulting problem ($9 \div 5 = \frac{9}{5} = 1\frac{4}{5} = 1.8$). They might say, "Every one degree change in Celsius is the same as 1.8 degrees of change in Fahrenheit." The equivalent for 71 degrees Celsius is 159.8 degrees Fahrenheit (158 + 1.8 = 159.8).

Some students may suggest that 10 pairs of temperatures are not necessary. They might suggest that you need only two pairs such as the first and last pair in the example list. Comparing the differences in these two pairs would give you the same unit ratio as found in doing the previously suggested procedure. A change of 90 degrees Fahrenheit is the same as a change of 50 degrees Celsius (Fahrenheit/Celsius = $\frac{90}{50} = \frac{18}{10} = \frac{9}{5} = \frac{1.8}{1}$). The recognition of this is very useful for those students who understand it. However, it is far along in the developmental process and not necessary for further understanding.

After students have thoroughly studied the information in chart form, have them make a scattergram of the information. If they are not familiar with coordinate graphing, some direct instruction will need to be done on this topic.

When the points are plotted, the students should recognize a pattern that is close to a line. Students may connect the points to make a broken-line graph or make a line-of-best-fit to emphasize this observation.

Students should then be asked to describe the line so someone else could reproduce it without seeing it. Generally they will respond that it is diagonal. It can be quickly demonstrated that there are many diagonal lines. If the students do not come up with a more precise means of describing the line, suggest that they note how much it goes up between each of the points, and how far it goes over between every point. This will produce a general "upness and overness" of the line, as illustrated on the following graph, with a shaded line. The line appears to have a general pattern of about ten up for every five over. Having looked at the patterns in the graph, the students should be asked to relate the patterns in the graph to patterns they found in the chart. Most students will recognize that the "upness" is the same as the average change in Fahrenheit, while the "overness" is the average change in Celsius. If they do not mention that the straightness of the line shows that both temperatures are changing consistently, ask them why the line is straight.

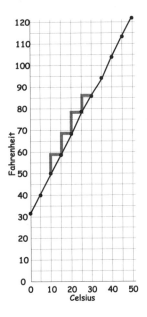

After the students have recognized that the chart and graph provide the same information but in different forms, focus their attention on the graph. Ask the students to determine a way to use the graph to predict the Celsius equivalent of 72 degrees Fahrenheit (room temperature). Since students are dealing with information they understand, they will be quick to see or learn that the graph can be used to interpolate an equivalent reading of about 23 degrees Celsius. Next they should be asked how to use the graph to determine the Fahrenheit equivalent of 71 degrees Celsius. Again students should recognize that the line on the graph can be extended and used to determine the conversion. When students do this they will find they are very close to the same solution they determined with the chart.

As students have more experience with activities of this type, they should come to recognize that the straighter the line formed from the data, the more reliable the prediction that can be made. It might also be brought to their attention that often they will be provided with a graph, but no charted data. It would be useful to have them generate a chart of information from a graph.

When students are secure in their understanding of charts and graphs, they will be ready to explore writing a function for the relationship. They should be encouraged to explain in words how they go about converting the value of one variable to its corresponding value of the other variable. When they can clearly explain this, the teacher can help translate their procedure into mathematical terms. This modeling will be enough guidance for the student who is ready to determine the mathematical function.

Using the temperature example, the students might be asked to come up with a way to calculate the Fahrenheit temperature if they were given a Celsius temperature. Generally students quite quickly suggest two things:

- Remembering part of the pattern from the graph or chart, they say, "Multiply the Celsius temperature by 9." Have the students check this conjecture. "Zero x 9 = 0 ... not very close to 32; 5 x 9 = 45 ... pretty close to what we should get; 10 x 9 = 90 ... way off; 15 x 9 = 135 ... this is getting worse. This process doesn't seem to be leading us the right way."

- A more reasonable suggestion that is based on an understanding of the patterns in the chart or graph would be, "Take the Celsius temperature and divide it by five to find how many fives are in it. Take that number and multiply it by nine because that is how many Fahrenheit degrees there are for every group of five Celsius degrees." Have the students check this conjecture by making a chart including a column for the predicted answers.

Students will be quick to realize this method is not working either. Before they quit have them make a fourth column to record how wrong their predictions are. They will quickly see they are always off about 32 degrees.

C	F	Predicted	Wrong
0	32	0	32
5	42	9	31
10	50	18	32
15	59	27	32
20	68	36	32

When asked how to correct for this, students will respond, "Add 32 degrees" to their prediction. At this point students can be shown how to write the function in mathematical form: $F = ((C \div 5) \times 9) + 32$. This function can be written in different forms depending on how the student understands it. A student who understood the unit ratio concept might write the function as: $F = (1.8 \times C) + 32$ or $F = \frac{9}{5}C + 32$.

When students have determined a method for calculating the conversion and have seen it in mathematical form, they should be asked how it is similar to patterns they found in the chart and graph. They will recognize how the division and multiplication, or the factor, is related to the numbers added to each column on the chart. These numbers also describe the "upness and overness" of the line on the graph, or its slope.

When students are comfortable in their understanding of the function they have written, they can use it to determine the answer to the original question, "What is the Fahrenheit equivalent to 70 degrees Celsius?" They can then check to see if this solution is similar to the ones they got from the graph and the chart.

As students work through a series of problems similar to this example, they will develop a thorough understanding of the interrelationships of the different representations. They will be able to interpret the information in any of the forms and be able to translate it into another form. Most of them will gain an ability to gather and organize data so that they can find connections.

Using Activities

In planning a unit that studies linear functions, the investigations should be completed in a sequence that allows the students to develop the concepts and make the connections between the multiple representations. Begin with activities that have less chance for error and allow the students to discover the patterns more easily. As they become experienced, introduce activities that tend to have more error. Finally provide problems that are linear but are not proportions so students gain experience in using addition in the functions.

It is hoped that teachers will use the strategies suggested and have students generate there own charts and graphs using graph paper. The teacher may model for students how to make a chart and graph on the early problems. As students become more competent, they can design the charts and graphs themselves.

Temperature Conversion

How do you convert a temperature in Celsius to one in Fahrenheit?

°C	°F
0	
5	
10	
15	
20	
25	
30	
35	
40	
45	
50	
70	
71	

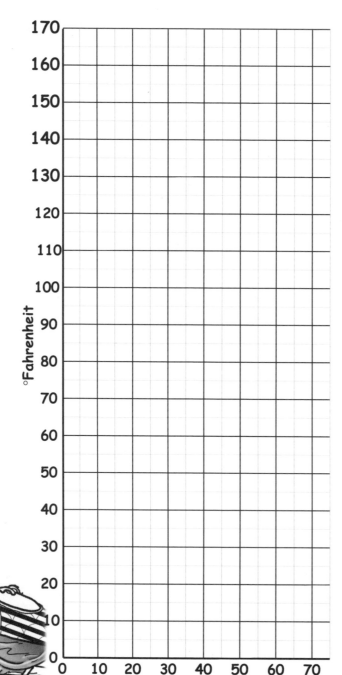

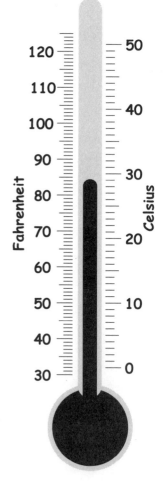

1. Using the sample thermometer, make a data table comparing the two tempeature scales. Display and label all information so a reviewer could easily identify the meaning of all data.

2. Convert your data to a broken-line graph or scattergram. Interpret the meaning of the graph for the reviewer. This is your chance to demonstrate how much you know about graphs.

3. Use your data table and/or graph to determine an equation that converts Celsius to Fahrenheit. Explain the methods you used to determine the equation and confirm that it is correct.

4. Using your data table, graph and/or equation, determine what 110 degrees Celsius would be in Fahrenheit. Explain how you got the solution.

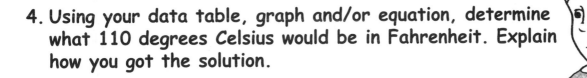

ALGEBRAIC UPS AND DOWNS

Topic
Algebra—Linear Functions

Key Question
How can the language of algebra be used to describe a simple elevator system?

Learning Goals
Students will:
- translate a simple elevator system into the language of algebra, and
- complete a table, draw a graph, and write an algebraic expression.

Guiding Documents
Project 2061 Benchmark
- *Symbolic equations can be used to summarize how the quantity of something changes over time or in response to other changes.*

NRC Standard
- *Mathematics is important in all aspects of scientific inquiry.*

NCTM Standards 2000*
- *Represent, analyze, and generalize a variety of patterns with tables, graphs, words, and, when possible, symbolic rules*
- *Investigate how a change in one variable relates to a change in another variable*
- *Use symbolic algebra to represent situations and to solve problems, especially those that involve linear relationships*
- *Explore relationships between symbolic expressions and graphs of lines, paying particular attention to the meaning of intercept and slope*

Math
Algebra
    linear equations

Science
Engineering
    counterweight

Integrated Processes
Observing
Collecting and recording data
Graphing data
Interpreting data

Materials
Scissors
Rulers
Empty 35 mm film canisters
Transparent tape

Background Information
The elevator described in this activity consists of a passenger box connected to a counterweight by a cable of constant length. The cable is stretched over a pulley connected to a source of power.

The relationship between the location of the elevator and the location of the counterweight is expressed algebraically by the equation $7 = X + Y$. X represents the floor location of the elevator, and Y represents the floor location of the counterweight. This equation is a member of the *Addition Family* of linear algebraic equations.

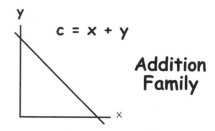

The manipulatives used in the activity give students a concrete tool useful for thinking about the elevator system. The manipulatives are designed to help students *translate* the physical elevator system into the language of algebra.

Management
1. Construct both the *Elevator Math Model* and the three-dimensional model and decide which model to present to students. One strategy would be to assign all students the *Elevator Math Model* and then assign the three-dimensional model to those students that need additional assistance.
2. To speed up student construction of either manipulative model, you may choose to precut the slits with a razor knife and precut the X-Y Strips.
3. Film processing centers are a source of free 35 mm film canisters.

Procedure
Constructing the Elevator Math Model
1. Distribute the student page.
2. Demonstrate for the students how to fold and crease the page along the lightly shaded line and

how to use the tips of a pair of scissors to cut slit *A* and slit *B*.

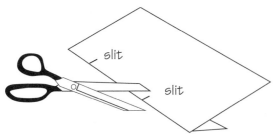

3. Instruct the students to fold and crease their pages and to carefully cut both slits in their pages.
4. Distribute an X-Y strip to each student.
5. Demonstrate for students how to insert the left end of the X-Y strip down, from the top of the page, into and through slit *B*.

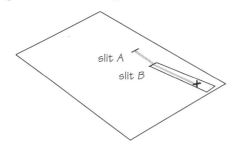

6. Show them how to push the X-Y strip, from the bottom of the page, up and through slit *A*.

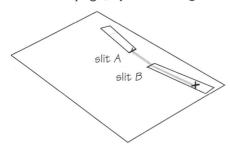

7. Tell the students to align the top and bottom edges of the model and check that the X-Y strip moves freely through the slits.

Constructing the 3-dimensional Model
1. Distribute one X-Y strip, three-dimensional model strip, and 35 mm film canister to each student.
2. Instruct the students to cut the slits (see step 2 above) in the three-dimensional model strip.

3. Show the students how to thread the X-Y strip through the three-dimensional model strip (see steps 5 and 6 above).
4. Show students how to make a simple loop of tape for neatly taping the pulley to the canister. Tell them to cut out the pulley and tape it to the end of the film canister.
5. Show students how to tape the top of the three-dimensional model strip to the rim of the film canister. Tell them that a single, short piece of tape applied between the two 6s works best.

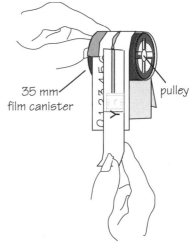

35 mm film canister   pulley

Using the Models
1. Use the *Overhead Transparency* page to explain the operation of the elevator.
2. Tell the students to adjust the X-Y strip so that the X symbol on the right side of the strip is positioned at 1 on the right side of the model.
3. Instruct the students to pull the strip to the left until the X symbol is positioned at 2 on the scale and record the position of Y in the table.
4. Have the students complete the table.
5. Instruct the students to graph the X-Y pairs.
6. Ask the students to write the rule that expresses the relationship between X and Y.

Discussion
1. What is the purpose of the elevator? [to transport people and materials to the various floors of the building]
2. What parts make up the elevator system? [the passenger car, the cable, the counterweight, the pulley, and the motor that powers the system]
3. When people use the word "elevator" in a conversation, what part of the system are they usually thinking of? [the passenger car]
4. What is there about the elevator system that varies or "changes"? [The number of people in the passenger car changes. The floor that the passenger car is on changes. The location of the counterweight changes.]
5. What is there about the elevator system that stays the same or remains constant? [The length of the cable remains constant.]

6. What number is usually assigned to the ground floor. [one]
7. Someone looks at your data table and asks, "What is X?" What's your reply? [the floor location of the passenger car]

   Someone looks at your table and asks, "What is Y?" What's your reply? [the floor location of the counterweight]
8. What number in your table represents the basement? [zero] What number represents the roof? [seven]
9. What true statement can you make about each of the coordinate pairs, (X,Y), on your graph? [The sum of the X and Y coordinates always equals seven.]
10. What rule would describe a similar elevator system in a 10-story building? [11 = X + Y]
11. What rule would describe a similar elevator system in a n-story building? [n + 1 = X + Y]
12. What does the location of the counterweight *depend upon*? [the location of the passenger car and the length of the cable]
13. What does the location of the passenger car *depend upon*? [the location of the counterweight and the length of the cable]
14. When riding in an elevator a lighted panel indicates the floor level of the elevator. Describe how the elevator "knows" what floor it is on. [Located somewhere in the elevator system is either a mechanical or electronic device that senses the location of the passenger car or counterweight.]

Solutions

X	0	1	2	3	4	5	6	7
Y	7	6	5	4	3	2	1	0

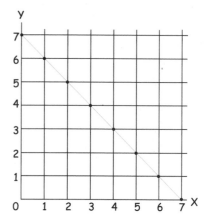

7 = X + Y

Extension

Challenge interested students to construct a counterweighted elevator from cardboard boxes, soup cans, and string.

ALGEBRAIC UPS AND DOWNS

The diagram shows the simple elevator system installed in a 6-story building (with basement and roof). The elevator system is a counterweight system. The "normal" weight of the elevator is balanced by the counterweight. This makes it possible to use a smaller, cheaper to run, electric motor to operate the elevator.

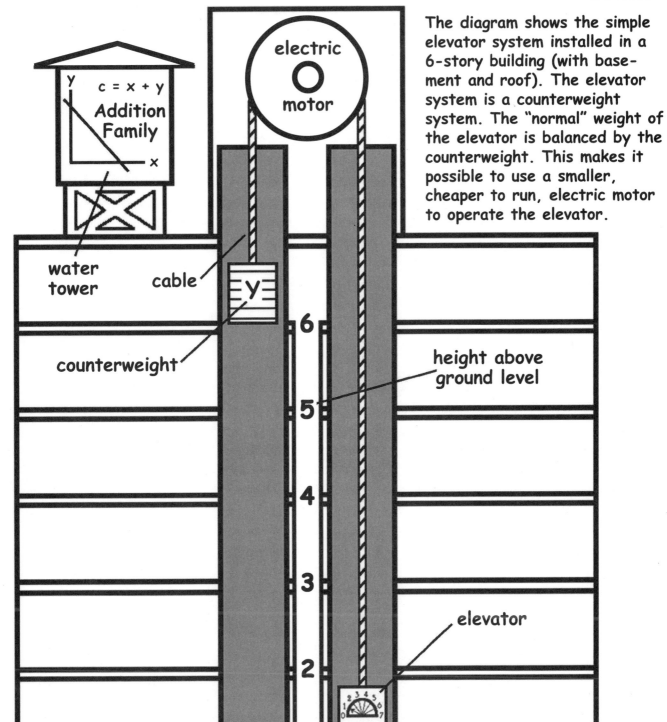

electric motor

Addition Family

$c = x + y$

water tower

cable

counterweight

height above ground level

elevator

ground level

basement

ALGEBRAIC UPS and DOWNS

Elevator Math Model

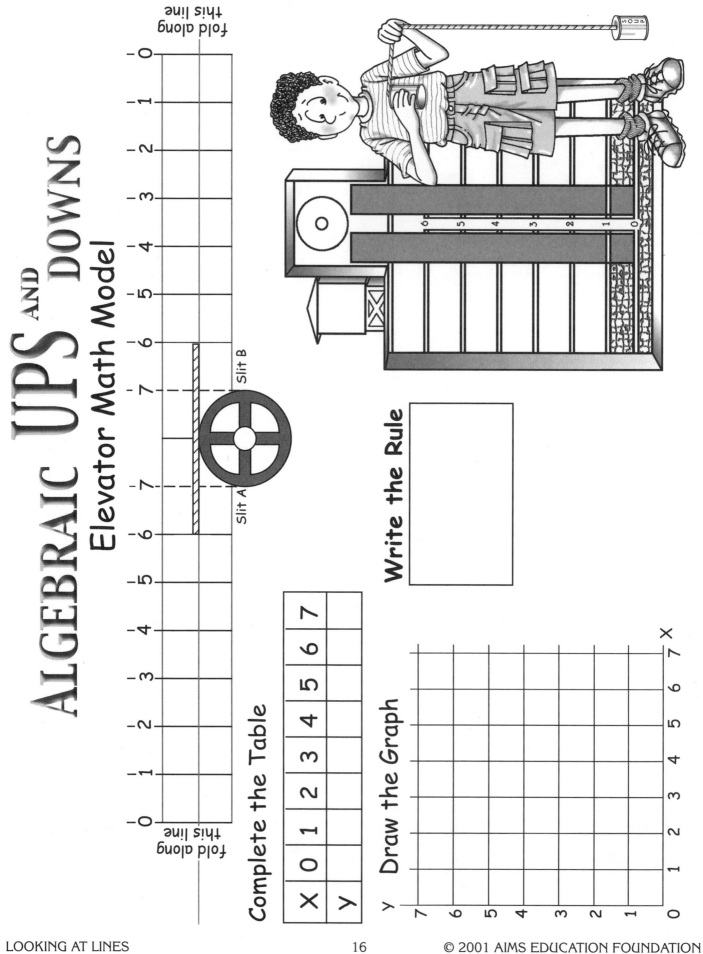

fold along this line

Slit B

Slit A

fold along this line

Complete the Table

X	0	1	2	3	4	5	6	7
y								

Write the Rule

Draw the Graph

3-Dimensional Model Strips

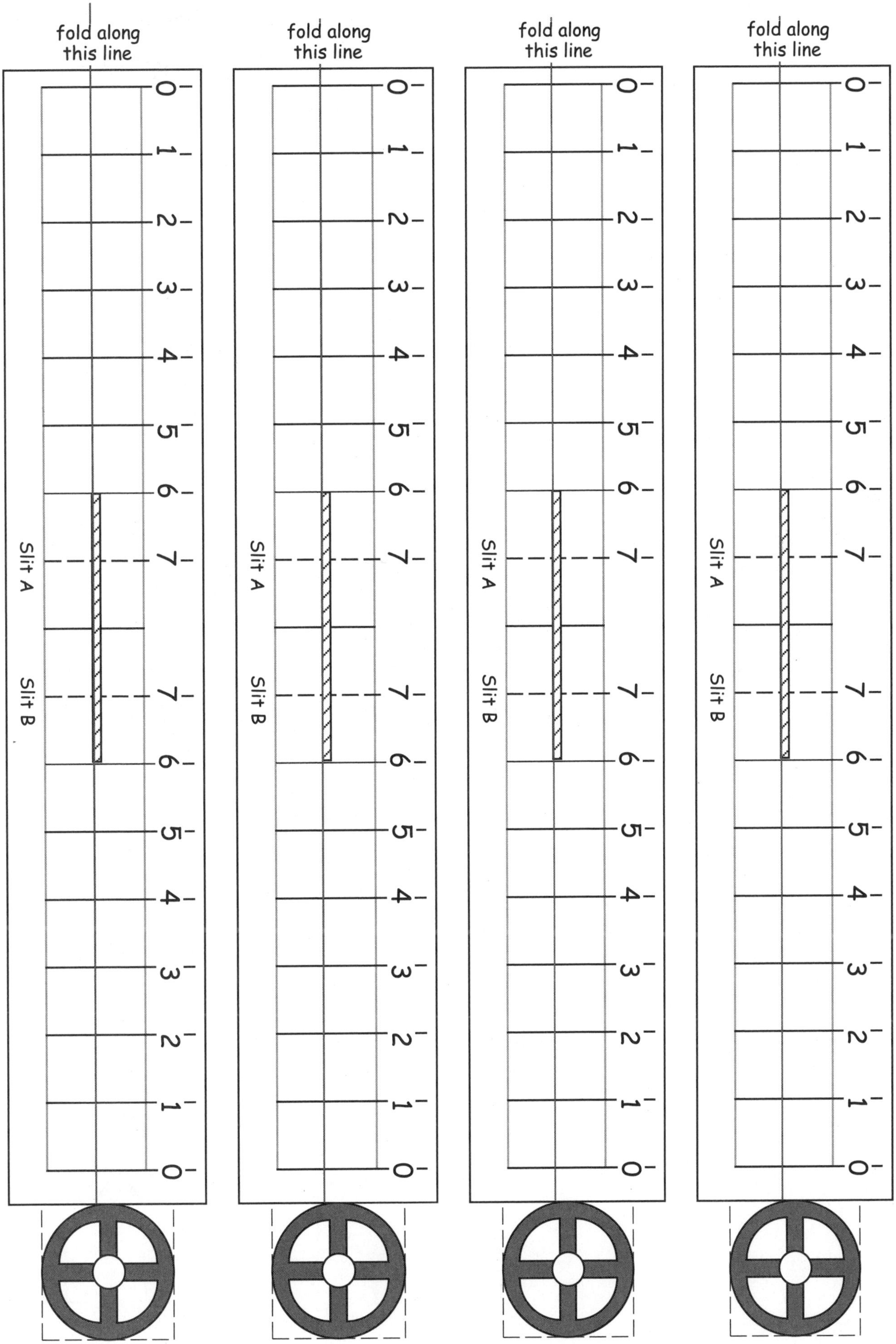

0 1 2 3 4 5 6 7 7 6 5 4 3 2 1 0

Slit A Slit B

0 1 2 3 4 5 6 7 7 6 5 4 3 2 1 0

Slit A Slit B

0 1 2 3 4 5 6 7 7 6 5 4 3 2 1 0

Slit A Slit B

0 1 2 3 4 5 6 7 7 6 5 4 3 2 1 0

Slit A Slit B

fold along this line

fold along this line

fold along this line

fold along this line

LOOKING AT LINES

17

© 2001 AIMS EDUCATION FOUNDATION

X-Y Strips

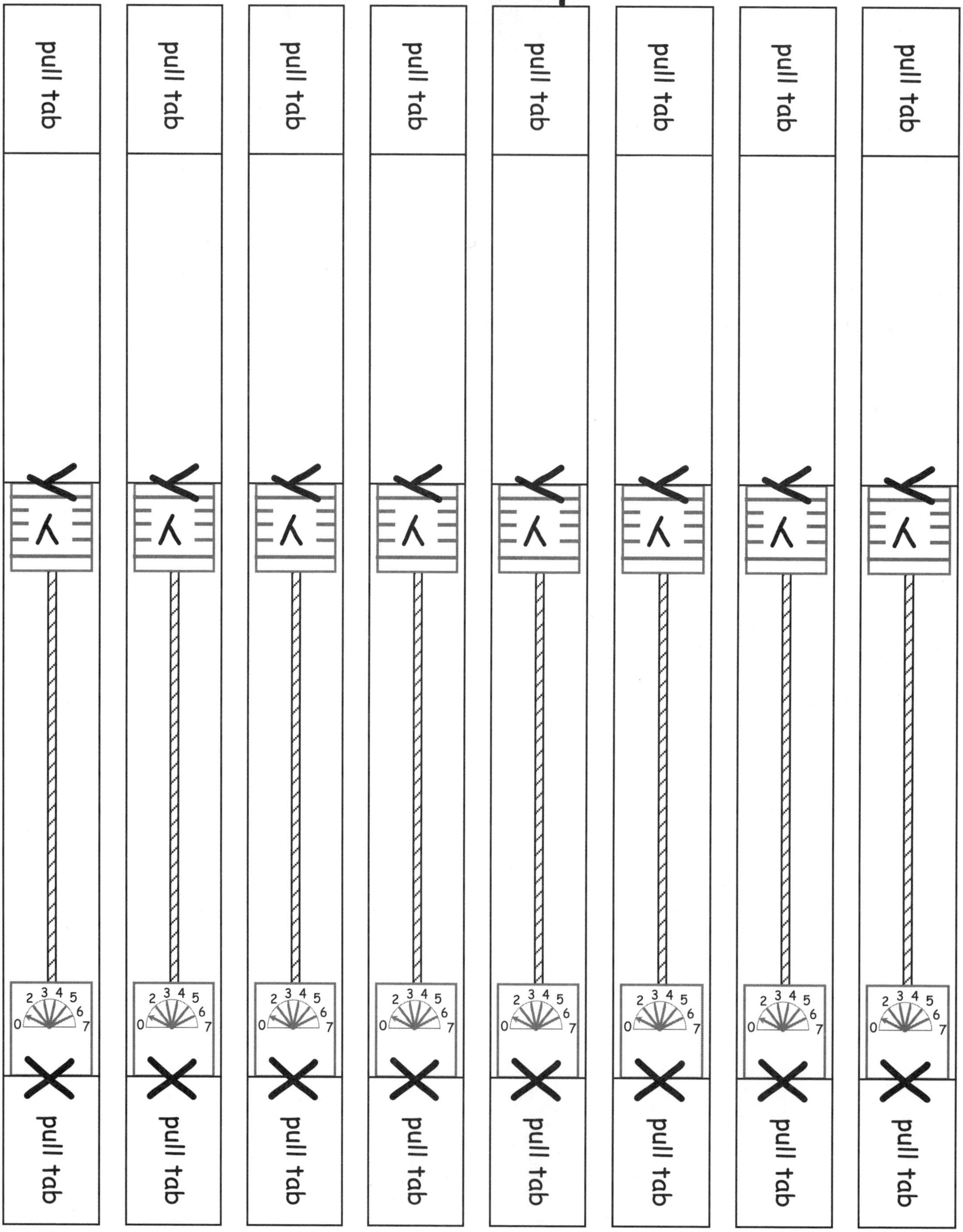

pull tab

pull tab

pull tab

pull tab

pull tab

pull tab

pull tab

pull tab

pull tab

pull tab

pull tab

pull tab

pull tab

pull tab

pull tab

pull tab

On the Level

Topic
Algebra—Linear Functions

Key Question
How can the language of algebra be used to describe data collected from an equal-arm balance?

Learning Goals
Students will:
- construct an equal-arm balance to collect data, and
- analyze data to discover the linear relationship.

Guiding Documents
Project 2061 Benchmark
- *Symbolic equations can be used to summarize how the quantity of something changes over time or in response to other changes.*

NRC Standard
- *Mathematics is important in all aspects of scientific inquiry.*

NCTM Standards 2000*
- *Represent, analyze, and generalize a variety of patterns with tables, graphs, words, and, when possible, symbolic rules*
- *Investigate how a change in one variable relates to a change in another variable*
- *Use symbolic algebra to represent situations and to solve problems, especially those that involve linear relationships*
- *Explore relationships between symbolic expressions and graphs of lines, paying particular attention to the meaning of intercept and slope*

Math
Algebra
  linear equations of the form $y = mx+b$, $m=1$, $b = 0$
  independent, dependent variable
  domain, range

Science
Physical science
  force and motion
    Law of the Lever
      torque
      lever arm (moment arm)
      equilibrium

Integrated Processes
Observing
Collecting and recording data
Inferring
Predicting
Generalizing

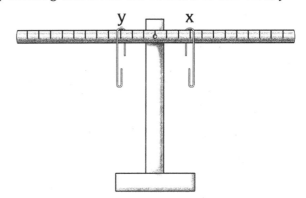

Materials
For each group:
  plastic, 10" drinking straw
  transparent tape
  jumbo-size paper clip
  2 regular paper clips
  3" x 6" piece of cardboard
  permanent marking pen
  scissors

Background Information
Mathematics
  The general form for the equation of a straight line is
$$y = mx + b$$
where *m* is the slope, and *b* is the y-axis intercept of the line.

  In this activity the slope m equals one, and the y-axis intercept equals zero. The equation for this straight line reduces to $y = x$.

  The equation $y = x$ is modeled by placing a single paper clip at position *x* on the right arm of the balance. A single clip is then placed on the left arm at the position *y* that levels the balance. In this case, $y = x$.

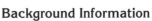

  A *function* is a set of ordered pairs (x, y) in which each value of *x* is paired with exactly one value of *y*. The first element of the ordered pair, x, is called the independent variable. The second element of the ordered pair, y, is called the dependent variable.

  The *domain* of a function is the set of *x* values specified for the function; the *range* is the resulting set of *y* values.

Science: (See *The Science of the Equal-arm Balance*.)

Management

1. This activity is designed to be done in groups of two or three.
2. Pre-punch one straw per group (see *Constructing an Equal-arm Balance*).
3. It is an important component of the activity that each group construct and adjust an equal-arm balance. If time or any other factor makes student construction impossible, construct one equal-arm balance per group.

Procedure

Have students construct an equal-arm balance (see *Constructing an Equal-arm Balance*).

Collecting and Analyzing Data

1. Instruct the students to hang one paper clip at the first mark (x=1) on the right arm of the balance. Tell them to hang one paper clip on the left arm of the balance and to carefully move the clip until the clip on the right arm is balanced. Tell them to record the position of the left-arm paper clip on the student page.
2. Instruct the students to move the right-side paper clip to the second mark (x=2) on the right arm of the balance. Tell them to carefully move the left paper clip until the clip on the right arm is again balanced and to then record its position in the data table.
3. Instruct the students to repeat this process until they have completed the data table for the positions x = 1, 2, 3, 4, 5, 6, 7, 8, 9, and 10.
4. Tell the students to graph the data, write the equation, and answer the questions on the student page.

Discussion

1. Explain the first data column, x=0 and y=0. [The equal-arm balance is constructed and adjusted to balance in a horizontal position when zero clips are on the right arm and zero clips are on the left arm.
2. What do you notice about the x and y values?
3. How do the x and y values in the table appear in the graph?
4. Look at the picture of the equal-arm balance on your student sheet. Why does the paper clip on the right arm of the equal-arm lever balance with a single clip placed on the left arm?

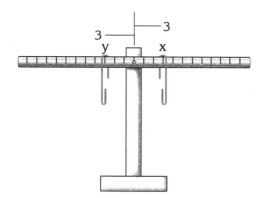

[Since the lever arm is balanced, the counterclockwise torques must equal the clockwise torques.]

counterclockwise torques	clockwise torques
$\tau = F \times d$	$\tau = F \times d$
$\tau(1) = 1 \times 3 = 3$	$\tau(1) = 1 \times 3 = 3$

3 torque units = 3 torque units]

Solutions

1.

x	0	1	2	3	4	5	6
y	0	1	2	3	4	5	6

7	8	9	10
7	8	9	10

2.

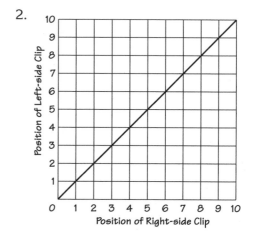

3. What is the equation of the line? [y = x]
4. What is the slope of the line? [1]
5. What is the y-axis intercept of the line? [0]
6. What is the independent variable? [x, the position of the clip on the right arm of the balance]
7. What is dependent variable? [y, the position of the clip on the left arm of the balance]
8. What is the domain? [The procedure imposes data collection at discrete, integer positions on the right arm of the balance. In this case, the domain is the set {0,1,2,3,4,5,6,7,8,9,10}. In reality, the clip can be placed at *any* position on the right arm of the balance. In this case, the domain becomes any *x* equal to or greater than zero and equal to or less than the length of the right arm.]
9. What is the range? [For the integer domain, the range is the set {0,1,2,3,4,5,6,7,8,9,10}. For the continuous domain, the range is {0 to n} where n equals the length of the right arm of the balance.]

20

10. What part of the equal-arm balance represents the independent variable? [the right arm]
11. What part of the equal-arm balance represents the dependent variable? [the left arm]
12. How is "slope" represented when using an equal-arm balance to model the equation y = x? [The coefficient of x, in this case one, represents the slope.]
13. What limits data collection? [The length of the straw used to make the equal-arm balance.]
14. On the graph, what does the line y = x tell you about the behavior of the equal-arm balance? [The line y = x represents the positions (ordered pairs) of the clips that balance the equal-arm balance.]

15. On the graph, what does the shaded region below the line y = x tell you about the behavior of the equal-arm balance? [The region below the line represents the positions (ordered pairs) of the clips that cause the equal-arm balance to lower the right arm.]
16. On the graph, what does the region above the line y = x tell you about the behavior of the equal-arm balance? [The region above the line repesents the positions (ordered pairs) of the clips that cause the equal-arm balance to lower the left arm.]

* Reprinted with permission from *Principles and Standards for School Mathematics*, 2000 by the National Council of Teachers of Mathematics. All rights reserved.

The Science of the Equal-arm Balance

At the same location on the Earth's surface, all bodies fall freely with the same acceleration g. By Newton's second law of motion, the force acting on a body equals the product of its mass, *m*, and its acceleration, *g*. This force, due to the attractive pull of gravity, is called *weight*. It follows that if, at the same point on the Earth's surface, the weights of two bodies are equal, their masses are also equal.

The *equal-arm balance* is a device that can accurately determine when the weights of two bodies are equal, and therefore when their masses are equal. A simple equal-arm balance can be constructed from a ten-inch plastic drinking straw and a few paper clips (see *Constructing an Equal-arm Balance*).

In the diagram below, a plastic drinking straw is attached to a vertical support by a straight pin through the straw's exact center. The straw is free to rotate around the axis of the pin. A single paper clip is hanging on the left arm and the balance is being gripped by its right arm to hold it level.

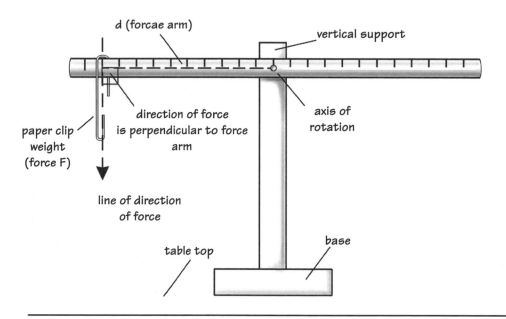

The force arm, *d*, is the perpendicular distance from the axis of rotation to a line drawn along the direction of the force.

The product of the magnitude of a force and its force arm is called the *moment*, the force about the axis. *Torque* is also another name for moment.

$$\text{moment} = F \times d$$

The effect of the moment acting on the left arm is to produce a counterclockwise rotation about the axis of the pin. If the grip on the right arm were released, the left arm of the straw would drop to the table top.

The paper clip on the left arm can be balanced by placing an identical clip on the right arm at an equal distrance from the rotation axis. The clip on the right arm produces a clockwise moment that counterbalances the counterclockwise moment prouced by the clip on the left arm.

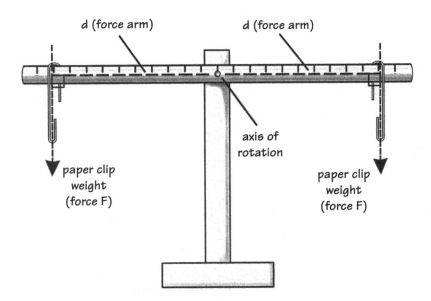

In general, for the straw to be balanced in the horizontal position, the sum of the moments acting in a clockwise direction must equal the sum of the moments acting in a counterclockwise direction.

In the diagram, a single clip at position 9 on the left arm balances two clips, one at position 3 and the other at position 6, on the right arm.

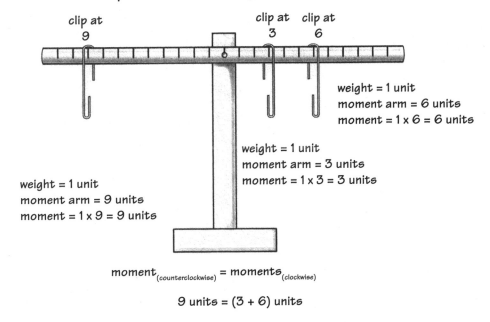

$$\text{moment}_{(counterclockwise)} = \text{moments}_{(clockwise)}$$

$$9 \text{ units} = (3 + 6) \text{ units}$$

If forces are expressed in gram-force units and lengths in centimeter, then the moments are expressed in gram-force x centimeter units.

Constructing an Equal-arm Balance

Materials:

1 plastic drinking straw, 10 inches
$\frac{1}{8}$" hole punch
transparent tape
jumbo-size paper clip
5 paper clips, regular size

3" x 6" piece of cardboard
ruler with centimeter divisions
permanent marking pen
scissors
glue stick

1. Locate the approximate center of the plastic drinking straw.

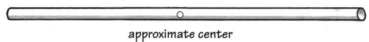

approximate center

2. Use a $\frac{1}{8}$" hole punch to make a hole at the center of the straw. (The straw will flatten when placed between the jaws of the hole punch but will spring back to its original shape when removed.)

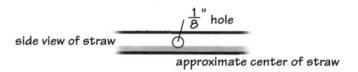

side view of straw

$\frac{1}{8}$" hole

approximate center of straw

3. Mark the straw at centimeter intervals, starting from the hole, to the left and right of the pinhole.

hole

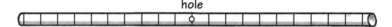

4. Open and bend the jumbo-size paper clip into a j-shape. Tape the j-shaped clip near the edge of a desk or table so that approximately one inch of the clip extends beyond the edge. Align the holes with the end of the clip and slide the straw onto the clip.

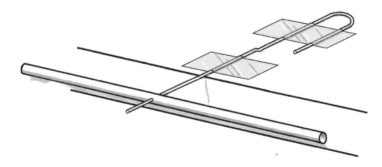

5. Use the scissors to carefully trim a very small piece from the low end of the straw. Do this until the straw is level (balanced).

6. Copy the *Equalizer Forks* page onto cardstock or cut out the pattern for a fork and trace its outline onto a stiff piece of cardboard. Cut out the fork and tape it to the side of the desk or table so that the up and down motion of the right arm of the straw is limited by the arms of the fork.

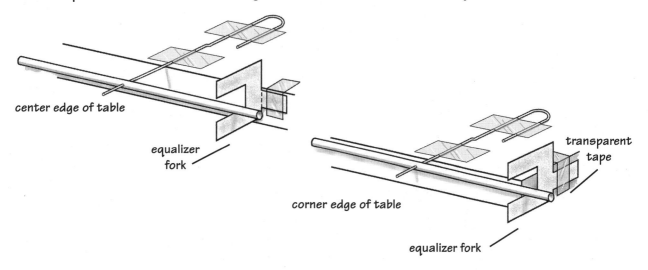

center edge of table

equalizer fork

transparent tape

corner edge of table

equalizer fork

The fork removes a lot of the frustration in tinkering with a system as sensitive as this one.

7. Bend three paper clips into the shape shown in the diagram. Hang the larger end on the straw. When you need to hang more than one clip at the same location, hang the additional clips on the lower loop.

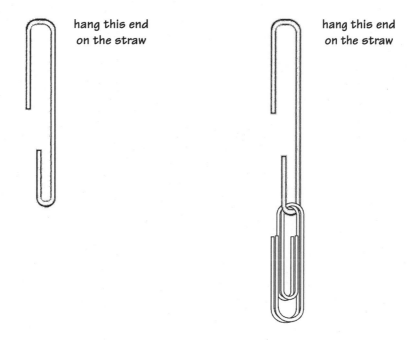

hang this end on the straw

hang this end on the straw

Equalizer Forks

Copy onto cardstock and/or trace the Equalizer Fork pattern
onto a piece of stiff cardboard.

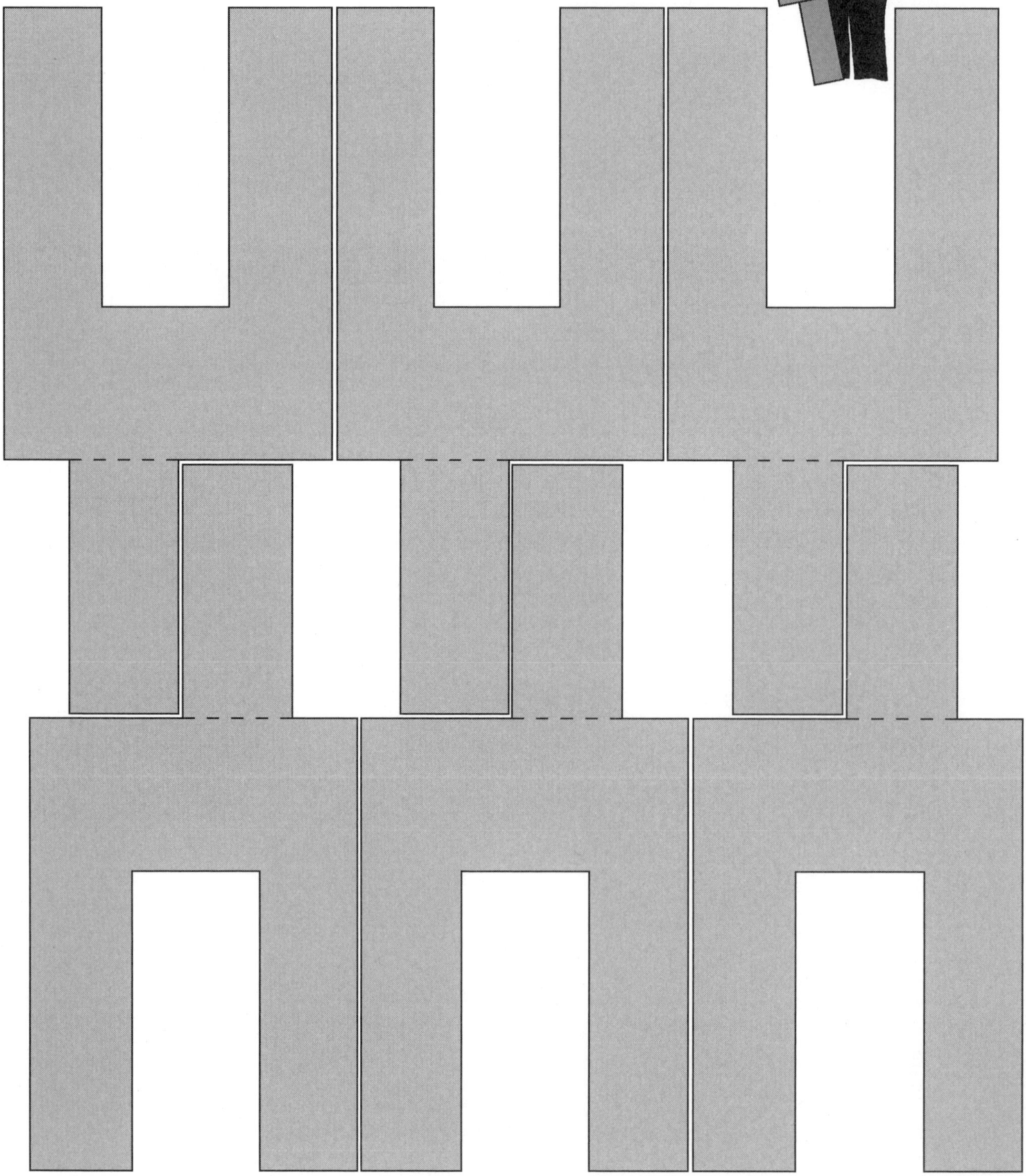

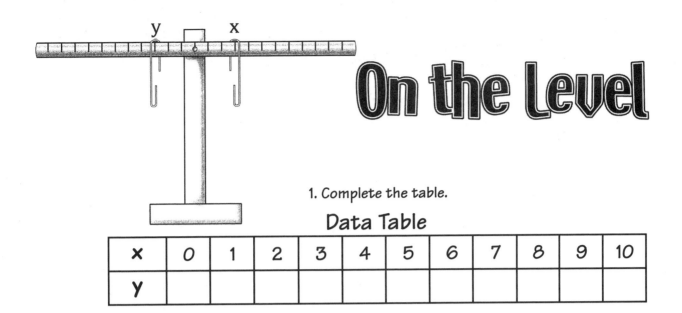

On the Level

1. Complete the table.

Data Table

x	0	1	2	3	4	5	6	7	8	9	10
y											

2. Draw the graph.

Graph

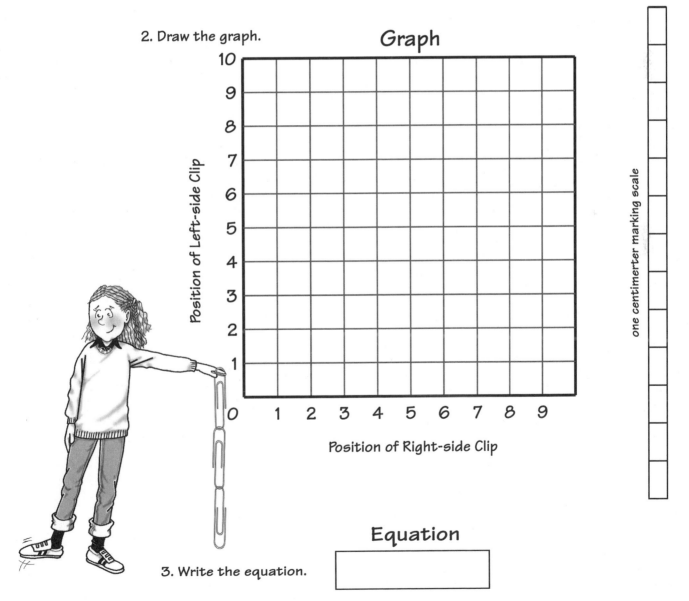

Position of Left-side Clip

Position of Right-side Clip

one centimerter marking scale

Equation

3. Write the equation.

On the Level

4. What is the slope of the line?

5. What is the y-intercept of the line?

6. What is the independent variable?

7. What is the dependent variable?

8. What is the domain?

9. What is the range?

The following are questions about how the equal-arm balance models the above linear equation.

10. What piece or pieces on the balance represent the independent variable?

11. What piece or pieces on the balance represent the dependent variable?

12. How is "slope" represented when using an equal-arm balance to model the equation y = x?

13. What limits data collection?

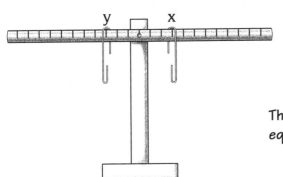

Equal-arm Balance

On the Level

The graph shown below describes the behavior of the equal-arm balance.

14. On the graph, what does the line y = x tell you about the behavior of the equal-arm balance?

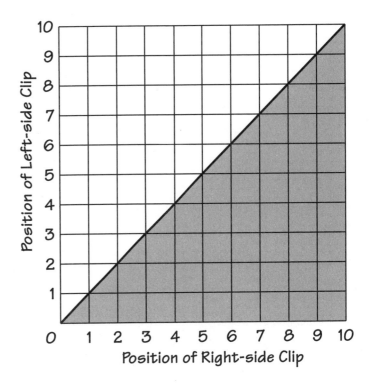

15. On the graph, what does the shaded region below the line y = x tell you about the behavior of the equal-arm balance?

16. On the graph, what does the region above the line y = x tell you about the behavior of the equal-arm balance?

On the Level II

Topic
Algebra—Linear Functions

Key Question
How can the language of algebra be used to describe data collected from an equal-arm balance?

Learning Goals
Students will:
- construct an equal-arm balance to collect data, and
- analyze data to discover the linear relationship.

Guiding Documents
Project 2061 Benchmark
- *Symbolic equations can be used to summarize how the quantity of something changes over time or in response to other changes.*

NRC Standard
- *Mathematics is important in all aspects of scientific inquiry.*

NCTM Standards 2000*
- *Represent, analyze, and generalize a variety of patterns with tables, graphs, words, and, when possible, symbolic rules*
- *Investigate how a change in one variable relates to a change in another variable*
- *Use symbolic algebra to represent situations and to solve problems, especially those that involve linear relationships*
- *Explore relationships between symbolic expressions and graphs of lines, paying particular attention to the meaning of intercept and slope*

Math
Algebra
    linear equation of the form $y = mx + b$,
        $m > 1$, $b = 0$
    independent, dependent variable
    domain, range

Science
Physical science
    force and motion
        Law of the Lever
            torque
            lever arm (moment arm)
            equilibrium

Integrated Processes
Observing
Collecting and recording data
Inferring
Predicting
Generalizing

Materials
For each group:
    plastic, 10" drinking straw
    transparent tape
    jumbo-size paper clip
    4 regular paper clips
    3" x 6" piece of cardboard
    permanent marking pen
    scissors

Background Information
Mathematics
    The general form for the equation of a straight line is
$$y = mx + b$$
where m is the slope and b the y-axis intercept of the line.

    In this activity the slope m is greater than 1, and the y-axis intercept equals zero. The equation for this straight line reduces to $y = mx$.

    The equation $y = mx$ is modeled by placing m paper clips at position x on the right arm of the balance and a single clip at position y on the left arm of the balance. In the diagram, three clips at position two on the right arm of the balance are balanced by a single clip at position six (3×2) on the left arm.

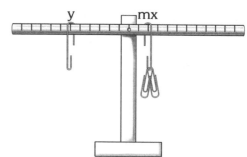

    A *function* is a set of ordered pairs (x, y) in which each value of x is paired with exactly one value of y.

    The first element of the ordered pair, x, is called the independent variable. The second element of the ordered pair, y, is called the dependent variable.

    The *domain* of a function is the set of x values specified for the function; the *range* is the resulting set of y values.

Science: (See *The Science of the Equal-arm Balance*, page 22.)

Management

1. This activity is designed to be done in groups of three or four.
2. Pre-punch one straw per group (see *Constructing an Equal-arm Balance,* page 24).
3. It is an important component of the activity that each group construct and adjust their own equal-arm balance. If time or any other factor makes student construction impossible, construct one equal-arm balance per group.

Procedure

Have students construct an equal-arm balance (see *Constructing the Equal-arm Balance,* page 24).

Collecting and Analyzing Data

1. Show students how to open one paper clip so that each end has a hook. Tell them to hang two clips on the smaller end and then hang the large end on the straw.

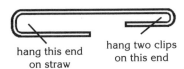

hang this end on straw

hang two clips on this end

2. Instruct the students to hang the three paper clips at the first mark (x=1) on the right-side arm of the balance. Direct them to hang one paper clip on the left-side arm of the balance and to carefully move the clip until the three clips are balanced. Tell them to record the position of the left-arm paper clip on the student page.
3. Instruct the students to move the right-side paper clips to the second mark (x=2) on the right-side arm of the balance. Tell them to carefully move the left paper clip until the three clips are again balanced and to then record its position in the data table.
4. Instruct the students to repeat this process until they have completed the data table for the right-arm positions x = 1, 2, 3, and 4.
5. Tell the students to graph the data, write the equation, and answer the questions on the student page.

Discussion

1. Explain the first data column, x=0 and y=0. [The equal-arm balance is constructed and adjusted to balance in a horizontal position when zero clips are on the right arm and an equal number (zero) clips are on the left arm.]

2. Look at the equal-arm balance on your student sheet. Why do the paper clips on the right arm of the equal-arm balance balance with a single clip placed on the left arm? [Since the lever arm is balanced, the counterclockwise torques must equal the clockwise torques.]

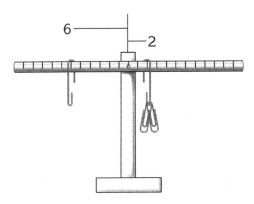

counterclockwise torques	clockwise torques
$\tau = F \times d$	$\tau = F \times d$
$\tau(1) = 1 \times 6 = 6$	$\tau(1) = 1 \times 2 = 2$
	$\tau(2) = 1 \times 2 = 2$
	$\tau(3) = 1 \times 2 = 2$

6 torque units = 6 torque units

3. What limited your collection of data? [the length of the straw] How could you remedy that? [Connect two or more plastic straws together to make an equal-arm balance.]

Solutions

1.

x	0	1	2	3	4
y	0	3	6	9	12

2.

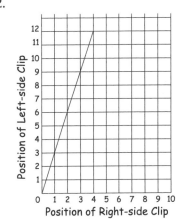

3. y = 3x
4. What is the slope of the line? [3]
5. What is the y-axis intercept of the line? [0]
6. What is the independent variable? [x, the position of the clip on the right arm of the balance]
7. What is dependent variable? [y, the position of the clip on the left arm of the balance]
8. What is the domain? [The procedure imposes data collection at discrete, integer positions on the right arm of the balance. In this case, the domain is the set {0,1,2,3,4}. In the continuous case, the domain becomes any x equal to or greater than zero and equal to or less than four.]
9. What is the range? [For the integer domain, the range is the set {0, 3,6,9,12}. For the continuous domain, the range is {0 to 12}.]
10. What part of the equal-arm balance represents the independent variable? [the right arm]
11. What part of the equal-arm balance represents the dependent variable? [the left arm]
12. How is "slope" represented when using an equal-arm balance to model the equation y = x? [The coefficient of x, in this case three, represents the slope.]
13. What limits data collection? [The length of the straw used to make the equal-arm balance.]

14. On the graph, what does the line y = 3x tell you about the behavior of the equal-arm balance? [The line y = 3x represents the positions (ordered pairs) of the clips that balance the equal-arm balance.]
15. On the graph, what does the shaded region below the line y = 3x tell you about the behavior of the equal-arm balance? [The region below the line represents the positions (ordered pairs) of the clips that cause the equal-arm balance to lower the right arm.]
16. On the graph, what does the region above the line y = 3x tell you about the behavior of the equal-arm balance? [The region above the line repesents the positions (ordered pairs) of the clips that cause the equal-arm balance to lower the left arm.]

Extension

Encourage interested students to connect two or three straws together to make an equal-arm balance that will collect more data.

Extension Activities

The *Extension* sections of the activities *On the Level II* and *On the Level III* ask students to construct a longer balance arm so that more data can be collected. Here are two methods for constructiong a longer balance arm.

1. **The first method** is to slit lengthwise a short section of plastic drinking straw to form a sleeve and then use the sleeve to join together two other sections of plastic straw.

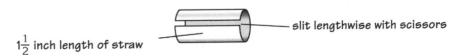

$1\frac{1}{2}$ inch length of straw — slit lengthwise with scissors

2. Wrap the sleeve around the ends of two drinking straws and push the two straws together, end-to-end.

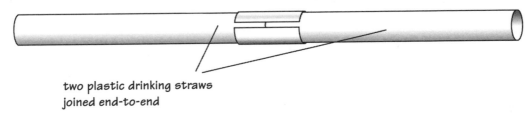

two plastic drinking straws
joined end-to-end

3. Secure the sleeve to the straws with pieces of transparent tape.

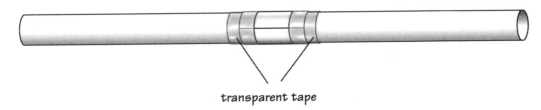

transparent tape

4. **A second method** makes use of the fact that the plastic drinking straws found in fast food outlets generally have different diameters. The smaller diameter straw slips easily but snugly inside the larger diameter straw.

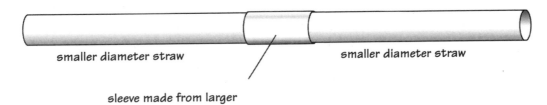

smaller diameter straw   smaller diameter straw

sleeve made from larger
diameter straw

5. Go to the *Constructing an Equal-arm Balance* instructions.

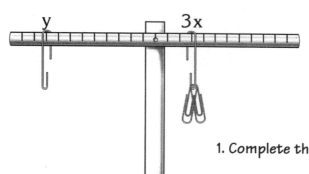

On the Level II

1. Complete the table.

Data Table

x	0	1	2	3	4
y					

2. Draw the graph.

Graph

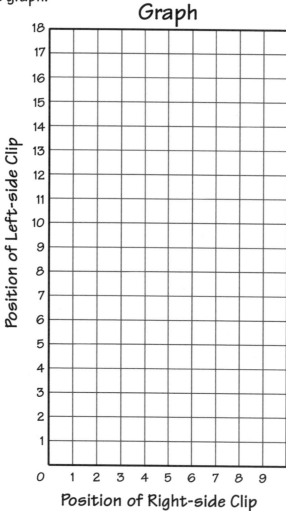

Position of Left-side Clip

Position of Right-side Clip

one centimerter marking scale

Equation

3. Write the equation.

On the Level II

4. What is the slope of the line?

5. What is the y-intercept of the line?

6. What is the independent variable?

7. What is the dependent variable?

8. What is the domain?

9. What is the range?

The following are questions about how the equal-arm balance models the above linear equation.

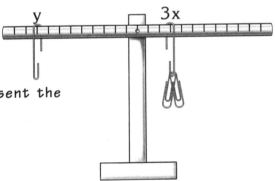

10. What piece or pieces on the balance represent the independent variable?

11. What piece or pieces on the balance represent the dependent variable?

12. How is "slope" represented when using an equal-arm balance to model the equation y = x?

13. What limits data collection?

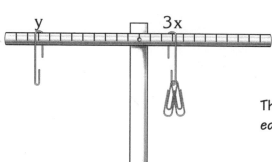

On the Level II

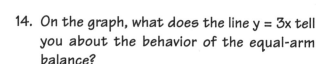

Equal-arm Balance

The graph shown below describes the behavior of the equal-arm balance.

14. On the graph, what does the line y = 3x tell you about the behavior of the equal-arm balance?

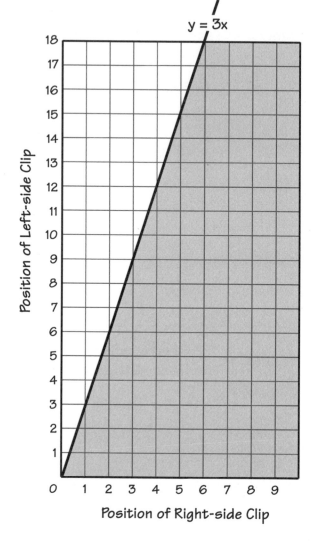

15. On the graph, what does the shaded region below the line y = 3x tell you about the behavior of the equal-arm balance?

16. On the graph, what does the region above the line y = 3x tell you about the behavior of the equal-arm balance?

Clipping Along

Topic
Algebra—Linear Functions, Rates

Key Question
You have a chain of standard paper clips and your friend has a chain of jumbo paper clips. If your friend told you the length of objects in jumbo clips, how could you change that number into standard clip lengths?

Learning Goals
Students will:
- measure the lengths of objects with standard and jumbo paper clips, and
- graph and analyze the data to develop their understanding of a proportional relationship as a linear function represented in graphic and symbolic forms.

Guiding Documents
Project 2061 Benchmarks
- *Organize information in simple tables and graphs and identify relationships they reveal.*
- *The graphic display of numbers may help to show patterns such as trends, varying rates of change, gaps, or clusters. Such patterns sometimes can be used to make predictions about the phenomena being graphed.*

NRC Standards
- *Use appropriate tools and techniques to gather, analyze, and interpret data.*
- *Mathematics is important in all aspects of scientific inquiry.*

NCTM Standards 2000*
- *Relate and compare different forms of representation for a relationship*
- *Use graphs to analyze the nature of changes in quantities in linear relationships*
- *Explore relationships between symbolic expressions and graphs of lines, paying particular attention to the meaning of intercept and slope*
- *Use symbolic algebra to represent situations and to solve problems, especially those that involve linear relationships*

Math
Proportional reasoning
Linear functions
Measuring
   length
Graphing

Integrated Processes
Observing
Collecting and recording data
Interpreting data
Drawing conclusions
Applying
Generalizing

Materials
Jumbo paper clips, 12 per group
Standard paper clips, 19 per group

Background Information
Conversion rates are factors by which you multiply one measurement unit to get a different type of unit. The conversion rate is determined by using a ratio to compare the quantity in one system to an equal value in the other system. When the ratio is reduced to a unit rate, with a one as the denominator, you have the conversion rate for the two types of measures.

Conversion rates can be represented as linear functions. The change in one system is proportional to the change in the related system. The comparison of corresponding values in both systems always give equivalent ratios numerically. Graphing pairs of corresponding values forms a straight line with a slope equivalent to the conversion rate. When the conversion is represented in symbolic form, the conversion rate becomes the coefficient with the independent variable.

For paper clips, the length of 9 standard clips is the same as 6 jumbo clips. The conversion ratio would be 9 standard clips to 6 jumbo clips (9/6). As a unit ratio this would be 1.5 standard clips for each (1) jumbo clip (1.5/1). The one in the denominator is assumed and the rate is recorded as 1.5 standard/jumbo. This functional relationship shows up in a coordinate graph with a line having a slope of 1.5, the conversion rate between the two systems. The number of standard clips (S) is a function of the number of jumbo clips (j). The function is symbolized with the conversion rate as a coefficient of (j): $S(j) = 1.5j$.

Management
1. This activity works well in groups of two with one partner measuring objects with a jumbo clip chain and the other measuring the same object with the standard clip chain.
2. To get more consistent results as a class, the teacher may choose to pre-select the items to be

measured by students. In choosing items, there needs to be a variety of lengths from one jumbo paper clip to 12 jumbo clips.

3. The investigation is divided into two parts. *Part A* has students develop the understanding of the linear nature of the conversion rate. *Part B* has students measure objects and graph the data to establish the linear nature of the function. Most students profit from both experiences. If a class has had a good deal of experience with proportions and rates, a teacher may choose to skip *Part A*.

Procedure

Part A

1. Distribute paper clips of both sizes and have student groups make a chain for each size of paper clip.
2. Pose the idea that lengths can be measured by chains of paper clips and have the students suggest what problems might arise if they used the chains they made.
3. Have students lay the chains side by side with one end of each chain matched with the other chain.
4. Ask students to observe and record how long in standard paper clips the given amount of jumbo clips is.
5. Have students make a coordinate graph of the data.
6. Discuss with students the patterns they see in the graph and their relation to the data. Have them consider how they can use the patterns to convert lengths in jumbo paper clip units to standard paper clip units. Have the students record their conversion method as an equation.
7. Use a jumbo chain to measure items that are not one of the given lengths. Have students determine the items' lengths in standard paper clips using their graph and equation, then check their answers with a standard clip chain.

Part B

1. Pose the *Key Question* and have students discuss how they might solve the problem.
2. Have student groups make a chain for both sizes of paper clips.
3. Using *Part B* activity sheet, have students measure and record the lengths of six objects in both standard and jumbo paper clip units.
4. Have students make a coordinate graph of the data.
5. Discuss the patterns they see in the graph and their relation to the data. Have them consider how they can use the patterns to convert lengths in jumbo paper clips to standard paper clip units. Have the students record the conversion patterns as equations.
6. Connect several jumbo chains and measure larger objects in the room and have students use their equations to determine the length in standard paper clip units. Several small chains can be connected and used to confirm the results.

Discussion

1. What patterns do you see in the chart? [For every two jumbo clips, there are three standard clips.]
2. How many times larger is the number of standard clips than the number of jumbo clips for any object? [1.5]
3. What patterns do you see in the graph? [The points make a straight line. For every jumbo you go to the right, you go up 1.5 standard clips.]
4. How do the patterns you found in the chart show up on the graph? [To stay on the line, you go up three standard clips and over two jumbo clips. To stay on the line, you go up 1.5 units for every one you go sideways.]
5. How could you use the patterns to determine the length of something in standard clips if you know its length in jumbo clips? [jumbo clips X 1.5 = standard clips ($1.5j=s$), interpolate or extrapolate the line on the graph.]
6. What are some types of measurement conversions that might be more practical than jumbo clips to standard clips?

Extensions

1. Make conversion rates for other standard units such as hex-a-link cubes, Unifix cubes, floor tiles. Develop charts, graphs, and equations to communicate the relationships.
2. Develop conversion rates to do estimations such as feet/step, centimeters/hand span, yards/arm span. Develop charts, graphs, and equations to communicate the relationships.

Clipping Along

Jumbo Clips Long	Standard Clips Long	Standard Clips for Each Jumbo Clip
2		
4		
6		
8		
10		
12		

STANDARD PAPER CLIPS

15

10

5

0

0   5   10   15

JUMBO PAPER CLIPS

Clipping Along

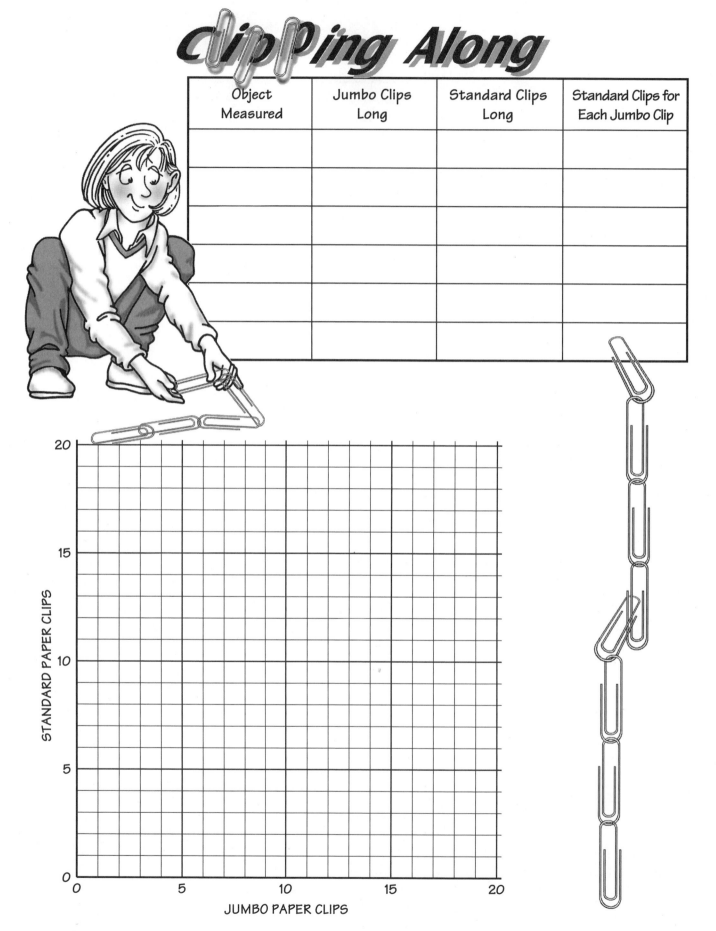

Object Measured	Jumbo Clips Long	Standard Clips Long	Standard Clips for Each Jumbo Clip

STANDARD PAPER CLIPS

20

15

10

5

0

0   5   10   15   20

JUMBO PAPER CLIPS

Functions IN CIRCLES

Topic
Circumference of a circle as a function of its diameter

Key Question
What can we learn about the circumference of a circle as a function of its diameter?

Learning Goals
Students will:
- deepen their understanding of diameters and circumferences of circles by using manipulatives;
- accurately measure diameters and circumferences of containers;
- construct an input/output table of the data, graph the data, and write a rule for the function in sentence and standard algebraic form; and
- recognize that the table, graph, and rule assign a value to pi and that the slope equals pi.

Guiding Documents
Project 2061 Benchmarks
- *The graphic display of numbers may help to show patterns such as trends, varying rates of change, gaps, or clusters. Such patterns sometimes can be used to make predictions about the phenomena being graphed.*
- *Graphs can show a variety of possible relationships between two variables. As one variable increases uniformly, the other may do one of the following: always keep the same proportion to the first, increase or decrease steadily, increase or decrease faster and faster, get closer and closer to some limiting value, reach some intermediate maximum or minimum, alternately increase and decrease indefinitely, increase and decrease in steps, or do something different from any of these.*
- *Mathematical ideas can be represented concretely, graphically, and symbolically.*
- *Organize information in tables and graphs and identify relationships they reveal.*

NCTM Standards 2000*
- *Represent, analyze, and generalize a variety of patterns with tables graphs, words, and, when possible, symbolic rules*

- *Relate and compare different forms of representation for a relationship*
- *Explore relationships between symbolic expressions and graphs of lines, paying particular attention to the meaning of intercept and slope*
- *Use graphs to analyze the nature of changes in quantities in linear relationships*
- *Model and solve contextualized problems using various representations, such as graphs, tables, and equations*
- *Understand relationships among the angles, side lengths, perimeters, areas, and volumes of similar objects*

Math
Function
Measurement
Graphing
Slope and pi (π)
Input/output data table construction
Development of a function rule
Proportional reasoning

Integrated Processes
Observing
Collecting and organizing data
Interpreting data
Generalizing

Materials
Metric rulers or meter sticks
Round cans or containers of various sizes
    (see *Management 4*)
Chart or butcher paper
Inflated basketball
Felt tip markers, optional

Background Information
   Students will approach the relationship between circumference and diameter from the perspective of functions. Three functional relationships of special interest exist in the circle: circumference as a function of the diameter, area as a function of the radius, and area as the function of the circumference or vice versa. Only the first of these, the circumference as a function of the diameter, is a linear function. It is that relationship which is the focus of this investigation.

   The study of a function can be done from three perspectives: patterns of input/output ordered pairs organized in a table, graphs of the ordered pairs, and a rule generalizing the functional relationship of output to input.

Pi (π) is the relationship of the circumference of a circle to its diameter. It is an irrational number. Its approximation is written as $\frac{22}{7}$ as a fraction or 3.1415... as its decimal equivalent. The approximation of 3.14 works very well in all but the most precise applications.

Students are often introduced to the circumference of a circle with the formula 2πr = C. They do not have any experience to connect with the formula so it tends to be meaningless and quickly forgotten or mixed up with other formulae.

Making a concrete graph from containers provides a valuable experience with which students can think about the relationship of circumference and diameter. They can come to see that the diameter and circumference of a circle increase proportionately.

The function rule is of the general form $f(x)$ = mx + y. In this case x is replaced by d, the diameter, the slope m is replaced by pi, and y = 0 since the line passes through the origin. C replaces f because the circumference is a function of the diameter. The function rule becomes:

$$C(d) = \pi d$$

This is read as "C of d is equal to pi times d."

Encourage students to see and discuss the relationship among the table, graph, and rule. They should develop the ability to visualize the graph just by looking at the table or rule, etc.

Management

1. Students will need to be familiar with measuring in centimeters, graphing, and the concept of function before beginning this activity.
2. They should work together in small groups of three or four.
3. Each group of students will need a large piece of butcher paper or chart paper on which to construct a graph. Be sure that the paper is wide enough for each of the containers you have selected.
4. Each group will need at least five or six round containers with different diameters. Empty coffee cans, soda cans, chip canisters, and pill bottles all work well. Lids do not work as well because they are harder to roll in a straight line.
5. You may want to have felt tip pens available for students to use as they create their graphs so that the lines will be easier to see. The markers can also be used for students to mark on the containers which is necessary to measure the circumference.

Procedure

1. Have each group construct a graph on a piece of chart paper or butcher paper. Guide them to use a straight edge to draw a horizontal axis just up from the bottom edge of the paper and label it Diameter. Have them make a vertical axis just in from the left edge of the paper and label it Circumference. (The intersection of the two axes in the lower left corner of the paper is the origin.)
2. Inform the students that for each container, they must find the point on the horizontal axis that corresponds with that object's diameter. Show them that they can do this by putting the diameter of the container on the horizontal axis with one end on the origin. Have them mark the other endpoint along the axis to show the distance of the diameter from the origin.
3. Direct the students to place the container on its side on the paper so that it may be rolled at a right angle to the horizontal axis, positioning it so it touches the horizontal axis at the endpoint of the diameter. Have them place a mark on the container where it touches the horizontal axis.
4. Instruct the students to roll the container one complete revolution until the mark is back on the paper. Have them mark a point at this position on the paper. (This point represents the relationship between the circumference and diameter of the can.) Caution students to keep the container rolling parallel to the vertical axis.
5. Have each group graph the points for all of their containers. A group's graph should look something like this:

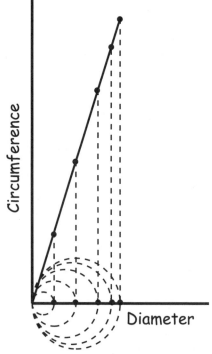

The dashed lines indicate the circumferences of the containers and the paths along which they were rolled.

6. Discuss what patterns can be seen in the graph and what information they give about the containers. [The graph forms a straight line, it goes

up as it goes right, the circumference is always bigger than the diameter, bigger diameters result in bigger circumferences, etc.]

7. Hand out the student sheets and have the students measure and record the diameters and circumferences of the containers using the graph they constructed.

8. After they have entered this information in the table, direct them to calculate and record the ratio of circumference to diameter for each of the containers, and then average the ratios. They should then complete the graph based on the numeric data.

9. When they have finished, have groups work together to answer the questions on the second student sheet.

10. When groups reach the final question, make an inflated basketball available for students to test their methods.

11. When all groups have completed both pages, close with a time of discussion where students can share what they learned about how the ratios compare to each other, what that says about circles, and how it is related to the graph.

Discussion

1. What type of function does the relationship of circumference to diameter represent and what evidence do you have to support your conclusion? [It is a linear function. The graph goes up in a straight line.]

2. What is the significance of the slope of the line in the graph? [The slope of the line is equal to pi, which is equivalent to the circumference over the diameter in any circle.]

3. How can the graph be used to predict the circumference given its diameter? [Determine where a given diameter would cross the line, and that is the circle's circumference.]

4. How can the graph be used to find the diameter of a circle given its circumference? [Find where a given circumference would cross the line, and trace that point down to the horizontal axis. That will give the circle's diameter.]

5. How do you know that this is a linear function? [The relationship between any (x, y) ordered pair that falls on the line is the same; the line goes up at a constant rate, etc.]

6. Have students share and discuss the sentences they have written relating the circumference to the diameter as a function.

7. As they share their translations, help students to refine them into proper algebraic language as necessary. [$C(d) = \pi d$]

8. In discussing how to determine the diameter of a basketball from its circumference, it is important to note that students must find its greatest girth. Have them discuss how they came to this conclusion and how they obtained the measure.

Extension

Measure the diameters of large circles on athletic fields and predict the circumferences. Then measure them to see if they are correct.

* Reprinted with permission from *Principles and Standards for School Mathematics*, 2000 by the National Council of Teachers of Mathematics. All rights reserved.

Functions

IN CIRCLES

How does the circumference of a circle compare to the diameter of a circle? To find out, record the diameter, circumference, and ratio of circumference to diameter for each container your group has. When you have recorded all of your containers, find the average ratio and record it at the bottom of the table. Plot each circumference and diameter on the graph and connect the points. All values on the graph are in centimeters.

Container	Diameter	Circumference	Ratio $\frac{C}{d}$
		Average	

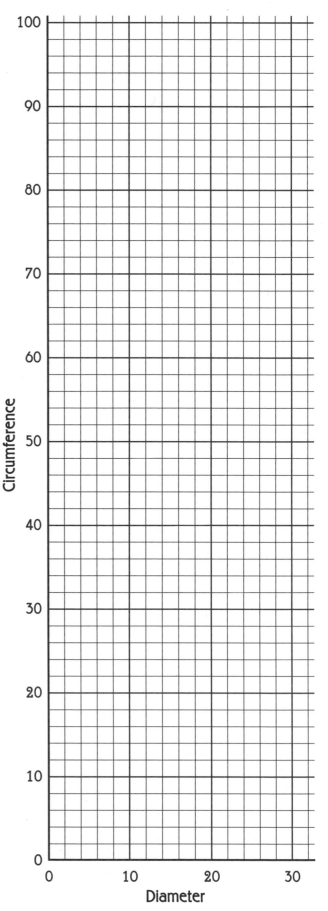

Functions

Answer the following questions after you have completed the first student sheet.

1. Please explain what type of function the relationship of circumference to diameter represents and what evidence you have to support your conclusion.

2. Write a sentence that relates circumference to diameter as a function.

3. Translate the sentence into standard algebriac language for linear functions.

4. What is the significance of the slope of the line in the graph?

5. How can the graph be used to predict the circumference given its diameter?

6. How can the graph be used to find the diameter of a circle given its circumference?

7. On the back side of this paper, explain how you could find the circumference and diameter of an inflated basketball. Test your process by finding the circumference and diameter of a real basketball.

Measuring Lines

Topic
Algebra—Linear Functions

Key Questions
How do centimeters compare to inches?

Focus
Students will measure a number of items in centimeters and inches to determine a conversion rate. They will make a scatter plot of the data and determine its equation to understand the functional nature of the proportion.

Guiding Documents
Project 2061 Benchmarks
• *The graphic display of numbers may help to show patterns such as trends, varying rates of change, gaps, or clusters. Such patterns sometimes can be used to make predictions about the phenomena being graphed.*
• *Mathematical statements can be used to describe how one quantity changes when another changes. Rates of change can be computed from magnitudes and vice versa.*

NRC Standard
• *Use appropriate tools and techniques to gather, analyze, and interpret data.*

NCTM Standards 2000*
• *Understand and use ratios and proportions to represent quantitative relationships*
• *Relate and compare different forms of representation for a relationship;*
• *Use symbolic algebra to represent situations and to solve problems, especially those that involve linear relationships*
• *Model and solve contextualized problems using various representations, such as graphs, tables, and equations*
• *Understand both metric and customary systems of measurement*

Math
Measurement
Proportional reasoning
Algebra
    linear functions
    graphing
    equations

Integrated Processes
Observing
Collecting and organizing data
Interpreting data
Generalizing

Materials
Rulers, metric and English standard
Tape measures, metric and English standard
Meter sticks
Yard sticks

Background Information
There are 2.56 cm in an inch. This relationship may be shown numerically by the ratio of centimeters to inches. It may be shown graphically as it forms a straight line going through the origin and having a slope of 2.56. It may be shown symbolically as cm = 2.56 x in.

Management
1. Students need to be familiar with measuring both in centimeters and inches. They should be able to measure to the nearest millimeter and the nearest eighth inch.
2. This activity can be completed in a 45–60 minute period.
3. Gather a variety of measuring tools so students may choose the one most appropriate for the task.
4. Before beginning the activity the teacher should choose how directed the investigation will be. Students could be free to choose a variety of objects to measure. The final results of all the students will be similar although the specific measurements

will vary. If more direction is required, all the students can measure the same set of objects. In this case all the numbers and conclusions should be the same.

Procedure

1. Have students discuss the *Key Question* and what they would need to know to determine how to change centimeters to inches. [measurements in centimeters and inches]
2. Allowing students to choose the appropriate measuring tool, have them measure a variety of objects in both centimeters and inches and record them.
3. Direct students to make a scatter plot of the measurements.
4. Have them discuss what patterns they find in the scatter plot and what the patterns tell them about the relationship of inches to centimeters.
5. Allow time for students to calculate the decimal ratio of the relationship of centimeters to inches and record it in the blank column on the chart.
6. Have them find the average ratio and make an equation to convert inches into centimeters and centimeters into inches.
7. To practice using the graph and/or conversion formula they constructed, tell the students the lengths of several objects in inches and invite them to convert the measures to centimeters.

Discussion

1. What patterns do you see in the graph? [forms a straight line, goes up as it goes to the right]
2. How could you use your graph to determine how many centimeters long something is if it were measured in inches? [complete and extend line, then extrapolate or interpolate]
3. What do the patterns tell you about how centimeters compare to inches? [consistent relationship, more than twice as many centimeters as inches]
4. How can you determine how many centimeters make an inch? [divide centimeter by inches]
5. From your data, about how many centimeters are there in an inch? [should average close to 2.56 cm/in]
6. How could use the average number of centimeters in an inch to change an inch measurement into a centimeter measurement? [multiply inches by 2.56]
7. Write a mathematical sentence for your conversion method. [cm = 2.56 x in]
8. How does the average amount of centimeters per inch show up on the graph? [For each inch to the right, you go up 2.56 cm on the graph.]

Extension

Make other types of measurements to determine conversion graphs and rates. (meters/feet, grams/ounces, milliliters/fluid ounces) Kilometer to mile data is included on a student page for this extension.

Measuring Lines

How do centimeters compare to inches?

Object	Inches	Centimeters

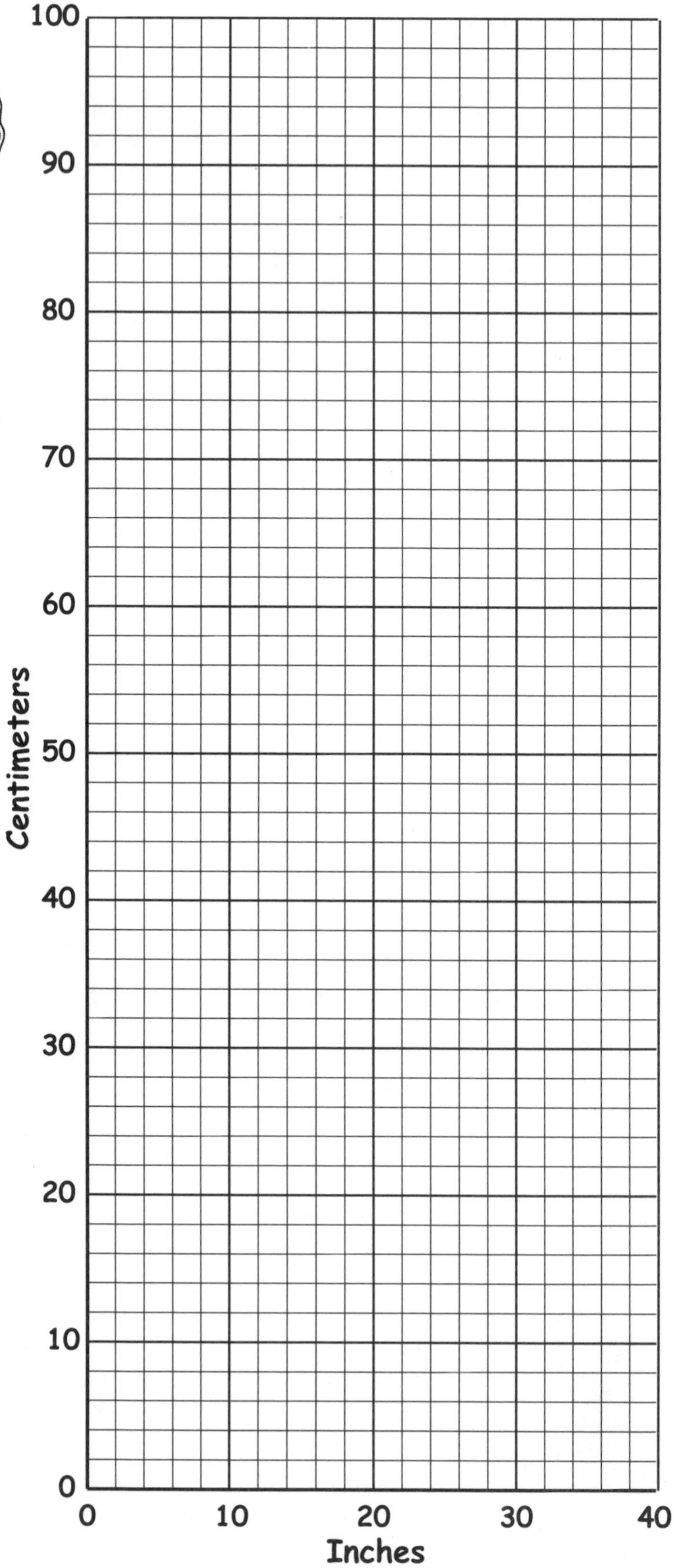

Centimeters (vertical axis: 0, 10, 20, 30, 40, 50, 60, 70, 80, 90, 100)

Inches (horizontal axis: 0, 10, 20, 30, 40)

Measuring Lines

TEN LONGEST ROAD AND RAILROAD TUNNELS IN THE UNITED STATES*
(Excluding subways)

	Tunnel/location	Length km	miles
1	Cascade, Washington	12.54	7.79
2	Flathead, Montana	12.48	7.78
3	Moffat, Colorado	10.00	6.21
4	Hoosac, Massachusetts	7.56	4.70
5	BART Trans-Bay Tubes		
	San Francisco, California	5.79	3.60
6	Brooklyn-Fattery, New York	2.78	1.73
7	E. Johnson Memorial, Colorado	2.74	1.70
8	Eisenhower Memorial, Colorado	2.72	1.69
9	Holland Tunnel, New York	2.61	1.62
10	Lincoln Tunnel I, New York	2.51	1.56

* The Top 10 of Everything Russell Ash. ©1994

Kilometers — 0 1 2 3 4 5 6 7 8 9 10 11 12 13

Miles — 0 1 2 3 4 5 6 7 8

Part Two:
Discovering Linear Functions In Science

Science phenomena in which linear functions are embedded exist in abundance. *Part Two* contains a small selection of activities that range over a broad spectrum. This variety will make students aware of the broad range of situations where linear functions can be found in the real world. Because students will be dealing with real-world situations, they must be careful in their counting and measuring to obtain the best possible results. All of the activities in this section deal with proportional relationships.

In *BBs in a Boat* students translate a simple weighted-straw system into the language of algebra. In the process they complete a data table, draw a graph, and write an algebraic expression. The manipulatives used in this activity give students a concrete tool and a representational tool useful for thinking about the floating straw. The manipulatives are designed to help students *translate* the physical system into the language of algebra.

Bounce Back! has students drop a ball from a known height and then observe and measure the height of successive bounces. The successive heights reached by a bouncing ball can be described by a linear relationship of the form $f(x) = mx + b$. The input variable is the height from which the ball is dropped and the output variable is the height of the resulting bounce. Students learn that the gravitational potential energy possessed by the ball because of its height relative to a reference level is converted in kinetic energy as it falls.

In *The Shadow Knows* students measure shadow lengths cast by objects of various heights to establish the understanding that the length of a shadow and the height of the object have the same proportion for all objects at a given time. The scatter graph (due to measurement errors) will contain points that lie close to a straight line which, if extended, passes through the origin.

In *Reflections Take a Turn* students study the relationship between the angle through which the reflection of a fixed beam of light is rotated and the angle through which the mirror is rotated. The independent, or input, variable is the angle of rotation of a vertical plane mirror and the dependent, or output, variable is the angle through which the reflected beam of light is rotated. This relationship is proportional so the equation has the form $y = mx$ since $b = 0$. The slope is the ratio of beam rotation to mirror rotation.

A Line on Pendulums is a study of the behavior of a simple pendulum. Frequency is measured as a function of time. Students learn that the *period* of a simple pendulum is the time it takes the mass to swing through one back-and-forth cycle and that the period remains constant for a given length of pendulum regardless of the amplitude of the swing. The frequency turns out to be proportional to time and the result is expressed by the equation $y = mx$.

Cubeprints has students use the language of algebra to describe the relationship between the number of identical blocks in a stack and the pressure the stack exerts at its base. The input variable is the number of cubes in the stack and the output variable is the pressure at the bottom of the stack.

In *Hooked on Algebra* students study the elasticity of a rubber band. Elasticity is the ability of a material to spring back to its original shape and size after it has been stretched. Students construct an apparatus for measuring how far a rubber band stretches as additional weights are suspended from it and measure the increase in length as a function of added weight. They discover that the relationship is proportional within the limit of elasticity.

The y-intercept takes a surprising and interesting form in *Up Periscope!* Linear functions are found in the most unusual real-world situations as this activity confirms. In this simple periscope, the path of the light and the distance it travels are modeled by a linear function.

Topic
Algebra—Linear Functions

Key Question
How can the language of algebra be used to describe the depth to which a weighted plastic straw sinks when placed in water?

Learning Goals
Students will:
- translate a simple weighted-straw system into the language of algebra; and
- complete a table, draw a graph, and write an algebraic expression.

Guiding Documents
Project 2061 Benchmark
- *Symbolic equations can be used to summarize how the quantity of something changes over time or in response to other changes.*

NRC Standard
- *Mathematics is important in all aspects of scientific inquiry.*

NCTM Standards 2000*
- *Represent, analyze, and generalize a variety of patterns with tables, graphs, words, and, when possible, symbolic rules*
- *Investigate how a change in one variable relates to a change in another variable*
- *Use symbolic algebra to represent situations and to solve problems, especially those that involve linear relationships*
- *Explore relationships between symbolic expressions and graphs of lines, paying particular attention to the meaning of intercept and slope*

Math
Algebra
    function
    linear equations
    domain
Variable
    formula for the volume of a cylinder

Science
Force
    equilibrium

Integrated Processes
Observing
Collecting and recording data
Graphing data
Interpreting data

Materials
Plastic drinking straws, $\frac{1}{4}$" diameter
Plastic clay
Scissors
BBs
12-ounce water cups
Permanent marking pen with a sharp tip
Magnet
Metric rulers

Background Information
A plastic drinking straw is weighted with enough BBs (usually three BBs) to make the straw float vertically when placed in water. The straw is then marked off in equal units. The end of the straw is then shortened with a pair of scissors until the straw floats vertically at a unit mark. This unit mark is the zero point marking the water level.

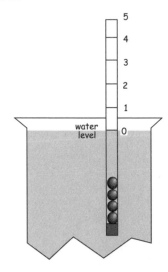

Since the straw is vertically at rest, the straw is in vertical equilibrium. According to Archimedes' Principle, the weight of the straw is equal to the weight of the volume of water displaced by the straw.

For a 0.25 inch diameter straw, the volume of a 1-cm long cylindrical section is

$$V = 0.3166 \text{ cm}^2 \times 1 \text{ cm}$$
$$V = 0.3166 \text{ cm}^3$$

The weight of this volume of water is 0.3166 gf. The weight of one BB is approximately 0.34 gf. To find the length of the cylinder of water equal to 0.34 gf, solve this proportion.

$$\frac{0.3166 \text{ gf}}{1 \text{ cm}} = \frac{0.34 \text{ gf}}{X \text{ cm}}$$

The unit marks are therefore 0.34/0.3166 or 1.07 cm apart.

Each BB added to the straw adds another cylinder-shaped volume of water to the total volume of displaced water. Add one BB to the straw and it floats at the next unit mark.

The relationship between the number of BBs added to the straw and the depth to which the straw sinks is expressed algebraically by the equation Y = X. X represents the number of BBs and Y represents the depth of the floating straw. This equation is a member of the *Division Family* of linear algebraic equations.

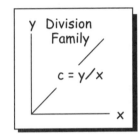

The manipulatives used in the activity give students a concrete tool and a representational tool useful for thinking about the floating straw. The manipulatives are designed to help students *translate* the physical system into the language of algebra.

Management

1. Construct both the *BBs in a Paper Boat* and the hands-on, *BBs in a Straw Boat* model. Decide whether to present one or both models to students. One strategy would be to present the math model during one class session and the hands-on model at a following session. Another strategy would be to present the *BBs in a Paper Boat* model to all students and then assign the hands-on model to those students that need additional assistance.
2. To speed up student construction, you may choose to precut the slits with a razor knife and precut the X-Y Strips. You may also choose to cut out the *Boat Strips* prior to teaching the lesson.
3. Plastic modeling clay will not dissolve in water. Do not attempt to use an oil-based clay as it will dissolve in water.
4. Keep the BBs under control with a magnet.
5. Keep a supply of paper towels handy for wiping up any spills.
6. The *Discussion* section applies to both models.

Procedure

Constructing the BBs in a Paper Boat Model
1. Distribute one *BBs in a Paper Boat* page to each student.

2. Demonstrate for the students how to fold and crease the page along the lightly shaded line and how to use the tips of a pair of scissors to cut slits A, B, C, and D.

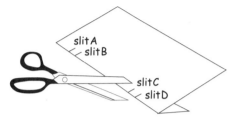

3. Instruct the students to fold and crease their pages and to carefully cut these slits in their pages.
4. Distribute a *Boat Strip* to each student.
5. Demonstrate for students how to insert the X end of the *Boat Strip* down into slit A and up through slit B, down through slit C, and up through slit D.

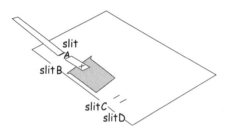

6. Instruct the students to insert the *Boat Strip* into and through the slits in the page.
7. Tell the students to adjust the strip so that the 0 symbol on the right side of the straw boat is positioned at the water level (Y) on the water container.
8. Instruct them to observe and record the position of X and Y (on the strip) in the X-Y table.
9. Have them pull the strip down until the X symbol is positioned at *1* on the scale and to observe and record the positions of X and Y in the table.
10. Instruct them to complete the table.
11. Have them graph the X-Y pairs.
12. Ask them to write the rule that expresses the relationship between X and Y.

Constructing the BBs in a Straw Boat Model
1. Distribute a *BBs in a Straw Boat* page to each student.
2. Instruct students to measure and cut a 13-cm length of plastic drinking straw.
3. Tell the students to roll a pinch of plastic clay into a ball and insert one end of the plastic straw into the ball of clay. Tell them to use their fingers to trim the excess clay from the end of the straw. Inform the students that this method creates a watertight plug in the end of the straw and maintains the cylindrical shape of the straw.

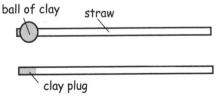

4. Instruct the students to place the clay end of the straw on the left side of the guide and, using a permanent marking pen, to mark the straw according to the scale printed on the guide.
5. Distribute 10 BBs to each student. (Placing the BBs on a magnet helps control the BBs.)
6. Distribute a plastic or paper cup of water to each student.
7. Instruct the students to add three BBs to the straw and to then float the straw in the cup of water. Tell them to note the first mark below the water line.

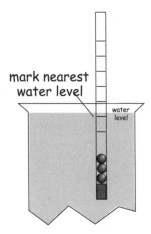

mark nearest water level

water level

8. Using scissors, tell the students to cut short, millimeter-length pieces off the end of the straw until the straw floats vertically at the mark. This mark is taken as the *zero* mark.

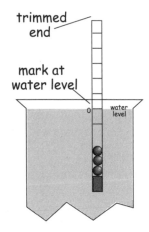

trimmed end

mark at water level

water level

9. Instruct the students to add a single BB to the straw and note the mark at which the straw floats. Tell them to record this data in the table.
10. Tell the students to continue to add BBs to complete as much of the table they can *without sinking the straw.*
11. Have the students graph the data in the table and then write the algebraic rule that describes the floating straw.

Discussion

1. Why were you unable to collect data for one or more values for *X* in the table? [The straw would sink if the fifth or sixth BB were added to the boat.]

2. Someone looks at your table and asks, "What is X?" What's your reply? [the number of BBs added to the straw]
3. Someone looks at your table and asks, "What is Y?" What's your reply? [the depth at which the straw floats]
4. Which is the *independent variable?* [X]
5. Which is the *dependent variable?* [Y]
6. What number in your table represents the unloaded straw? [0]
7. What true statement can you make about each of the coordinate pairs, (X, Y), on your graph? [The X coordinate equals the Y coordinate.]
8. Over what domain does your table, graph, and rule accurately describe the straw boat?
9. What would you do to extend the domain? [build a bigger boat]
10. If the weight of each BB doubled, how would the rule change?
11. If the weight of each BB were halved, how would the rule change?
12. What does the level at which the straw floats *depend upon?* [the number of BBs added to the straw]
13. Real boats float and sink. What information related to this activity would you believe important for naval engineers and ship captains to know?

Solutions
7.

X	0	1	2	3	4	5	6
y	0	1	2	3	4	5	6

8.

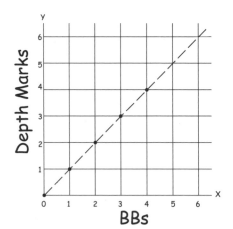

9.

$$Y = X$$

BBs in a Paper Boat

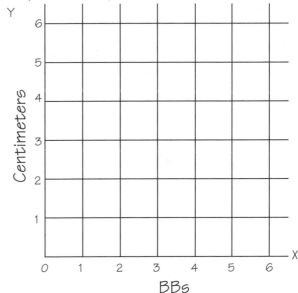

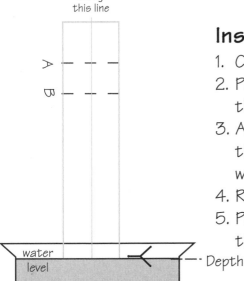

fold
along
this line

A

B

water
level

Depth

water
container

C

D

0
1
2
3
4
5

BBs

fold along
this line

Instructions:

1. Cut slits A, B, C, and D.
2. Push the X end of the Boat Strip, down through slit A, up through slit B, down through slit C, and up through slit D.
3. Adjust the strip so that the O symbol on the right side of the straw boat is positioned at the water level (Y) on the water container.
4. Record the position of X and Y in the X-Y table.
5. Pull the strip down until the X symbol is positioned at 1 on the scale. Record the positions of X and Y in the table.

6. Complete the table.

X	0	1	2	3	4	5	6
Y							

7. Graph the X-Y pairs.

Y

Centimeters

6
5
4
3
2
1

0   1   2   3   4   5   6   X

BBs

8. Write the rule.

Boat Strips

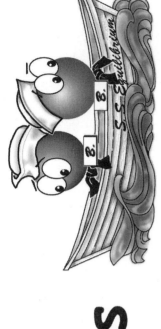

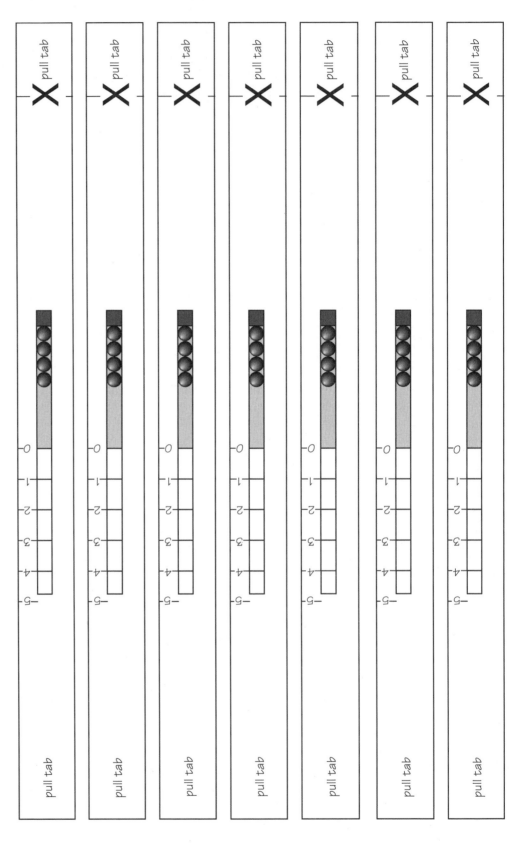

BBs in a Straw Boat

1. Measure and cut a 13-cm length of plastic drinking straw. Use the marking guide in step 3.
2. Roll a pinch of plastic clay into a ball. Insert one end of the plastic straw into the ball of clay. Use your fingers to trim the excess clay from the end of the straw. The clay should form a water-tight plug in the end of the straw. The cylinder shape of the straw must be maintained.

ball of clay   straw

clay plug

3. Place the clay end of the straw on the left side of the guide shown below, and using a permanent marking pen, mark the straw according to the scale printed on the guide.

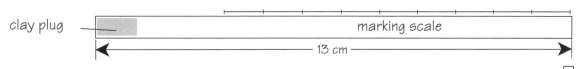

clay plug   marking scale

◄──────── 13 cm ────────►

4. Add three BBs to the straw and float the straw in a cup of water. Note the first mark below the water level.
5. Using scissors, cut short, mm-length pieces off the end of the straw until the straw floats vertically at the mark. This mark is taken as the zero mark.
6. Add one BB to the straw and note the level at which the straw now floats. Make a record of this in the appropriate column in the table below.

mark nearest water level

water level

trimmed end

mark at water level

water level

7. Complete the table.

X	0	1	2	3	4	5	6
Y							

8. Graph the X-Y pairs.

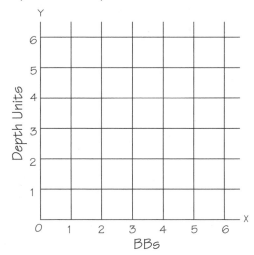

Depth Units

BBs

9. Write the rule.

Topic
Algebra—Linear Functions

Key Question
How can the language of algebra be used to describe how the bounce of a ball is related to the height from which the ball is dropped?

Learning Goals
Students will:
- collect and graph discrete data,
- discover the relationships of linear functions to a real-world situation, and
- write a linear function rule for the data.

Guiding Documents
Project 2061 Benchmarks
- *Mathematical ideas can be represented concretely, graphically, and symbolically.*
- *Tables and graphs can show how values of one quantity are related to values of another.*
- *Organize information in simple tables and graphs and identify relationships they reveal.*

NCTM Standards 2000*
- *Represent, analyze, and generalize a variety of patterns with tables, graphs, words, and, when possible, symbolic rules*
- *Investigate how a change in one variable relates to a change in another variable*
- *Use symbolic algebra to represent situations and to solve problems, especially those that involve linear relationships*
- *Explore relationships between symbolic expressions and graphs of lines, paying particular attention to the meaning of intercept and slope*

Math
Algebra
  linear equation of the form y = mx + b
    domain
    range
Measurement
  length

Science
Physical science
  gravity
    gravitational potential energy
    kinetic energy
    coefficient of restitution

Integrated Processes
Observing
Collecting and recording data
Inferring
Predicting
Comparing and contrasting
Generalizing

Materials
For each group:
  one meter stick
  ball that bounces (tennis, table tennis, golf, superball)
  calculator

Background Information
Mathematics

The successive heights reached by a bouncing ball can be described by a linear relationship of the form y = mx + b. The independent (Input) variable is the height from which the ball is dropped, and the dependent (Output) variable is the bounce height.

For any given ball and surface, the ratio of Bounce Height to Drop Height is constant. With the Drop Height as the independent variable and the Bounce Height as the dependent variable, the slope *is* the ratio of Bounce Height to Drop Height.

The relationship between Drop Height and Bounce Height is proportional. The equation that represents the relationship has the form y = mx since b = 0. Again the slope *m* is the ratio of Bounce Height to Drop Height.

Science

Gravitational potential energy is the energy an object possesses because of its height relative to a reference level. The greater the height, the greater the potential energy. A ball held above a fixed horizontal surface possesses gravitational potential energy. When dropped, the gravitational potential energy (GPE) is converted to *kinetic energy* which is the energy an object possesses due to its motion. The faster an object is moving, the greater its kinetic energy (KE). At the moment the ball strikes the surface, its GPE is at a minimum and its KE is at a maximum. For the ball to bounce back to its original height after colliding with the surface, its KE would have to be exactly equal to its original GPE. But energy has been lost to air resistance and the deformation to the ball that occurred at impact. The ball will therefore bounce back to some fraction of its original height.

In physics, a quantity called the *coefficient of restitution, e*, is defined by the formula

$$\sqrt{\dfrac{h_2}{h_1}}$$

where h_1 is the drop height and h_2 is the bounce height.

In this activity students find the square of the coefficient of restitution.

Management

1. This activity is designed to be done in groups of three or four. One can hold the meter stick, one can drop the ball, one can observe the bounce, and one can record the height of the bounce.
2. To observe the height of the bounce more accurately, the students should hold a piece of paper or cardstock at eye level in front of the meter sticks. When the ball bounces, move the paper to the highest point the *bottom* of the ball reaches. By sighting over the paper, the students can more easily read the measurement on the meter stick. The observers must be at eye level with the ball at its highest point of bounce. This means the observers might have to get on their hands and knees to make the observations.
3. It is advisable to have all students use a hard tile or cement floor as their bouncing surface.
4. It is best to start measurements at a height of 100 cm and work down to the 20 cm height. The lower drop heights are more difficult to observe and measure.

Procedure

1. Distribute the *Bounce Back! Data Table* page.
2. Instruct one student in each group to stand the meter stick vertically with the zero end on the floor.
3. Tell the student in each group that will drop the ball to place the bottom of ball at the 100 cm mark of the meter stick.
4. Instruct the remaining students to observe and record the bounce height in cm (distance from the floor to the highest point the bottom of the ball reaches at the peak of its bounce).
5. Tell the groups to repeat twice more for a total of three trials.
6. Have the groups repeat this procedure for each of the remaining four dropping heights.
7. Distribute a calculator to each group. Instruct the groups to sum and average the three trials for each drop height.
8. Tell the groups to divide the average bounce height by the drop height and record the result for each drop height.

9. Distribute the *Bounce Back! Graph* page. Instruct the students to graph the average bounce height for each of the five dropping distances.
10. Distribute the *Bounce Back! Questions* page. Instruct the students to answer the questions.

Discussion

1. Did the ball bounce as high or higher than the point from which it was dropped? [No. A ball will never bounce back to its original drop height.]
2. What are some reasons that might explain why a ball cannot bounce back to its drop height? [A small but non-zero energy loss due to air resistance, the energy absorbed by the collision of the ball with the floor, and the energy lost to deforming ball when it collides with the floor. If a ball actually bounced higher than its drop, it would eventually bounce into outer space.]
3. Compare the graphs and equations for different ball types. (Different ball types will have different Bounce Height to Drop Height ratios, i. e., different slopes.)
4. What is the independent (Input) variable? [Drop Height] What is the dependent (Output) variable? [Bounce Height]
5. Describe the relationship between the independent and dependent variables. [The Bounce Height is some fraction of the Drop Height.]
6. Is the relationship between the independent and dependent variables proportional? Explain. [The graph does pass through the origin (0,0). The Bounce Height is zero cm if the Drop Height is zero cm.]
7. What is the slope? [The Bounce Height ÷ Drop Height numbers show what portion of the drop height the ball is able to bounce up to.]
8. For any one ball, would you expect each of these numbers to be about the same or different? [For the same ball and surface, the ball should bounce a fixed proportion of the drop height.]
9. If the ratio of bounce height to drop height is 0.5, use a formula to compute the bounce height if the ball is dropped from a height of 10 feet. [5 feet] What is the bounce height for this same ball on the third bounce? [$1\frac{1}{4}$ feet]
10. Explain why the graph for each ball type falls below the $y=x$ line. [The y=x line represents the graph for a perfect bouncing ball, i.e., a ball that always bounces back to its original drop height.]

Extensions

1. Repeat the activity with a different balls.
2. Inflate a basketball with different amounts of air pressure. Find the relationship of air pressure to bounce height.

---

* Reprinted with permission from *Principles and Standards for School Mathematics,* 2000 by the National Council of Teachers of Mathematics. All rights reserved.

Data Table

Select a ball and surface to which it will be dropped. At each of the listed Drop Heights, observe, measure, and record the Bounce Height for each of three trials.

Find the average Bounce Height for each of the Drop Heights.

For each Drop Height, divide the average Bounce Heights by the drop heights.

Bounce Back Data Table					
Type of ball: _____ Type of surface: _____					
Drop Height cm	20	40	60	80	100
Bounce Height cm — Trial 1					
Trial 2					
Trial 3					
Sum					
Average					
Bounce Height ÷ Drop Height					

BOUNCE BACK!

Graph

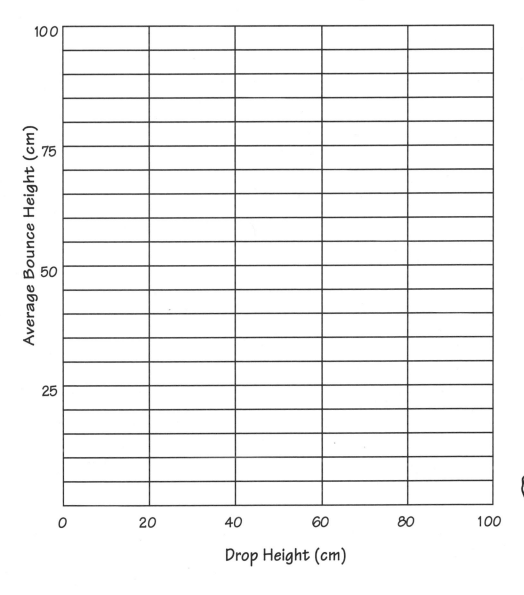

Average Bounce Height (cm)

100

75

50

25

0   20   40   60   80   100

Drop Height (cm)

Write the equation for your graph.

BOUNCE BACK!

Questions!

1. Identify and justify your answer:

   a. Independent variable (Input):

   b. Dependent variable (Output):

2. Describe the relationship between the dependent and independent variable.

3. Is the relationship between the dependent and independent variables proportional? Please explain.

4. What is the slope? Please explain.

5. Use your equation to compute the Bounce Height for the third bounce when the Drop Height equals 60 cm.

Shadow Lines

Topic
Algebra—Linear Functions

Key Question
How can you determine the height of an object from its shadow?

Learning Goal
Students will measure shadow lengths cast by objects of various heights to establish the functional relationship between the length of a shadow and the height of the object at any given time.

Guiding Documents
Project 2061 Benchmarks
- *Organize information in simple tables and graphs and identify relationships they reveal.*
- *The graphic display of numbers may help to show patterns such as trends, varying rates of change, gaps, or clusters. Such patterns sometimes can be used to make predictions about the phenomena being graphed.*

NRC Standards
- *Most objects in the solar system are in regular and predictable motion. Those motions explain such phenomena as the day, the year, phases of the moon, and eclipses.*
- *Use appropriate tools and techniques to gather, analyze, and interpret data.*
- *Mathematics is important in all aspects of scientific inquiry.*

NCTM Standards 2000*
- *Understand and use ratios and proportions to represent quantitative relationships*
- *Relate and compare different forms of representation for a relationship*
- *Use symbolic algebra to represent situations and to solve problems especially those that involve linear relationships*
- *Model and solve contextualized problems using various representations, such as graphs, tables, and equations*

Math
Algebra
    linear functions
Proportional reasoning

Measuring
    length

Science
Earth science
    terrestrial motions
        light and shadows

Integrated Processes
Observing
Collecting and recording data
Interpreting data
Drawing conclusions
Applying
Generalizing

Materials
Tape measures

Background Information
At any given time of the day, all the ratios of the heights of objects to the lengths of their shadows will be the same. This happens because sunlight travels in nearly parallel lines. For every object, the ground, the rays of light, and the line perpendicular to the ground through the highest point of that object form a triangle. These triangles are similar for all objects because all their corresponding sides are parallel.

The proportional aspect of these similar triangles makes it possible to determine the height of a tall object. A smaller object and its shadow are used to determine the proportion of object height to shadow length. This ratio is then applied to the tall object's shadow to determine its height.

All proportions are linear in nature. One variable changes proportionally to the other variable. Graphically proportions will form straight lines with slopes equal to the proportional relationships. Lines formed by proportions always pass through the origin of the graph. The symbolic representation of a proportion simply has the ratio of the proportion as the coefficient of the independent variable.

At any single point in time, the height of an object can be determined from the length of the shadow cast by the object. The height of an object is a function of its shadow's length. By multiplying the shadow's length by the ratio of proportion, the coefficient of the independent variable, or the slope of the line formed by the data, gives the object's height

Management

1. This activity must be done on a sunny day on a level surface which has unobstructed sunlight during the activity period. The area should be in the proximity of a tall object such as a flagpole, light pole, telephone pole, etc., which will cast a shadow onto level ground.

2. Prior to the activity, the teacher will need to identify objects in the activity area which will cast a shadow onto a level surface and the heights of which are easily measured. Such objects might include basketball goals, fence posts, benches, garbage cans, etc. If there are not enough objects in the area, the teacher may need to have students bring out objects such as waste paper baskets, chairs, boxes, cans, etc. There needs to be one object for each group.

3. Form eight or nine small groups to collect the data. The rest of the activity is done as a class with the groups sharing their data.

4. It is critical that measurement be taken accurately. Have students place a finger on top of the object and wiggle their finger until they can identify the spot by observing the shadow. Make sure students measure the height vertically to the ground from the identified point. The shadow length is measured from this point directly below the point from which the longest shadow is cast.

Procedure

1. As a class discuss the *Key Question* along with questions such as:
   - How do shadows change during the day?
   - How do shadows change with the seasons?
   - How are shadows of different objects different from each other? How are shadows of different objects similar to each other?

2. Separate the class into groups and provide them with tape measures.

3. Take the students to the selected area.

4. Have each group find an object to measure, verifying that its height and shadow length can be measured. Have the students measure and record the height of the object. A ninth group can be assigned to measure the shadow of the tall object in the area. If a ninth group is not available, the teacher will need to measure the length of this shadow.

5. At a given signal from the teacher, one student from each group should place a finger at the end of the object's shadow and keep it there until the other members measure this point's distance from the position directly under the place where the height of the object was measured.

6. Return to the classroom and have each group share the height and shadow length of their object.

7. Have students make a scatter plot of the data. An appropriate scale will need to be determined for the graph.

8. Have students discuss what pattern they see in the graph and what the pattern represents.

9. Ask students to explain where they think the tall object would be located on the graph. Ask them how they could use the graph and the shadow's length to determine the height of the tall object.

10. Have students compare the height to the shadow by completing the ratio column on the chart. The students should notice that this ratio is very similar for each of the objects.

11. Have the students state in their own words what this ratio is telling them about the height of the object and its shadow.

12. Ask how this ratio describes the line in the graph. [Every time the line goes over one space to the right, it goes up the number of spaces of the ratio. The slope of the line is the ratio.]

13. Ask students how they would use the ratio to predict the height of an object that casts a 65 cm shadow. ... 100 cm shadow. ... the length of the tall object's shadow.

14. Have the students translate their method of determining the object's height into an equation.

15. Have students calculate the height of the tall object using its shadow's length. Using their equation and comparing it to the graph.

Discussion

1. What patterns do you see in the graph? [points form a straight line]

2. How could you use the graph to figure out the height of something if you knew its shadow length?

3. What pattern do you see in the ratios comparing the height to shadow length? [almost the same]

4. What does the average ratio tell you about the height of an object and its shadow length? [how many times greater the height is than the shadow length]

5. How does the average ratio show up on the graph? [Every time the line goes over one space to the right, it goes up the number of spaces of the ratio. The slope of the line is the ratio.]

6. Describe how you could you use the ratio to determine the height of an object if you knew the length of its shadow?

7. Write you method of determining the height of an object from the shadow as an equation. [height (y) = avg. ratio (m) x shadow length (x) ; $y = mx$]

8. Now that it is later and the sun is in a different position, how would you expect the ratio to change if you did this activity again?

9. If you were given a meter stick and a tape measure, how would you measure a very tall pole?

Extensions

1. Go out at different times of the day and see if there is any pattern to the ratios. [The largest height to shadow ratio will be at solar noon with the ratio decreasing in value more rapidly as you get farther away from noon.]

2. Give students a meter stick and tape measure and have them apply what they have learned by measuring the heights of different objects using shadows.

* Reprinted with permission from *Principles and Standards for School Mathematics*, 2000 by the National Council of Teachers of Mathematics. All rights reserved.

LOOKING AT LINES   65

Shadow Lines

Time of day _____

Measure the height of an object and its shadow. Find the average ratio for the data.

Shadow (cm)	Height (cm)	Ratio: $\dfrac{\text{Height}}{\text{Shadow}}$
	Average Ratio	

Tall Object

Shadow Lines

Make a scatter plot of the data.

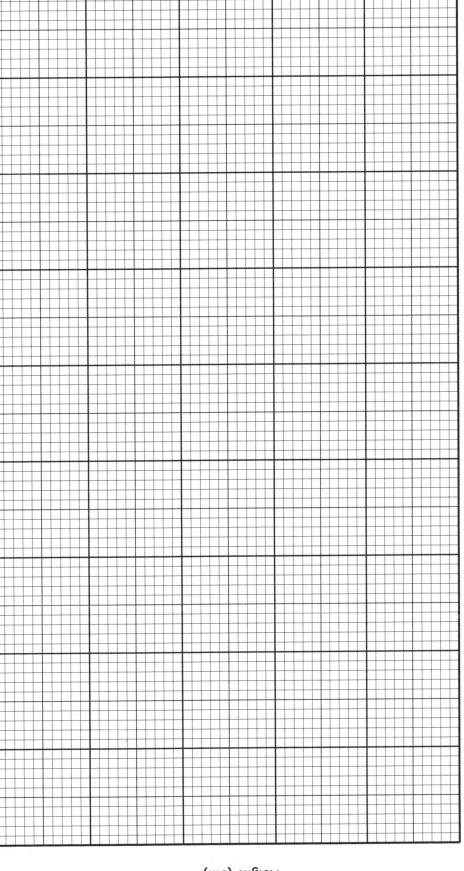

Height (cm)

Shadow Length (cm)

Reflection Takes a Turn

Topic
Algebra—Linear Functions

Key Question
How can the language of algebra be used to describe the relationship between the angle the reflection of a fixed beam of light is rotated through when the mirror is rotated.

Learning Goals
Students will:
- construct a simple device, using a single plane mirror, for measuring the rotation of a reflected beam of light;
- collect, record, and graph mirror rotation and beam rotation data;
- write a linear function rule for data; and
- discover the relationships of linear function to a real-world situation.

Guiding Documents
Project 2061 Benchmarks
- *Mathematical ideas can be represented concretely, graphically, and symbolically.*
- *Tables and graphs can show how values of one quantity are related to values of another.*
- *Organize information in simple tables and graphs and identify relationships they reveal.*

NCTM Standards 2000*
- *Represent, analyze, and generalize a variety of patterns with tables, graphs, words, and, when possible, symbolic rules*
- *Investigate how a change in one variable relates to a change in another variable*
- *Use symbolic algebra to represent situations and to solve problems, especially those that involve linear relationships*
- *Explore relationships between symbolic expressions and graphs of lines, paying particular attention to the meaning of intercept and slope*

Math
Algebra
    linear equation of the form $y = mx + b$
        domain
        range

Geometry
    line
    angle
Measurement
    angle

Science
Physical science
    plane reflection
        law of reflection

Integrated Processes
Observing
Collecting and recording data
Inferring
Predicting
Comparing and contrasting
Generalizing

Materials
For each group:
    one plane mirror

Background Information
Mathematics
    The reflection of a fixed beam of light off a rotating mirror can be described by a linear relationship of the form $y = mx + b$. The independent (Input) variable is the angle of rotation of a vertical plane mirror and the dependent (Output) variable is the angle through which the reflected beam of light is rotated.

    The relationship between mirror rotation and beam rotation is proportional. The equation that represents the relationship has the form $y = mx$ since $b = 0$. The slope is the ratio of beam rotation to mirror rotation.

Relationship Proof

A light beam is fixed to strike a plane mirror at an angle perpendicular (normal) to the mirror.

Prove: $\beta = 2\alpha$ (see diagram below)

Let α = the counterclockwise rotation of the mirror. Then, since vertical angles are equal, $\alpha = \alpha_1$.

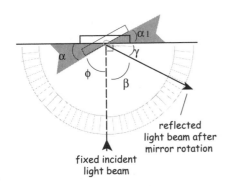

reflected
light beam after
mirror rotation

fixed incident
light beam

The new angle of incidence is symbolized by ϕ. The new angle of reflection equals $\alpha_1 + \gamma$. By the law of plane reflection, $\phi = \alpha_1 + \gamma$.

In the diagram, $\phi = 90° - \alpha$. Therefore, $90° - \alpha = \alpha_1 + \gamma$.

Since $\alpha = \alpha_1$, $90° - \gamma = 2\alpha$.

But $\beta = 90° - \gamma$ therefore $\beta = 2\alpha$ and β is the angle through which the beam has been rotated.

This proves that the beam rotates through twice the angle the mirror is rotated.

Science

The law of plane reflection states that the angle of incidence is equal to the angle of reflection. In the diagram, a beam of light strikes a plane mirror at an incident angle α and is reflected at a reflected angle ϕ. The incident and reflected angles are measured from a line perpendicular to the mirror. This line is called the *normal*. The angles, as measured from the mirror, are also equal.

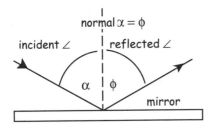

normal $\alpha = \phi$

incident $\angle$ reflected $\angle$

α ϕ

mirror

Management

1. This activity is designed to be done in groups of two.
2. To observe the beam rotation accurately, the student has to be careful in placing the mirror along the *mirror lines* that appear on the student page.
3. Taping the student page to the desk or table top helps eliminate alignment errors.

Procedure

1. Distribute the *Reflection Takes a Turn* page. Tell students to tape the corners of the page to the desk or table top.
2. Instruct students to stand the mirror vertically with the lower right edge near the small circle labeled *pivot*. The image of the circle should be approximately $\frac{1}{4}$ inch from the right edge of the mirror.
3. Tell the students to align the bottom edge of the mirror along the line labeled $x = 0°$. Tell them that the visual cue that informs them that they have properly aligned the mirror is that the image of the flashlight and its light beam is in a straight line with the flashlight and beam printed on the page.
4. Explain to the students that this position of the mirror (along the $x = 0°$ *line*) is the starting position of the mirror. Since the mirror has yet to be rotated from its starting point, the light beam has not been rotated. Tell the students to record 0° in the y row of the $x = 0°$ column of the data table.
5. Have the students hold the right side of the mirror on the pivot point and rotate the left side of the mirror until the bottom edge of the mirror aligns with the line labeled $x = 10°$, which represents a mirror rotation of 10°. Instruct them to observe, in the mirror, the reflection of the flashlight beam (see diagram below). This *mirror image* is directed back to the viewer's right along the same line a beam of light would actually be reflected. Tell them to read and record the angle (20°) through which the reflection of the fixed beam has been rotated.

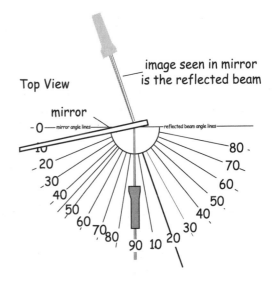

image seen in mirror
is the reflected beam

Top View

mirror

6. Instruct students to repeat this procedure for the mirror rotation angles listed in the independent variable (x) row of the table.
7. Distribute the *Reflection Takes a Turn Graph* page. Instruct the students to graph the data in the data table.
8. Distribute the *Reflection Takes a Turn Questions* page. Instruct the students to answer the questions.

Solutions

Table

x mirror rotation	0°	10°	20°	30°	40°	45°
y beam rotation	0°	20°	40°	60°	80°	90°

50°	60°	70°	80°	85°
100°	120°	140°	160°	170°

Graph

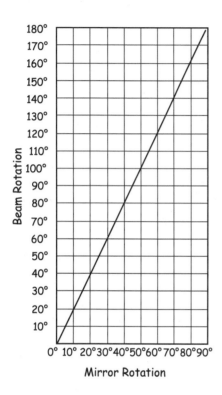

Mirror Rotation

Questions

1. What's the independent (Input) variable? [The angle through which the mirror is rotated. [It's what I *change*, or cause to happen in the investigation.] What's the dependent (Output) variable? [It's the change in direction (angle) of the reflected beam that I observe.]

2. The angle through which the reflected beam is rotated is related to the angle through which the mirror is rotated. The graph shows this relationship to be linear.

3. The graph passes through the origin (0,0) therefore the relationship is proportional.

4. The slope of the graph is the ratio of the angle through which the beam rotates to the angle through which the mirror rotates.

5. The slope shows that the beam rotates through twice the angle the mirror rotates. Therefore, $y = 2x$.

6. The relationship is continuous. The domain D is the angle rotation of the mirror. The mirror can be rotated through any angle, from 0° to 360°.

The resulting beam rotations range from 0° through <180°.

Extensions

1. Laser Pointer **Demonstration**.
   As a teacher demonstration only (laser pointers may cause eye damage if used incorrectly), show students how the light beam from a laser pointer reflects off a plane mirror according to the rule discovered as a result of doing this activity.
   Good results are obtained by setting the laser pointer on a quarter-inch thick book and slightly tilting the mirror towards the paper. A thin red line can be easily seen overlaying the reflected beam line printed on the page.

2. Assign the geometric proof to students. (See *Background Information—Mathematics*.)

3. Several popular computer screen savers continuously reflect a ball off the sides of the screen. The mathematics contained in the graphics program that computes the angle of reflection knowing the angle of incidence uses basic geometric principles.
   In the diagram, the angle of incidence of the ball with the top edge of the screen equals α. Through what angle must the heading (direction) of the ball turn in order to reflect the ball according to the law of plane reflection? Use the diagram. [turn angle = 2α]

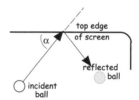

The diagram below shows how the answer to the question is derived.

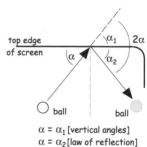

$\alpha = \alpha_1$ [vertical angles]
$\alpha = \alpha_2$ [law of reflection]

4. Use the Logo programming language to write a set of procedures that dynamically models plane reflection. Several free versions of Logo are available on the internet. Do a search with keyword "Logo."

Reflection Takes a Turn

Stand mirror vertically with the bottom right edge near the central dot. Rotate bottom edge of mirror, keeping mirror vertical, until bottom edge falls along one of the mirror lines. Look at the image of the flashlight beam in the mirror and determine the rotation angle of the light beam.

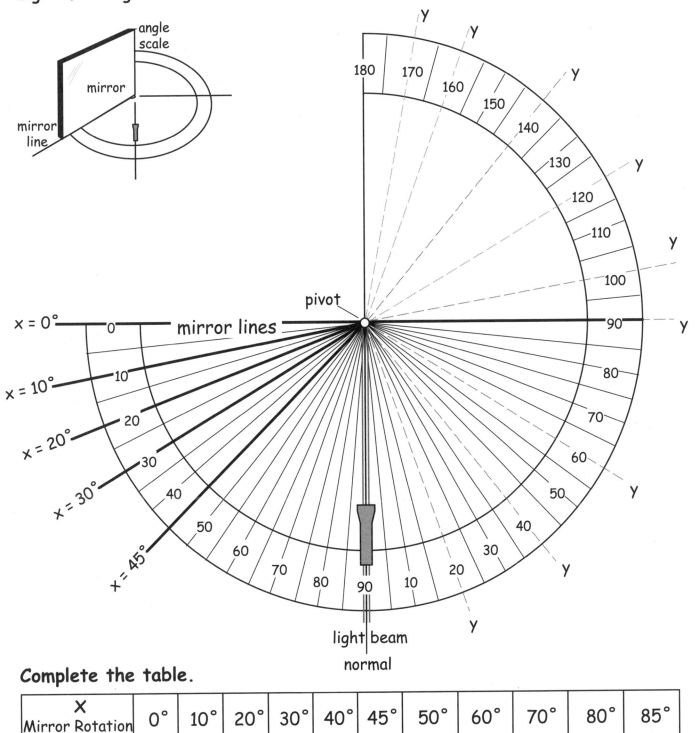

Complete the table.

X Mirror Rotation	0°	10°	20°	30°	40°	45°	50°	60°	70°	80°	85°
y Beam Rotation											

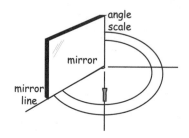

angle scale

mirror

mirror line

Reflection Takes a Turn
Graph

Complete the graph.

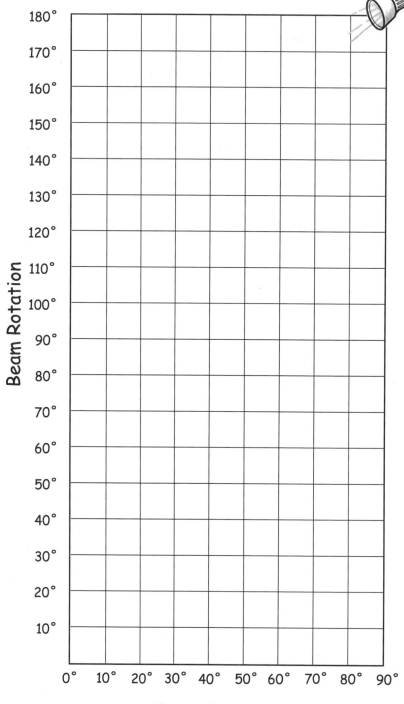

Beam Rotation

180°
170°
160°
150°
140°
130°
120°
110°
100°
90°
80°
70°
60°
50°
40°
30°
20°
10°

0° 10° 20° 30° 40° 50° 60° 70° 80° 90°

Mirror Rotation

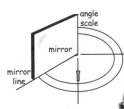

Reflection Takes a Turn

Questions

1. Identify and justify your answer:

   a. Independent variable (Input):

   b. Dependent variable (Output):

2. Describe the relationship between the dependent and independent variable.

3. Is the relationship between the dependent and independent variables proportional? Please explain.

4. What is the slope? Please explain.

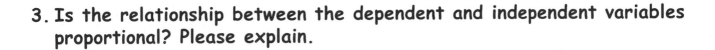

5. Write the equation for the relationship.

6. Is the relationship discrete or continuous?

   What is the domain?

   What is the range?

A Line on Pendulums

Topic
Algebra—Linear Functions

Key Question
What is the relationship between the number of cycles a pendulum makes and the elapsed time the pendulum swings?

Learning Goals
Students will:
- make a simple pendulum, and
- measure the pendulum's frequency as a function of time.

Guiding Documents
Project 2061 Benchmarks
- *Symbolic equations can be used to summarize how the quantity of something changes over time or in response to other changes.*
- *Mathematically ideas can be represented concretely, graphically, and symbolically.*
- *Tables and graphs can show how values of one quantity are related to values of another.*
- *Organize information in simple tables and graphs and identify relationships they reveal.*

NRC Standard
- *Mathematics is important in all aspects of scientific inquiry.*

NCTM Standards 2000*
- *Represent, analyze, and generalize a variety of patterns with tables, graphs, words, and, when possible, symbolic rules*
- *Investigate how a change in one variable relates to a change in another variable*
- *Use symbolic algebra to represent situations and to solve problems, especially those that involve linear relationships*
- *Explore relationships between symbolic expressions and graphs of lines, paying particular attention to the meaning of intercept and slope*

Math
Algebra
   relationship
   function
   domain, range
   linear equation

Science
Physical science
   periodic motion
     pendulum

Integrated Processes
Observing
Collecting and recording data
Inferring
Predicting
Comparing and contrasting
Generalizing

Materials
For each group:
   nylon fishing line, approximately 30 inches
   1 lead fishing line weight, 6–9 ounce
   1 binder clip
   watches or clocks with a second hand

Background Information
A Simple Pendulum

A simple pendulum consists of a mass, *m,* tied to the end of a light piece of line of length, *L,* that is fixed at its upper end. The *amplitude* of the motion is measured by the maximum angle of swing.

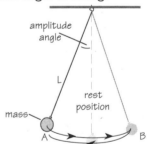

The *period* of a simple pendulum is the time it takes the mass to swing through one back-and-forth cycle. In the diagram, the period is the time it takes the mass to swing from point *A* to point *B* and back to point *A*. The symbol for the period of a simple pendulum is *T.* One divided by T is the frequency (cycles per time).

The period of a simple pendulum does not depend upon the mass. The period depends upon the *length* of the string. The longer the string, the longer the period; the shorter the string, the shorter the period. The period of a simple pendulum *is a function of its length.*

Set a simple pendulum swinging. Due to friction, the amplitude angle will decrease. But, and this is the essence of a simple pendulum, the *time* required to complete one back-and-forth cycle *remains constant.* As the pendulum swings, the amplitude decreases but so does the average velocity of the object. Therefore, the period remains constant. Galileo discovered the equal times property of a simple pendulum.

In this activity, students will count and record, at 30-second intervals, the number of cycles completed by a simple pendulum. The graph of the independent variable, time, versus the dependent variable, the number of cycles, will approximate a straight line.

Management
1. Make one simple pendulum for each group of three to four students.
2. To make a simple pendulum, tie one end of a 30-inch length of nylon fishing line to a lead fishing weight. Tie the other end to one of the handles on a binder clip.

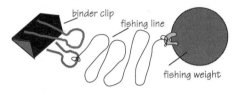

binder clip
fishing line
fishing weight

Procedure
1. Demonstrate to the students how to attach the binder clip to the pages in a book. The clip needs to be attached as shown so that the pendulum swings in a direction parallel to the edge of the table.

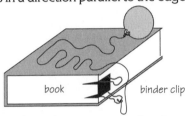

book   binder clip

2. Show students how to set the book near the edge of a desk or table. If necessary, stack one or more books on top of the first book to steady the pendulum.
3. Demonstrate to students how to stand to the side of the book, pull the weight straight back (not to either side), and release the weight to start the pendulum swinging.

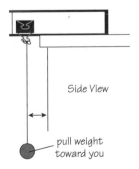

Side View

pull weight toward you

4. Distribute one simple pendulum to each group.
5. Instruct the students to set up and test the pendulum so that it swings parallel to the edge of the table.

6. Distribute the student pages and watches.
7. Tell the groups to select one student to monitor the watch or clock and report 30-second intervals, one student to count softly but clearly the number of cycles, and another student to record the number of cycles they hear the counter say at 30-second intervals.
8. Tell the students to draw the straight line on the graph that connects the origin with the number of cycles counted at 300 seconds.
9. Have them plot the remaining data points.

Discussion
1. Describe your graph. [straight line]
2. Use the number of cycles counted at 300 seconds to compute the slope (rise over run) of the line. (answers will vary)
3. What does the slope of the line tell you about the pendulum? [the number of cycles per second—the frequency]
4. How would you compute the period (T) of the pendulum? [$T = 1/f$ where f is the frequency]
5. What does the period tell you about the pendulum? [the time per one cycle]
6. What changes did you observe? [The number of cycles increased with time, the amplitude angle decreased, the weight seemed to move slower, etc.]
7. What can you conclude about the pendulum after doing this activity. [The frequency remained constant.]
8. Write the equation for the line. [$y=mx$]
9. Why does it make sense to draw the straight line through the data points? [The slope of the line that connects the origin with the y value at 300 seconds represents the *average* which is true for every point on the line.]
10. What is your hypothesis as to why the number of cycles, the frequency, remained constant? [As the amplitude angle decreased, so did the length of the arc traveled by the weight. But, as the amplitude angle decreased, so did the speed of the weight. These decreases must be such that the ratio of distance-to-velocity (time) remained constant. In other words, the weight could travel the shorter distance at a reduced speed in the same interval of time.]

Extension
Repeat this activity for longer and shorter lengths of fishing line.

A Line on Pendulums

Graph

Time (sec)	Cycles
0	
30	
60	
90	
120	
150	
180	
210	
240	
270	
300	

Write the equation.

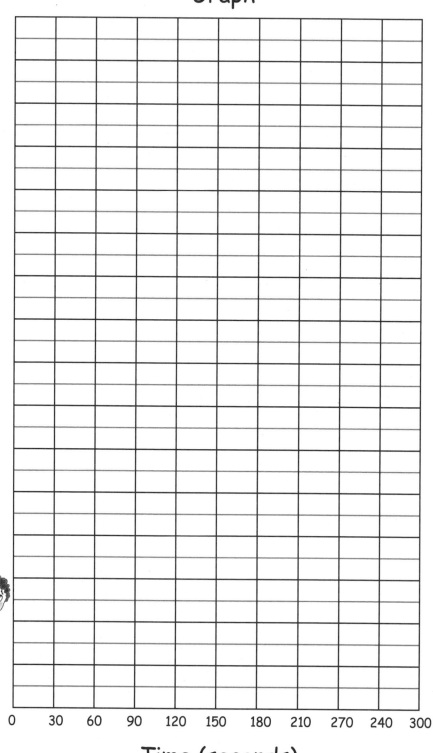

Cycles

0   30   60   90   120   150   180   210   270   240   300

Time (seconds)

CUBEPRINTS

Topic
Algebraic—Linear Functions

Key Question
How can the language of algebra be used to describe the relationship between the height of a stack of identical cubes and the pressure at the base of the stack?

Learning Goals
Students will:
- collect and record data,
- graph data, and
- use the language of algebra to write an equation that describes the relationship between the number of identical blocks in a stack and the pressure the stack exerts at the base of the stack.

Guiding Documents
Project 2061 Benchmarks
- *Mathematically ideas can be represented concretely, graphically, and symbolically.*
- *Tables and graphs can show how values of one quantity are related to values of another.*
- *Organize information in simple tables and graphs and identify relationships they reveal.*
- *Symbolic equations can be used to summarize how the quantity of something changes over time or in response to other changes.*

NRC Standard
- *Mathematics is important in all aspects of scientific inquiry.*

NCTM Standards 2000*
- *Represent, analyze, and generalize a variety of patterns with tables, graphs, words, and, when possible, symbolic rules*
- *Investigate how a change in one variable relates to a change in another variable*
- *Use symbolic algebra to represent situations and to solve problems, especially those that involve linear relationships*
- *Explore relationships between symbolic expressions and graphs of lines, paying particular attention to the meaning of intercept and slope*

Math
Algebra
  linear equation of the form y=mx + b, m = 1 and b = 0
Geometry
  area

Science
Physical science
  pressure
    force per unit area

Integrated Processes
Observing
Collecting and recording data
Graphing data
Interpreting data

Materials
For each group:
  six identical cubes of wood, plastic, or any other material

Background Information
Mathematics
  The pressure at the bottom of a stack of identical cubes can be described by a linear relationship of the form y = mx + b. The independent (Input) variable is the height of the stack of cubes and the dependent (Output) variable is the pressure (see *Science*) at the bottom of the stack.

  The relationship between the height of the stack of cubes and pressure is proportional. The equation that represents the relationship has the form y = mx since b = 0. The slope *m* is the ratio of pressure to the height of the stack of cubes.

  The relationship would not be proportional if a square-shaped rod of height *b* (with a unit-area footprint) were the base on which additional cubes were stacked.

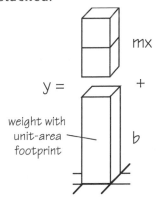

Science
  Pressure is defined as the force acting on a unit of area.

$$pressure = \frac{force}{area}$$

Place a unit cube on a flat surface. The bottom face of the cube comes into contact with one square unit of area of the surface.

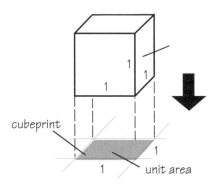

Gravity pulls on the cube with a force equal to the weight of the cube. This force is evenly distributed over the area of contact (the footprint) between the cube and the surface. A unit cube with one unit of weight exerts one unit of pressure on one unit of area.

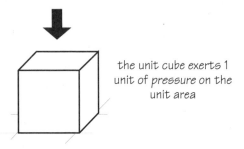

the unit cube exerts 1 unit of *pressure* on the unit area

A stack of blocks can also be used to define pressure in a fluid, like water. Start with a tall stack of blocks. The pressure on the top face of the top block is zero since there's no force (neglecting air pressure) acting on the top face. Slip a piece of paper below the top-most block. There's one unit of pressure at this level in the stack. Slip the paper under the second block from the top. Now there's two units of pressure, two blocks deep.

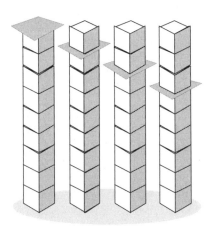

Continue this process down the stack of blocks until you reach the bottom face of the lowest block in the stack.

Management
1. Organize students into groups of two or three.
2. Any math manipulative that can be stacked (like identical pattern blocks) can be substituted for the cubes. Assign the pattern block a weight of one unit and the area of a face one unit of area.

Procedure
1. Distribute the *Data Table and Graph* page and six cubes to each student or pair of students.
2. Tell the students to place one cube on the figure where indicated. Instruct them to compute the pressure the cube exerts on the figure's chest and record its value in the table.
3. Tell them to repeat the process, adding one cube at a time, for the remaining cubes.
4. Instruct the students to graph the data in the table.
5. Distribute the *Cubeprints Questions* page for the students to complete.

Discussion
1. Someone looks at your data table and asks, "What is X?" What's your reply? [the height of the stack of cubes]
2. Someone looks at your data table and asks, "What is Y?" What's your reply? [the pressure at the bottom of the stack]
3. Identify the independent (Input) variable. [height of stack] Identify the dependent (Output) variable. [pressure]
4. The block-stacking process can be likened to the construction of a skyscraper. Beginning with a strong foundation, story upon story is added until the building is completed. Why is a strong foundation important? [The need for a strong foundation arises from the pressure the total weight of the building exerts on the foundation.]

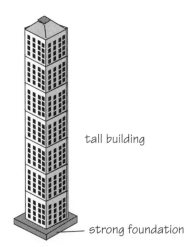

tall building

strong foundation

5. Why does it hurt when someone steps on your toe? [The relationship between force and area explains why it hurts when someone stands on your big toe.

Their weight (a large force) is distributed over a small area (your big toe) and the pressure could be high enough to break one or more bones in your toe!]

6. Describe the sensations you experience when swimming to the bottom of a swimming pool. How do they apply to this lesson? [The deeper you dive, the taller the stack of water above you. Therefore, the greater the pressure you feel, particularly on your ear drums.]

7. Imagine lying flat on the floor and having cubes of concrete stacked on your chest. Describe the sensations you would experience.

8. Why wouldn't you want an elephant to step on your foot?

9. Look around you, what examples of "pressure" can you find? [Any object setting on any surface is exerting a pressure on that surface equal to the weight of the object (found with a bathroom scale) and the area of contact between the object and the surface.]

Extensions

1. Determine the mass of ten wooden cubes (or ten identical pattern blocks) and find the average mass per cube. Round this value to the nearest gram. The *weight* (force) on a one gram mass, where g (the acceleration due to gravity) has the standard value of 9.8 m/s^2 is called one gram-force (1 gf) Compute the area of one face of the cube. With this information, repeat the activity. For example, to the nearest gram, a 2-cm cube weighs five grams. The area of one face of the cube is 4 square centimeters. The cube exerts a pressure of 5 gf/4 cm^2 which equals a pressure of 1.25 gf/cm^2.

This is the data table for a stack of these cubes.

cubes	0	1	2	3	4	5	6
pressure	0	1.25	2.5	3.75	5	6.25	7.5

This is the graph. Note the slope of the line generated by the data is greater than one.

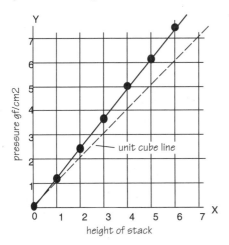

2. Discuss the results of this activity if it were performed by an astronaut on a space shuttle mission. [The astronaut and the cubes are weightless. Each cube has a mass of five grams but zero weight. Therefore, one cube or a stack of cubes would exert zero pressure.]

3. The pressure at the bottom of a stack of cubes is directly proportional to the density of the material from which the cube is made. Following is a chart that gives the densities of various solid and liquid materials. Make a graph that shows the pressure at the bottom of a stack of cubes made from the various materials. Notice that water graphs as y = x. What does the slope of the graph for each of the other materials represent? [the density of the material]

Densities	
Material	Density (gm/cm^3)
Aluminum	2.7
Brass	8.6
Copper	8.9
Gold	19.3
Ice	0.92
Iron	7.8
Lead	11.3
Platinum	21.4
Silver	10.5
Steel	7.8
Mercury	13.6
Ethyl alcohol	0.81
Benzene	0.90
Glycerin	1.26
Water	1.00

Solutions

1.

Height of stack	0	1	2	3	4	5	6
pressure	0	1	2	3	4	5	6

2.

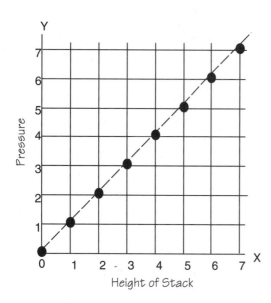

Y

Pressure

Height of Stack

3. x = y

Cubeprints Questions
1. Identify and justify your answer:
   a. Independent variable (Input): [height of stack] [I can stack as many blocks as I choose, in whatever order I choose.]

   b. Dependent variable (Output): [pressure at the bottom of the stack] [The pressure at the bottom of the stack is determined by the height of the stack.]
2. Describe the relationship between the independent and dependent variables. [The pressure is equal to the height of the stack of cubes, or the pressure at the bottom of the stack of cubes *is directly proportional* to the height of the stack of cubes.]
3. Explain why the relationship between the independent and dependent variables are proportional. [The graph passes through the origin (0, 0). In other words, the pressure is zero if the number of cubes is zero.]
4. What is the slope? [The pressure ÷ the number of cubes. The slope equals the pressure exerted by one cube.]

*   Reprinted with permission from *Principles and Standards for School Mathematics,* 2000 by the National Council of Teachers of Mathematics. All rights reserved.

80

CUBEPRINTS

Data Table and Graph

Complete the table.

height of stack	0	1	2	3	4	5	6
pressure							

Draw the graph.

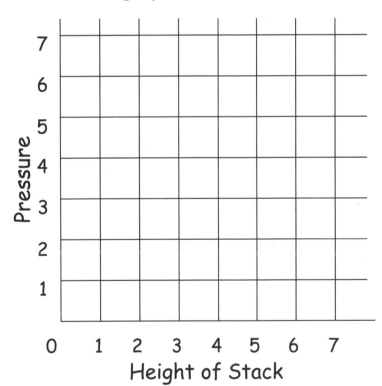

"Stack 'em up!"

Write the rule.

CUBEPRINTS

Questions

1. Identify and justify your answer:

   a. Independent variable (Input):

   b. Dependent variable (Output):

2. Describe the relationship between the dependent and independent variable.

3. Is the relationship between the dependent and independent variables proportional? Please explain.

4. What is the slope? Please explain.

5. Use your equation to compute the pressure at the bottom of a stack of 1000 cubes.

Hooked on Algebra

Topic
Algebra—Linear Functions

Key Question
How can the language of algebra be used to describe a stretched rubber band?

Learning Goals
Students will:
- construct an apparatus for measuring how far a rubber band stretches as additional weights are suspended from the rubber band,
- measure the increase in length as a function of added weight, and
- graph and analyze collected data.

Guiding Documents
Project 2061 Benchmarks
- *Symbolic equations can be used to summarize how the quantity of something changes over time or in response to other changes.*
- *Mathematical ideas can be represented concretely, graphically, and symbolically.*
- *Tables and graphs can show how values of one quantity are related to values of another.*
- *Organize information in simple tables and graphs and identify relationships they reveal.*

NRC Standard
- *Mathematics is important in all aspects of scientific inquiry.*

NCTM Standards 2000*
- *Represent, analyze, and generalize a variety of patterns with tables, graphs, words, and, when possible, symbolic rules*
- *Investigate how a change in one variable relates to a change in another variable*
- *Use symbolic algebra to represent situations and to solve problems, especially those that involve linear relationships*
- *Explore relationships between symbolic expressions and graphs of lines, paying particular attention to the meaning of intercept and slope*

Math
Measuring
   length
   force (applied weight)
Graphing
   interpreting graphs
Computing percent of error
Algebra
   linear equation of the form $y = mx + b$
   domain, range

Science
Physical science
   elasticity
      elastic limit
   force
      equilibrium (balance between elastic and gravitational forces)

Integrated Processes
Observing
Comparing and contrasting
Collecting and recording data
Inferring
Predicting
Generalizing

Materials
For each group:
   paper metric measure and system pointer from student page
   1 thin rubber band (see illustration on plan page)
   1 jumbo paper clip
   10 regular paper clips (13 if 2-pound tubs are used)
   1- or 2-pound margarine or similar tub (large enough to hold 325 grams of masses)
   set of masses totaling 325 grams
   transparent tape

Background Information
Science
   Elasticity is the ability of a material to spring back to its original shape and size after it has been stretched. It is the property whereby a material changes its shape and size under the action of opposing forces and recovers its original configuration when the forces are removed.

   All substances have some elasticity. Familiar

All substances have some elasticity. Familiar materials that have a greater degree of elasticity include the springs of an automobile, rubber balls, rubber bands, springs in watches, and the elastic cartilage between the vertebrae of the spinal column.

Englishman Robert Hooke (1635-1703) called the force acting upon a material the *stress* and the *elongation* it produces the *strain*. He found that as long as the elastic limit of a body is not exceeded, the strain produced is proportional to the stress causing it. This is known as *Hooke's Law*. In the ideal, according to this law, the value of {stress divided by strain} is a constant. This also means that the graph of (strain, stress) will always be a straight line, as is typical in relationships that are directly proportional.

Force is measured in *newtons*. At this level of understanding, it is sufficient to provide an approximate idea of the magnitude of a newton. The downward force exerted by the Earth's gravity on a mass of 1 kilogram is 9.8 newtons. On a mass of 100 grams it is .98 newtons. A rounded-off version is used in the table and graph of this investigation. Thus, the force acting on 100 grams is shown as 1.00 newton rather than 0.98 newton.

In this investigation the Earth's downward gravitational pull on the masses will cause the rubber band to stretch until it is in equilibrium with the upward elastic force exerted by the rubber band itself. As long as we remain within the elastic limit of the material (rubber band), we can use the graph to predict the elongation that will be produced by any force. When the results are graphed, they will look something like this:

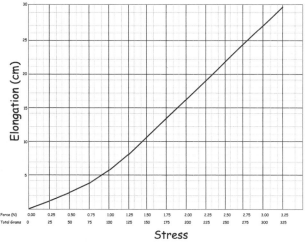

In the first part of the graph there is a slight deviation from the straight line predicted by Hooke's Law. This is probably due to the complex nature of the rubber (band) molecule. However, once a certain point is reached (approximately after 75 grams have been added), the rubber band begins to behave very much as predicted by Hooke's Law. Students will see this as they construct their broken-line graphs. The remainder of the graph will approximate a straight line. Deviations are due primarily to the accuracy of the data and the slightly irregular behavior of the rubber band.

Mathematics

A *function* is a set of ordered pairs (x, y) in which each value of *x* is paired with exactly one value of *y*. The *domain* of a function is the set of *x* values specified for the function; the *range* is the resulting set of *y* values.

Note that in the graph, the stress is along the horizontal axis and the strain is along the vertical axis. This conforms to the generally accepted procedure in which the manipulated variable is graphed along the horizontal axis and the responding variable along the vertical axis. However, in subsequent elasticity investigations, strain will be graphed along the horizontal axis and stress along the vertical axis. This exception to the rule is made to conform with the stress-over-strain definition of the *elastic constant*. This exception is necessary to produce the correct values for the elastic constant.

Management

1. This activity is designed to be done in groups of four.
2. Prior to using this investigation, collect enough one- and/or two-pound margarine or similar tubs to supply one to each group. Plastic tubs are preferred. They also provide convenient, permanent storage for all of the parts of the system. Note that two-pound tubs will require four paper clips for each arm instead of three.
3. It is an important component of the activity that each group construct and adjust their own system. This provides experience in translating a two-dimensional drawing (the square in the *AIMS Model of Learning*) into a three-dimensional system (the circle).

Procedure

1. Teach or review the *Background Information* with the students and clarify the meaning of all terminology.
2. Distribute the sets of materials required for constructing the system. If possible, use thin rubber bands, as illustrated; avoid thicker and wider bands, since they do not stretch enough to be appropriate.
3. Instruct students to stretch the rubber bands a dozen times to fully activate their elasticity.
4. Distribute the student pages. Have the students of each group construct a system, using the plan shown on the first student page. Tell them to secure the system pointer in a horizontal position by taping it securely to the paper clip through which it is threaded. Instruct them to carefully adjust the metric scale by raising or lowering it

until the system pointer points to zero. Finally, tell them to tape the paper strip (on which the metric scale is mounted) to the table.

5. Direct students to find the total elongations as force is increased in 0.25 newton intervals. Have them enter the data into *Table 1*. Tell them to continue the procedure until the total force is 1.75 newtons.

6. Before continuing, instruct each student to graph the data up to this point on the *Hooked On Algebra Graph* page using a **solid** broken line. Graph the ordered pairs (total force, total stretch).

7. Ask students to use a **dashed** line to predict graphically the elongation that will result when the total forces of 2.00, 2.25, 2.50, 2.75, 3.00, and 3.25 newtons have been reached *(step 3)*.

8. Invite students to read and interpret the graphs they just drew and record the predictions in *Table 2 (step 4)*.

9. Have students find the actual elongations by resuming the addition of masses, and record the data *(step 5)*.

10. Tell students to graph this actual data with a **solid** line *(step 6)*.

11. Ask them to now find and record the difference between the predicted and actual elongation at each level of force *(step 7)*.

12. Explain to students that to find the percent of error they will need to divide the difference by the actual elongation at the same level of force *(step 8)*.

13. Tell the students to inspect the graph and record over what domain (Stress values) the graph is fairly linear.

14. While still in groups, have students compare their predictions with the experimental results and record their observations. They may or may not wish to use the percentage of error as a basis of this comparison. Then, have them study their completed graphs and make observations based on them *(steps 9 and 10)*. Since similar rubber bands were used, there should be general agreement among the graphs.

15. Have each group tape the rubber band to the graph and store it for use in the next activity, which will appear in a future issue.

16. Review the *Background Information* with the whole class, clarifying any remaining questions. Emphasize that Hooke's Law is stated in the ideal, so there will always be a difference between the computed prediction and the actual measurement. In applications, materials and processes contain impurities and imperfections that impact the results.

Discussion

1. In what ways are the graphs (solid-line and dashed line) similar? What does this mean?

2. In what ways are the two graphs different from one another?

3. How well were you able to predict the elongation of the rubber band when asked to do so? (You may wish to encourage students to use the percentage of error to help in the explanation.) Why do you think you were able to predict with any degree of accuracy? [The strain is a function of the stress that is on the rubber band.]

4. Does each of the graphs have a section that approximates a straight line? If so, through what range is it straight? (In pilot-testing it usually began at 0.75 or 1.00 newtons and continued through 2.75 or 3.00 newtons.)

6. What does a straight line mean in this context? [application of Hooke's Law]

Extensions

1. Discuss the fact that everything is elastic to some extent. Make two lists, one of materials we think of as elastic and one of materials with which we do not usually connect elasticity.

2. Repeat the activity with a different size or thickness of rubber band. How do the resulting data differ?

3. How does the thickness of the rubber band change as force is increased?

4. List applications of Hooke's Law in everyday life. [bungey jumps, hitting tennis balls, elastic waistbands, balloons]

* Reprinted with permission from *Principles and Standards for School Mathematics,* 2000 by the National Council of Teachers of Mathematics. All rights reserved.

Hooked on Algebra

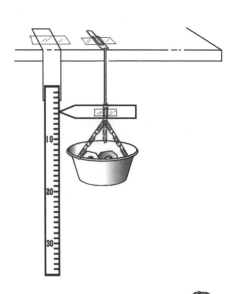

Does a rubber band stretch in a predictable manner when stress is applied?

Select the rubber band to be tested and stretch it a dozen times before inserting it into the system shown at the right.

Adjust the metric scale so the system pointer points to zero on the scale. Tape into place.

I'm hooked on Algebra !

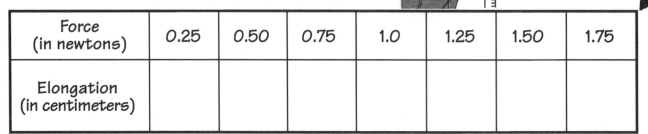

1. Complete this table.

Force (in newtons)	0.25	0.50	0.75	1.0	1.25	1.50	1.75
Elongation (in centimeters)							

2. Construct a SOLID broken line graph on Page 3 using the data in the table above.

3. Using a DASHED broken line graph, make a graphical prediction to indicate the elongation when total force reaches 2.00 to 3.25 newtons.

4. Read and interpret the graph to determine the elongation predicted for each level of force. Enter this data in Line A below.

	Force (in newtons)	2.00	2.25	2.50	2.75	3.00	3.25
A	Predicted elongation (in centimeters)						
B	Actual elongation (in centimeters)						
C	Difference between prediction and actual						
D	Percent of error (C ÷ B)						

5. Find the actual elongations. Enter data in Line B.

6. Graph this actual data, using a SOLID broken line graph.

7. Find the difference between the predicted and actual elongations. Enter in Line C.

8. Compute the percent of error by dividing this difference (Line C) by the actual elongation (Line B).

9. Over what domain is the graph fairly linear?

10. Study your graph. What observations can you make about the manner in which the rubber band stretches?

Hooked on Algebra

Graph

Elongation (cm)

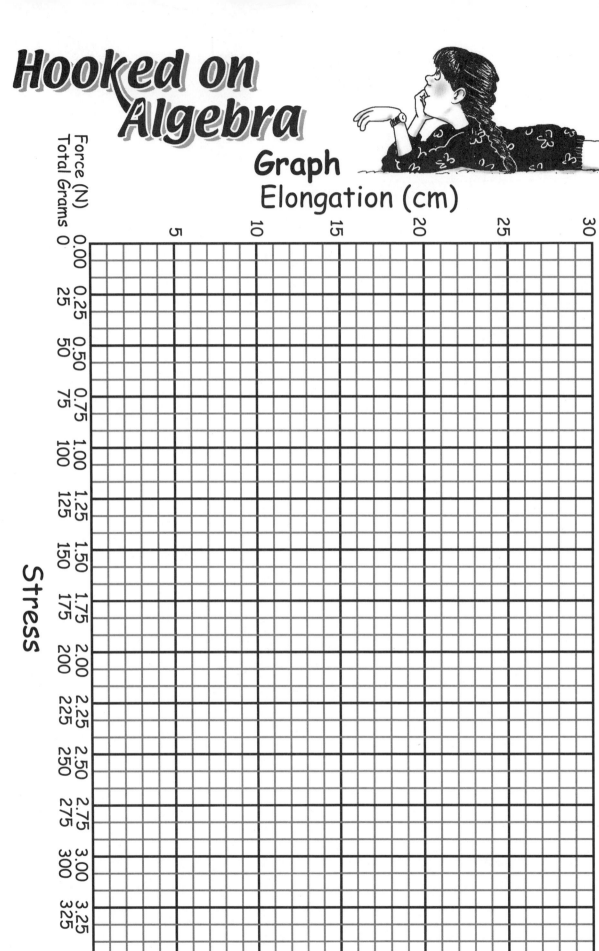

Force (N)
Total Grams

Stress

The Rubber Band System

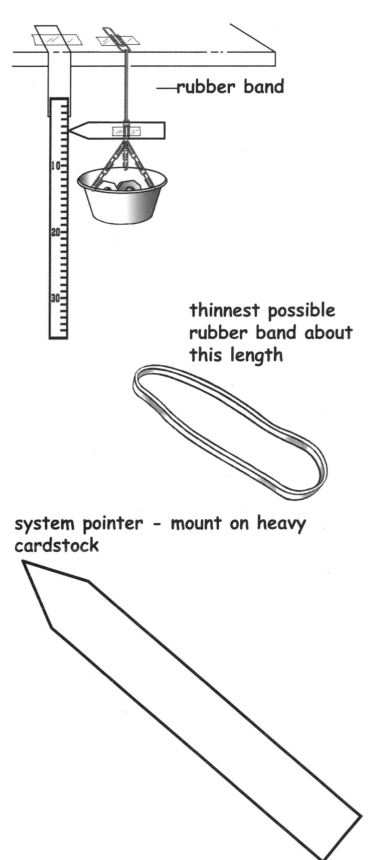

—rubber band

10

20

30

thinnest possible
rubber band about
this length

system pointer - mount on heavy
cardstock

22	44	66
21	43	65
20	42	64
19	41	63
18	40	62
17	39	61
16	38	60
15	37	59
14	36	58
13	35	57
12	34	56
11	33	55
10	32	54
9	31	53
8	30	52
7	29	51
6	28	50
5	27	49
4	26	48
3	25	47
2	24	46
1	23	45

Topic
Algebra—Linear Functions

Key Question
How does the language of algebra describe the relationship between the distance an object is located in front of the first mirror in a simple periscope and the distance the *image* of the object appears to be located behind the second mirror in the periscope?

Learning Goals
Students will:
- construct a working model of a simple periscope,
- collect and record data,
- graph data, and
- use the language of algebra to write an equation that describes the relationship between the distance an object is located in front of the first mirror in a simple periscope and the distance the image of the object *appears* to the viewer to be located behind the second mirror in a simple periscope.

Guiding Documents
Project 2061 Benchmarks
- *Mathematically ideas can be represented concretely, graphically, and symbolically.*
- *Tables and graphs can show how values of one quantity are related to values of another.*
- *Organize information in simple tables and graphs and identify relationships they reveal.*
- *Symbolic equations can be used to summarize how the quantity of something changes over time or in response to other changes.*

NRC Standard
- *Mathematics is important in all aspects of scientific inquiry.*

NCTM Standards 2000*
- *Represent, analyze, and generalize a variety of patterns with tables, graphs, words, and, when possible, symbolic rules*
- *Investigate how a change in one variable relates to a change in another variable*
- *Use symbolic algebra to represent situations and to solve problems, especially those that involve linear relationships*
- *Explore relationships between symbolic expressions and graphs of lines, paying particular attention to the meaning of intercept and slope*

Math
Algebra
linear equation of the form $y = mx + b$, $m = 1$, and $b \neq 0$

Science
Physical science
reflection from a plane mirror
mirror image

Integrated Processes
Observing
Collecting and recording data
Graphing data
Interpreting data

Materials
For each group:
plane mirror
medium-sized binder clip
Reflect/View
centimeter ruler
scissors
transparent tape or glue sticks

Background Information
Science:
A simple periscope is a z-shaped structure containing two plane mirrors. In a simple periscope, light is reflected off an object to a plane mirror fixed in the top of the periscope. The light path is turned through 90° and directed down the shaft of the periscope where it's reflected a second time into the eye of the viewer.

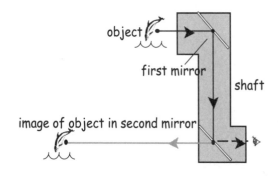

Mathematics:

Let *x* equal the distance the object is located in front of the first mirror. Let *b* equal the distance from the first mirror to the second mirror. In the simple periscope, the distance *b* is a constant.

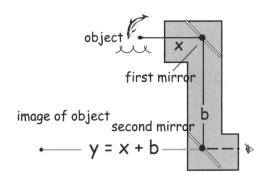

Let *y* equal the linear distance the image of the object appears to the viewer to be located behind the second mirror. Then the linear equation, $y = x + b$ describes the relationship between object distance and image distance.

Line symmetry and congruent triangles can be used to explain why $y = x + b$.

Construct the mirror lines and locate the image of the object in the first mirror and then the image of that image, as reflected by the second mirror. A Reflect/View or a geometric compass can be used to locate the images.

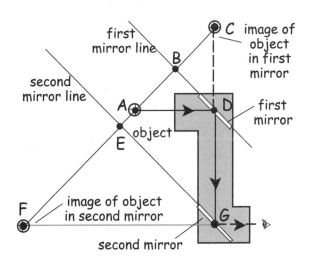

In the diagram, DABD is congruent (symbol ≈) to DCBD (side, angle, side = side, angle, side). Therefore the line segment AD is equal to the line segment CD. DFAG ≈ DCAG (side, angle, side = side, angle, side). Therefore the line segment FG is equal to the line segment CG. But the line segment FG is equal to the sum of the line segments CD and DG.

Management

1. Organize students into groups of two or three.
2. It's important that the first two pages are taped to the desk or table top so that they lie as flat as possible. Untaped pages can buckle up and create inaccuracies in the data collection process.
3. It's also important that the mirror and Reflect/View are aligned as accurately as possible to the locations printed on the student page. Flat pages and accurate mirror alignment make for accurate data collection.
4. Use the binder clip as a mirror stand.
5. Copy the *Dolphin Stand-up Figures* page. Cut out two dolphin figures for each group of students. Any other stand-up object, like a bent paper clip, can be substituted for the dolphin figure.

Procedure

1. Distribute the first two student pages.
2. Instruct each group to cut along the dashed line on the second page, fit the second page to the bottom of the first page, and then tape or glue the pages together.
3. Tell the students to place the mirror and the Reflect/View at the locations indicated.
4. Distribute two stand-up dolphin figures to each group.
5. Instruct the students to place one dolphin figure at the 14 cm mark on the scale in front of the first mirror. Tell them to look directly *through* the Reflect/View at about a 45° angle and locate the position on the centimeter scale the image appears to be located behind the Reflect/View. Inform them that the second dolphin figure might help them accurately locate the image. Tell them to record the image distance in the data table.
6. Instruct students to collect and record data for the remainder of the table.
7. Tell the students to measure and record the distance *b* (in cm) separating the mirror and the Reflect/View.
8. Distribute the *Questions About Your Periscope* page and ask students to record their answers on the page.

Discussion

1. Does the distance the eye is in front of the Reflect/View affect the distance the image appears behind the Reflect/View? [no]
2. What's the most commonly known use for a periscope? [in submarines—Periscopes are used whenever there is the need to look at something from a concealed or protected position. Military uses include installation in sea and land vehicles (especially tanks). Periscopes are used in nuclear physics laboratories to observe radioactive reactions. They are also used in industrial plants to observe and monitor manufacturing processes.]

3. What is the effect of *b*, the distance separating the two mirrors in a simple periscope, on how far away an object appears to be located? [In most cases, *b* can be ignored. For example, if a ship as seen through a periscope appears to be one mile away, the distance separating the two mirrors of the periscope is small in comparison.]

4. Two historical events that captured the world's attention and ushered in new technological eras made use of the periscope.

   On May 21, 1927, Charles A. Lindbergh completed his 33 hour and 30 minute solo flight across the Atlantic ocean in his single engine airplane, the "Spirit of St. Louis." A fuel tank filled the front of the airplane thereby blocking his forward view. A periscope was installed so that he could look around the tank to see ahead of the airplane.

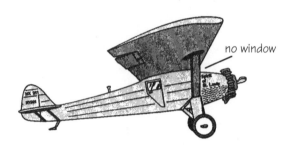

no window

   On February 28, 1962, astronaut John Glenn flew a Mercury space capsule into space to become the first American to orbit the Earth. Astronaut Glenn could look forward by extending a periscope from the side of the capsule. When not in use, the periscope could be retracted back into the space capsule.

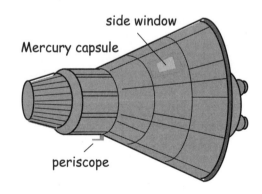

side window

Mercury capsule

periscope

Solutions

1.

Data Table								
x (cm)	14	13	12	11	10	9	8	7	6
y (cm)	27	26	25	24	23	22	21	20	19

2.

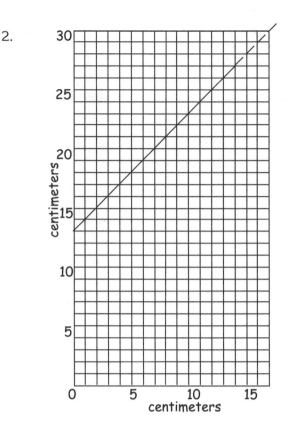

3. $y = x + 13$

Questions About Your Periscope
1. What is the independent variable? [x]
2. What does the independent variable represent? [the distance the object is in front of the first mirror]
3. What is the dependent variable? [y]
4. What does the dependent variable represent? [the distance the image appears to be located behind the Reflect/View]
5. What is the y-intercept on the graph? [13]
6. What is the measure (in cm) of *b*? [13 cm]
7. What does the y-intercept represent? [the distance separating the two mirrors]
8. For any simple periscope, why will the y-intercept always be greater than zero? [To make the y-intercept zero, the first mirror would have to be placed directly on top of the second mirror thereby destroying the usefulness of the device.]

* Reprinted with permission from *Principles and Standards for School Mathematics,* 2000 by the National Council of Teachers of Mathematics. All rights reserved.

uP Periscope

image distance

Complete the table.

Data Table									
X (cm)	14	13	12	11	10	9	8	7	6
Y (cm)									

Draw the graph.

(Ruler scale on left, from 16 to 36)

36
35
34
33
32
31
30
29
28
27
26
25
24
23
22
21
20
19
18
17
16

(Graph: vertical axis "centimeters" labeled 5, 10, 15, 20, 25, 30; horizontal axis "centimeters" labeled 0, 5, 10, 15)

uP Periscope

object distance

Write the Rule

14

13

12

11

10

9

8

6

16

15

14

13

12

11

10

9

8

7

6

5

4

3

2

1

INCOMING !

Reflect/View

mirror

b

b = _____ cm

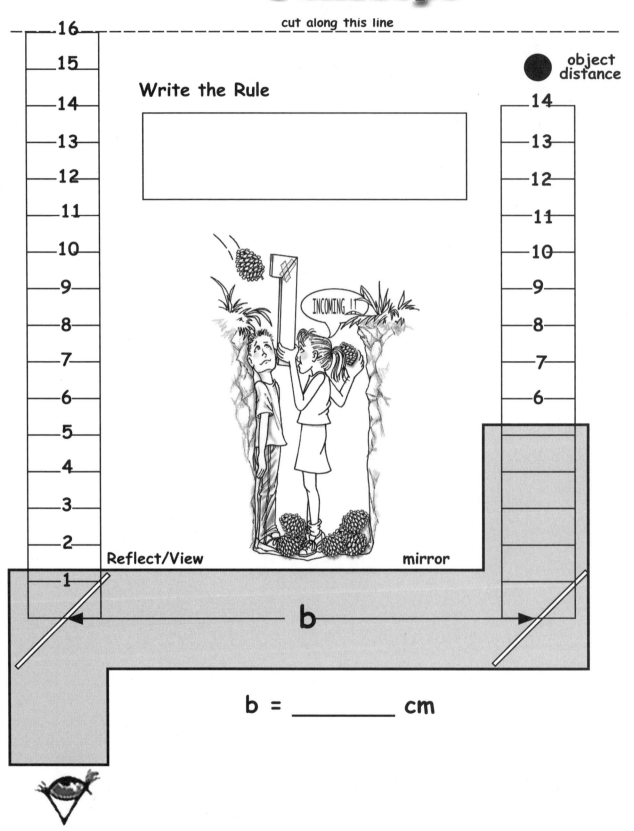

uP Periscope

Dolphin Stand-up Figures

Cut along solid lines, score and fold along dashed lines.

uP Periscope

Questions About Your Periscope

1. What is the independent variable?

2. What does the independent variable represent?

3. What is the dependent variable?

4. What does the dependent variable represent?

5. What is the y-intercept?

6. What is the length (in cm) of *b*.

7. What does the y-intercept represent?

8. Explain why, for any simple periscope, the y-intercept will always be greater than zero.

Part Three:
Constructing and Reading Data Tables and Graphs

Students are well served if they possess proficiency in the construction and reading of data tables and graphs. As they increase in their proficiency, they are freed to concentrate more fully on the phenomena under investigation. The activities in *Part Three* are designed to provide intensive practice in the development of the following skills:

- discovering and extending numerical patterns
- building data tables from patterns and graphs
- constructing graphs based on data or rules
- reading slope and y-intercept from graphs and rules
- writing verbal descriptions of patterns
- writing algebraic rules for patterns
- reading and translating graphs into rules
- distinguishing between proportional and non-proportional relationships based on data tables, graphs, or rules.

In the *AIMS Model of Functions* the foregoing processes represent movement from the triangle to the square and hexagon and from the square to the triangle and hexagon. Students should be able to chart the path they are following on the model from one form to the other as they move through the activities.

The three *Zap-It!* activities are designed to provide *periodic* practice and review of the processes involved in building data tables and translating number patterns into graphs, verbal rules, and algebraic rules. Interspersed at strategic times will help students hone these basic skills.

Graphing Functions requires students to read and interpret graphs. The sequence from graphs to rules, slope, and y-intercept is often given too little emphasis and needs to be an integral part of every student's experience. It models how the interpretation of graphs in other situations can be used to enrich the experience.

Topic
Algebra—Linear Functions

Key Question
What can we learn about functions from sets of ordered pairs and their graphs?

Learning Goals
Students will:
- look for a pattern in the set of ordered pairs;
- write additional ordered pairs using the pattern;
- build a table of the ordered pairs,
- graph the ordered pairs on the coordinate plane;
- determine slopes and y-intercepts;
- write a statement describing the pattern in set of ordered pairs; and
- write an expression for the linear function based on the written statement.

Guiding Documents
Project 2061 Benchmarks
- *Symbolic equations can be used to summarize how the quantity of something changes over time or in response to other changes*
- *Tables can show how values of one quantity are related to values of another*
- *Organize information in simple tables and graphs and identify relationships they reveal*
- *Graphical display of numbers may make it possible to spot patterns that are not otherwise obvious.*

NRC Standard
- *Mathematics is important in all aspects of scientific inquiry.*

NCTM Standards 2000*
- *Represent, analyze, and generalize a variety of patterns with tables, graphs, words, and, when possible, symbolic rules,*
- *Investigate how a change in one variable relates to a change in a second variable.*
- *Relate and compare different forms of representation for a relationship,*
- *Use graphs to analyze the nature of changes in quantities in linear relationships,*
- *Use symbolic algebra to represent situations and to solve problems, especially those that involve linear relationships,*

- *Explore relationships between symbolic expressions and graphs of lines, paying particular attention to the meaning of intercept and slope,*
- *Recognize and generate equivalent forms for simple algebraic expressions and solve linear equations.*
- *Express mathematical relationships using equations*

Math
Functions
Linear equations
Tables of ordered pairs
Graphs on the coordinate plane

Integrated Processes
Observing
Collecting and recording data
Graphing data
Analyzing data
Interpreting data

Materials
Student sheets

Background Information
Zap-It! activities are designed to provide practice
- in searching for patterns in sets of ordered pairs,
- graphing the results,
- writing statements describing the patterns, and
- writing linear function rules.

The goal is to provide an opportunity for students to master these processes.

The values of m and b in the linear function rule distinguish linear functions from each other. In real-world situations m and b are linked to the particular aspects that are under study. The rate of change m shows up as the slope of a line. The constant b is where the line intercepts the $f(x)$ axis. It is the output for the input 0.

Writing statements that describe patterns is an especially important skill too often neglected. Students need to acquire the ability to describe patterns in clearly understandable terms.

Procedure
1. Hand out the student sheets and go over the instructions as a class.
2. If necessary, do one or two problems together to insure that students understand the procedure.

3. Have students work together in small groups to complete the student pages.
4. Close with a time of class discussion and sharing.

Discussion
Compare the various graphs and answer the following with a general statement summarizing the result:
1. How do the numerical values of m influence the graphs?
2. How do the numerical values of b influence the graphs?

Extension
A blank master is included for use by the teacher or students to create additional problems. For example, students could be challenged to create as many different types of graphs as possible and to compare and contrast them as a means for further clarifying the role that m and b play in the linear function equation.

* Reprinted with permission from *Principles and Standards for School Mathematics, 2000* by the National Council of Teachers of Mathematics. All rights reserved.

Solutions
Zap-It 1
The last two entries in part a are student choices. The phrasing in part c will vary.

1. a. (3,5), (5,7), (7,9)...

   b.

   c. 2 is added to each input number.

   d. $f(x) = x + 2$

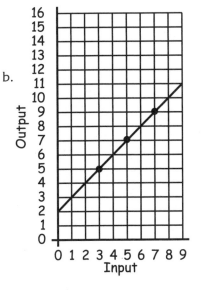

2. a. (6,3), (8,5), (9,6)...

   b.

   c. 3 is subtracted from each input number

   d. $f(x) = x - 3$

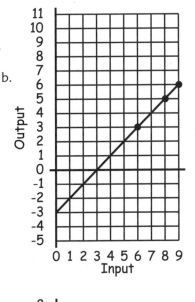

3. a. (2,6), (3, 9), (5, 15)...

   b.

   c. The input number is multiplied by 3

   d. $f(x) = 3x$

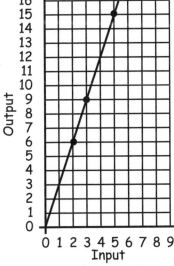

4. a. (5,0), (1,4), (7,-2)...

   b.

   c. The input number is subtracted from 5.

   d. $f(x) = {}^-x + 5$

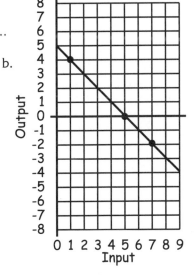

5. a. (1,⁻5), (3,⁻1), (5,3)...

b.

c. 7 is subtracted from 2 times the input number

d. $f(x) = 2x - 7$

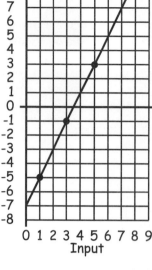

6. a. (3,10), (5,16), (1,4)...

b.

c. 1 is added to 3 times the input number

d. $f(x) = 3x + 1$

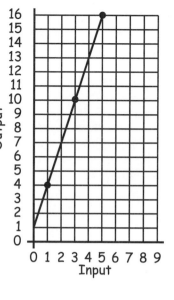

7. (2,7), (6,15), (4,11)...

b.

c. 3 is added to twice the input number

d. $f(x) = 2x + 3$

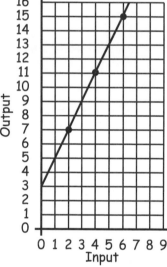

8. a. (8,⁻1), (4,3), (0,7)...

b.

c. The input number is subtracted from 7.

d. $f(x) = ⁻x + 7$

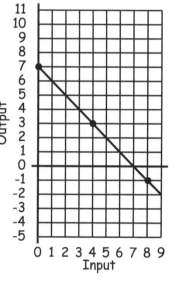

Zap-It 2

1.a. (2,5), (5,11), (7,15)...

b.

c. 1 is added to 2 times the input number.

d. $f(x) = 2x + 1$

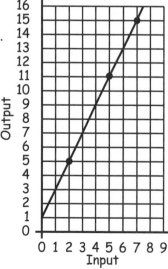

2. a. (4,14), (2,8), (3,11)...

b.

c. 2 is added to 3 times the input number.

d. $f(x) = 3x + 2$

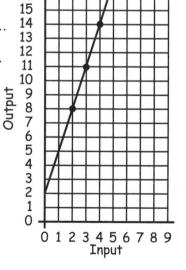

3. a. (2,⁻2), (4,⁻1), (8,1)...

b.

c. 3 is subtracted from one-half the input number.

d. $f(x) = .5x - 3$

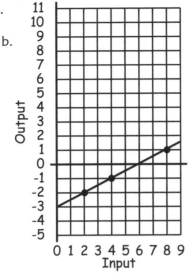

4. (2,4), (6,⁻4), (4,0)...

b.

c. 2 times the input number is subtracted from 8.

d. $f(x) = ⁻2x + 8$

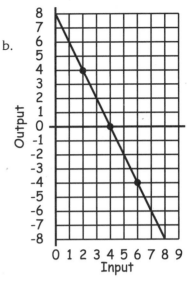

5. a. (2,1), (8,13), (5,7)...

b.

c. 3 is subtracted from 2 times the input number.

d. $f(x) = 2x - 3$

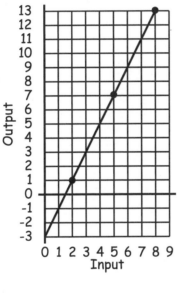

6. a.(2,4), (5,10), (8,16)...

b.

c. The input number is doubled.

d. $f(x) = 2x$

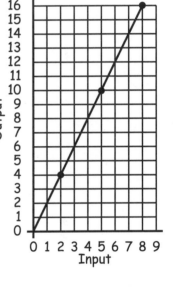

7. a. (0,12), (3,3), (5,-3)...

b.

c. 3 times the input number is subtracted from 12.

d. $f(x) = ⁻3x + 12$

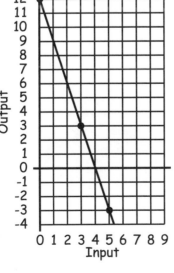

8. a. (2,3), (5,9), (7,13)...

b.

c. 1 is subtracted from 2 times the input number.

d. $f(x) = 2x - 1$

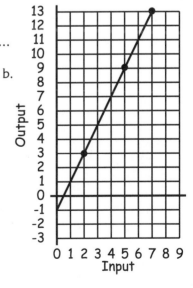

Zap-It 3

1.a. (0,7), (4,⁻5), (2, 1)...

b.

c. 3 times the input number is subtracted from 7.

d. $f(x) = ⁻3x + 7$

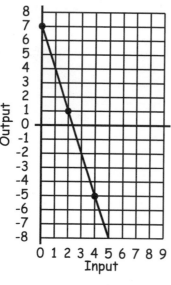

2. a. (5,13), (2,4), (1,1)...

b.

c. 2 is subtracted from 3 times the input number.

d. $f(x) = 3x - 2$

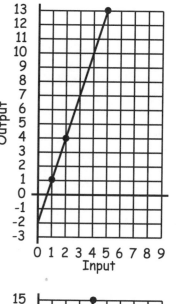

3. a (1,⁻3), (3,1), (5,5)...

b.

c. 5 is subtracted from 2 times the input number.

d. $f(x) = 2x - 5$

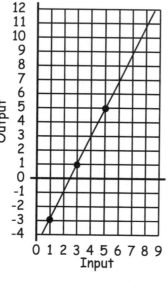

4. a. (3,11), (4,15), (2,7)...

b.

c. 1 is subtracted from 4 times the input number.

d. $f(x) = 4x - 1$

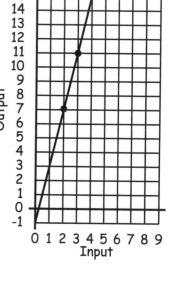

5. a. (6,⁻4), (0,8), (4, 0)...

b.

c. 2 times the input number is subtracted from 8.

d. $f(x) = ⁻2x + 8$

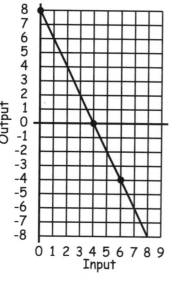

6. a. (4,4), (1,⁻2), (6,8)...

b.

c. 4 is subtracted from 2 times the input number.

d. $f(x) = 2x - 4$

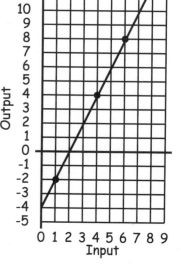

7. a. (8,13), (2,4), (4,7)...

b.

c. 1 is added to 1.5 times the input number.

d. $f(x) = 1.5x + 1$

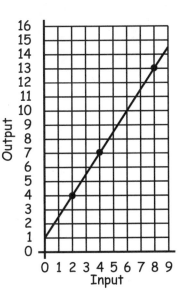

8. a. (1,11), (5,⁻1), (3,5)...

b.

c. 3 times the input number is subtracted from 14.

d. $f(x) = ⁻3x + 14$

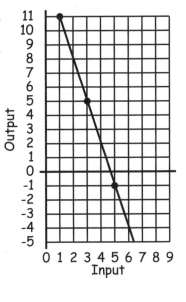

Zap-It 1

Zap-It has a secret process to determine output numbers for input numbers. It selects a different process for each problem. Zap-It works like this:

1. To enter an input number press any 0 to 9 number key.
2. Zap-It displays the corresponding output number on the screen.
3. Zap-It continues to use the same secret process for the entire problem.

Your challenge is to discover the secret process that is used in the three examples. Input numbers are shown inside heavy black circles; output numbers appear on the screen. Use the secret process to show the output numbers for the remaining two examples.

   a. Enter the five (input, output) number pairs in the table.
   b. Use the number pairs to build a graph.
   c. In you own words describe the secret process.
   d. Translate your description into algebraic shorthand using x to represent input and f(x) to represent output. The general form is:

$$f(x) = mx + b$$

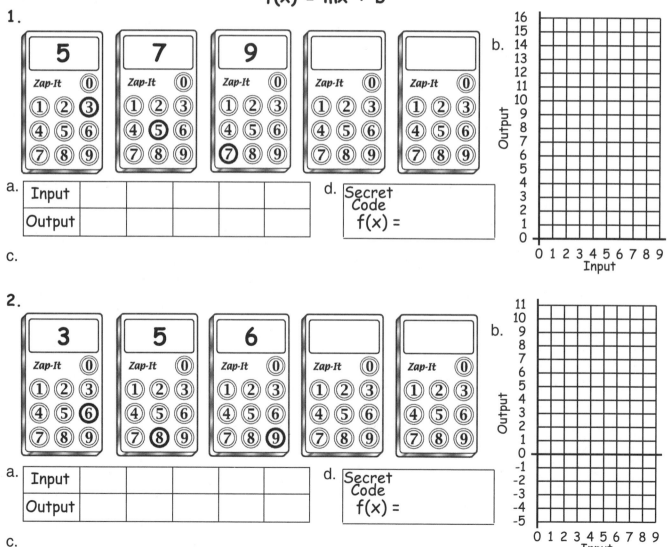

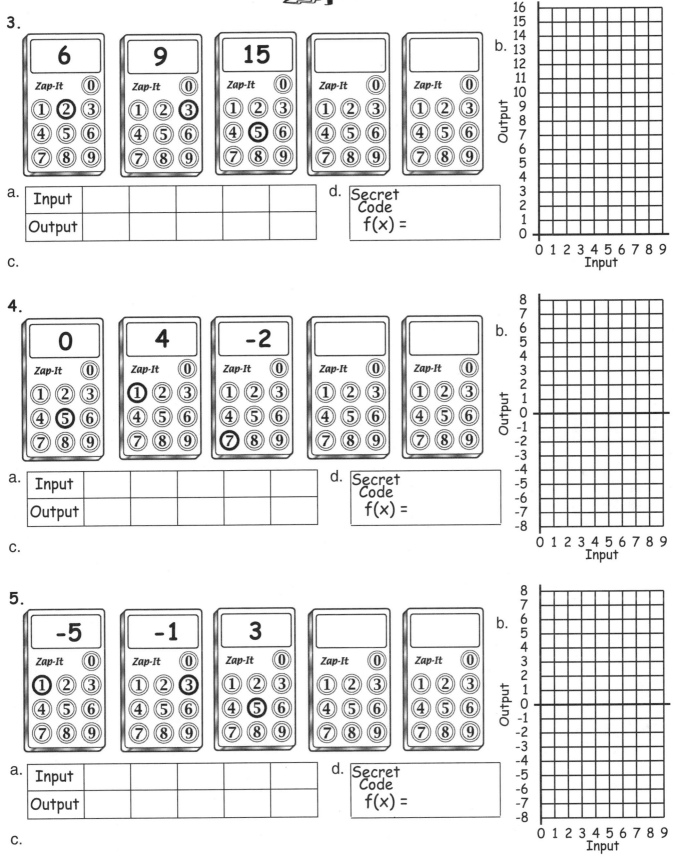

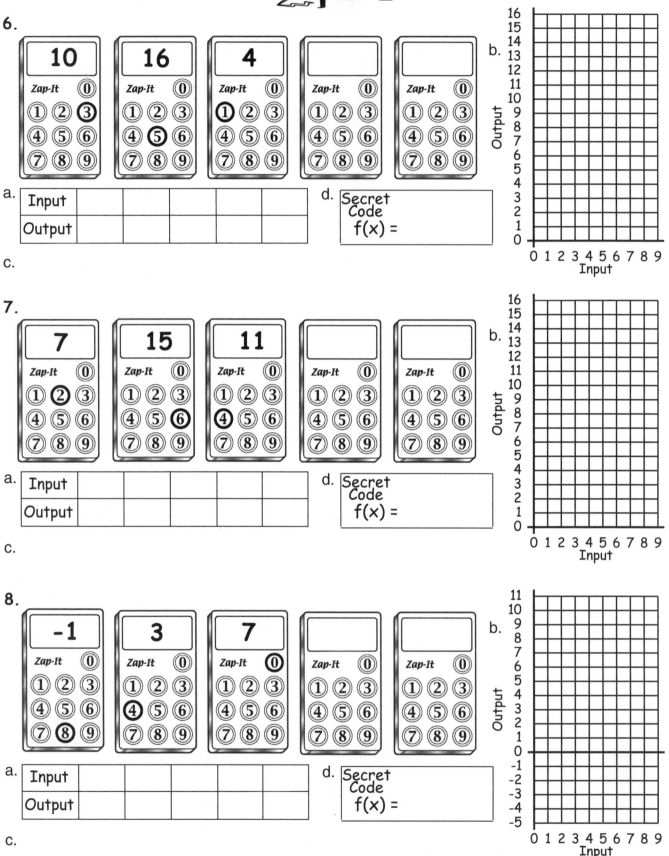

6.

| 10 | 16 | 4 | | |

a.
Input					
Output					

c.

d. Secret Code
f(x) =

b.

7.

| 7 | 15 | 11 | | |

a.
Input					
Output					

c.

d. Secret Code
f(x) =

b.

8.

| -1 | 3 | 7 | | |

a.
Input					
Output					

c.

d. Secret Code
f(x) =

b.

Zap-It 2

Zap-It has a secret process to determine output numbers for input numbers. It selects a different process for each problem. Zap-It works like this:

1. To enter an input number press any 0 to 9 number key.
2. Zap-It displays the corresponding output number on the screen.
3. Zap-It continues to use the same secret process for the entire problem.

Your challenge is to discover the secret process that is used in the three examples. Input numbers are shown inside heavy black circles; output numbers appear on the screen. Use the secret process to show the output numbers for the remaining two examples.

a. Enter the five (input, output) number pairs in the table.
b. Use the number pairs to build a graph.
c. In you own words describe the secret process.
d. Translate your description into algebraic shorthand using x to represent input and f(x) to represent output. The general form is:

$$f(x) = mx + b$$

1.

5	11	15		

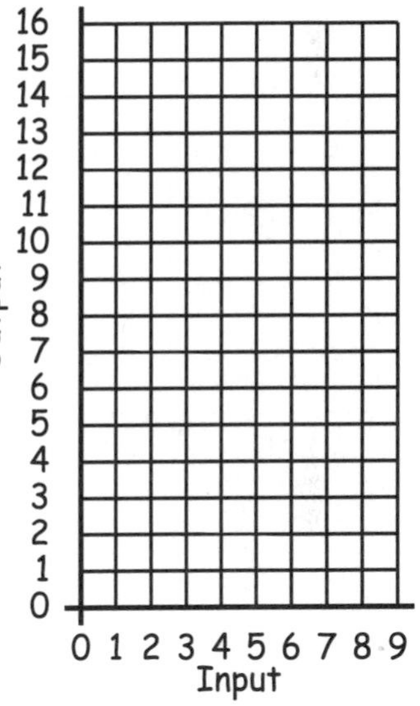

a.

Input					
Output					

b.

d. Secret Code
   f(x) =

c.

2.

14	8	11		

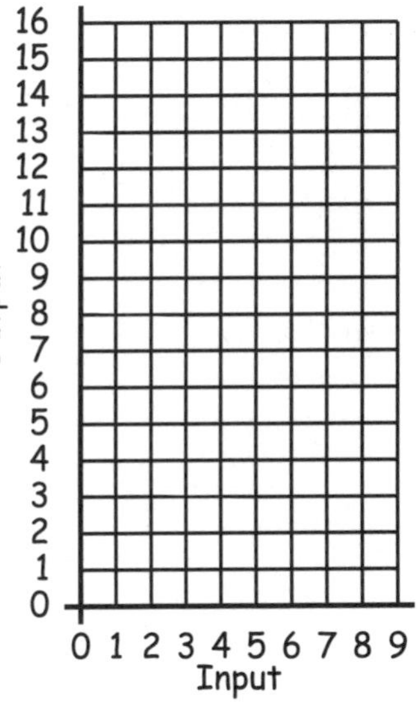

a.

Input					
Output					

b.

d. Secret Code
   f(x) =

c.

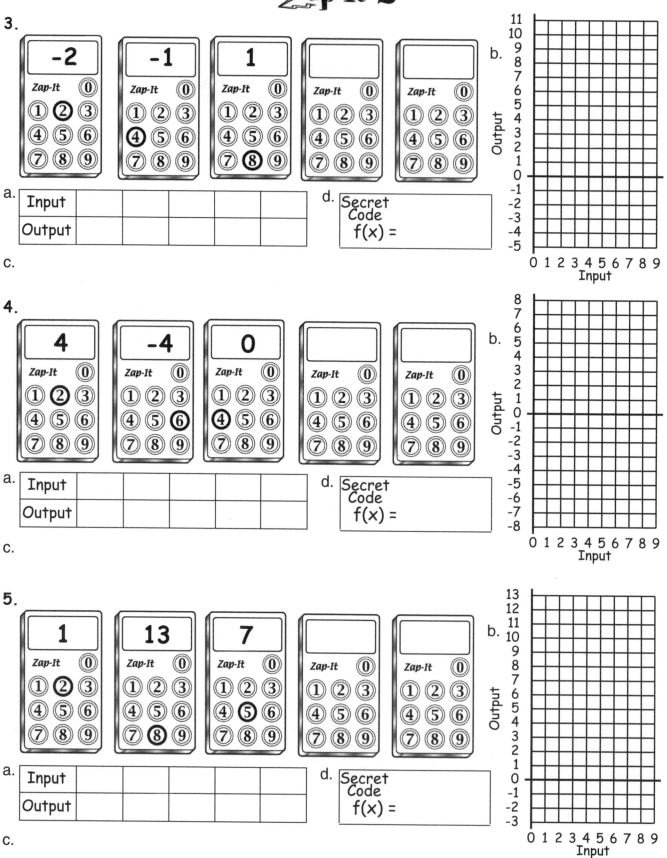

Zap-It 2

3.

Displays: -2, -1, 1, [blank], [blank]

a.
Input					
Output					

d. Secret Code f(x) =

b. (graph, Output -5 to 11, Input 0 to 9)

c.

4.

Displays: 4, -4, 0, [blank], [blank]

a.
Input					
Output					

d. Secret Code f(x) =

b. (graph, Output -8 to 8, Input 0 to 9)

c.

5.

Displays: 1, 13, 7, [blank], [blank]

a.
Input					
Output					

d. Secret Code f(x) =

b. (graph, Output -3 to 13, Input 0 to 9)

c.

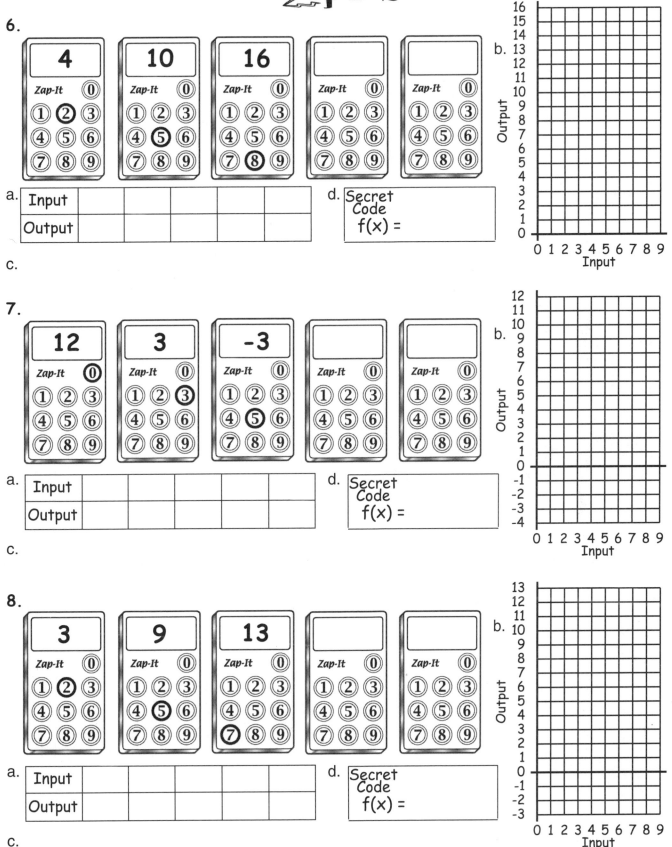

6.

| 4 | 10 | 16 | | |

a.

Input					
Output					

c.

d. Secret Code
f(x) =

7.

| 12 | 3 | -3 | | |

a.

Input					
Output					

c.

d. Secret Code
f(x) =

8.

| 3 | 9 | 13 | | |

a.

Input					
Output					

c.

d. Secret Code
f(x) =

Zap-It 3

Zap-It has a secret process to determine output numbers for input numbers. It selects a different process for each problem. Zap-It works like this:

1. To enter an input number press any 0 to 9 number key.
2. Zap-It displays the corresponding output number on the screen.
3. Zap-It continues to use the same secret process for the entire problem.

Your challenge is to discover the secret process that is used in the three examples. Input numbers are shown inside heavy black circles; output numbers appear on the screen. Use the secret process to show the output numbers for the remaining two examples.

a. Enter the five (input, output) number pairs in the table.
b. Use the number pairs to build a graph.
c. In you own words describe the secret process.
d. Translate your description into algebraic shorthand using x to represent input and f(x) to represent output. The general form is:

$$f(x) = mx + b$$

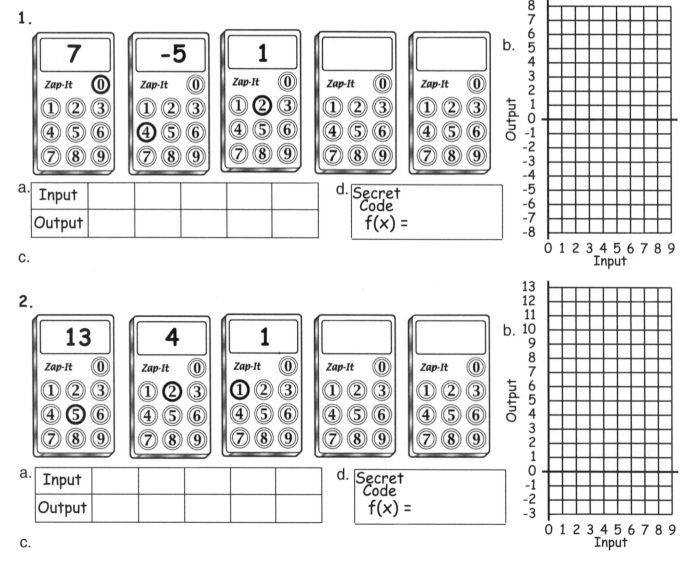

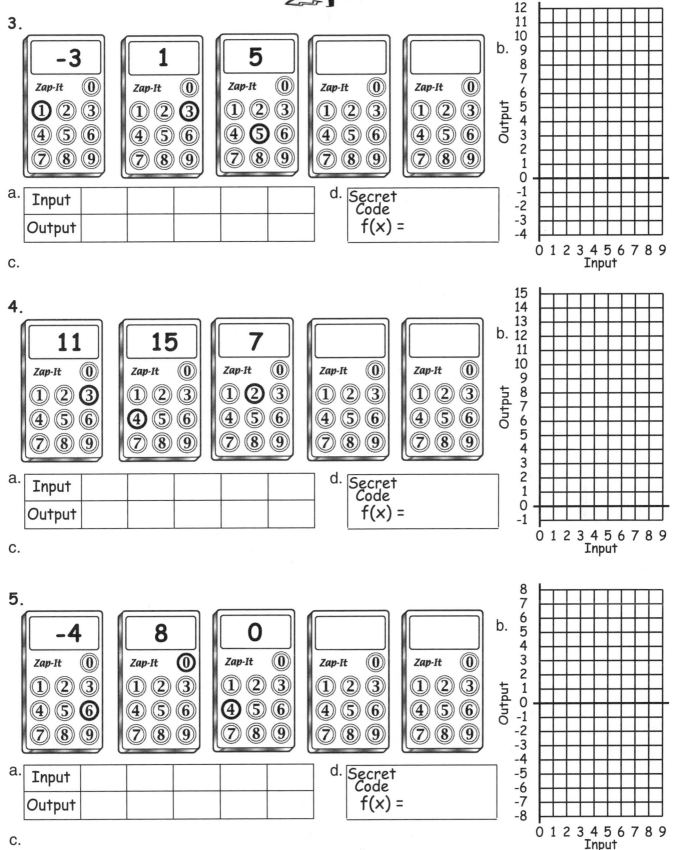

3.

-3   1   5

a.

Input					
Output					

c.

d. Secret Code
   f(x) =

4.

11   15   7

a.

Input					
Output					

c.

d. Secret Code
   f(x) =

5.

-4   8   0

a.

Input					
Output					

c.

d. Secret Code
   f(x) =

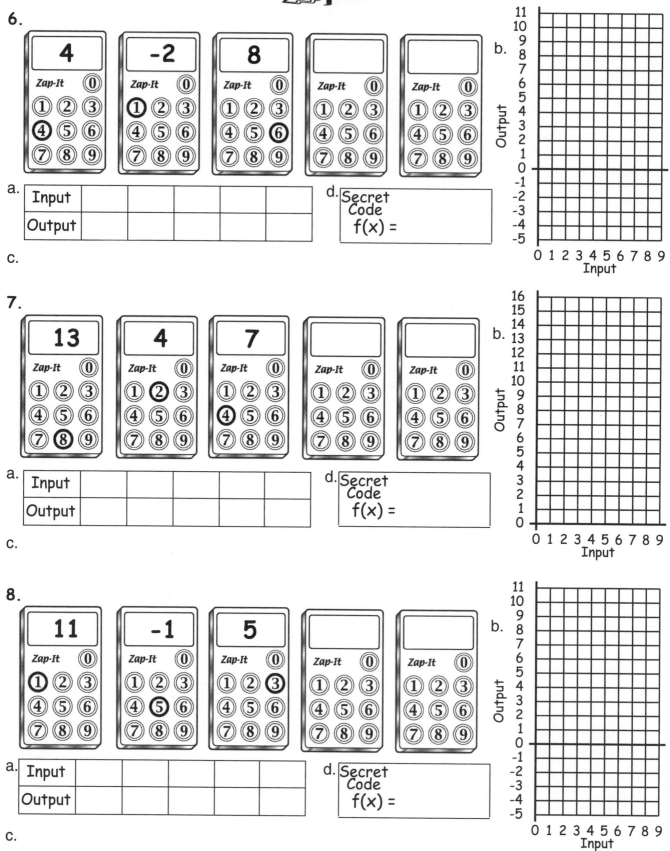

6.

| 4 | -2 | 8 | | |

a.

Input					
Output					

c.

d. Secret Code
f(x) =

7.

| 13 | 4 | 7 | | |

a.

Input					
Output					

c.

d. Secret Code
f(x) =

8.

| 11 | -1 | 5 | | |

a.

Input					
Output					

c.

d. Secret Code
f(x) =

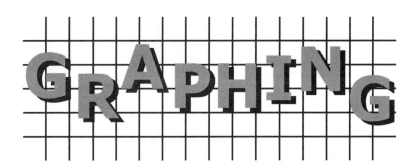 **FUNCTIONS**

Topic
Algebra—Linear Functions

Key Questions
How can you write the function rule (equation) for a line based on the graph of that line?
How can you graph a line based on the function rule of that line?

Learning Goals
Students will:
- determine the slope and crossing point on the vertical axis from the graph and use this to write the linear function rule.
- sketch the graph of a linear function from its function rule.

Guiding Documents
Project 2061 Benchmarks
- *Mathematical ideas can be represented concretely, graphically, and symbolically.*
- *Mathematical statements can be used to describe how one quantity changes when another changes.*

NCTM Standards 2000*
- *Represent, analyze, and generalize a variety of patterns with tables, graphs, words, and, when possible, symbolic rules*
- *Understand relations and functions and select, convert flexibly among, and use various representations for them*
- *Interpret representations of functions of two variables*
- *Relate and compare different forms of representation for a relationship*
- *Develop an initial conceptual understanding of different uses of variables*
- *Explore relationships between symbolic expressions and graphs of lines, paying particular attention to the meaning of intercept and slope*
- *Use symbolic algebra to represent situations and to solve problems, especially those that involve linear relationships*
- *Use graphs to analyze the nature of changes in quantities in linear relationships*
- *Investigate how a change in one variable relates to a change in a second variable*

Math
Linear function rules
Linear function graphs

Integrated Processes
Observing
Interpreting data
Relating
Generalizing

Materials
Student sheets
Rulers

Background Information
This activity deals with the relationship of graphs and symbolic expressions. Students will interpret graphs of linear functions into symbolic statements and symbolic statements into graphs. The purpose is to sharpen these skills so that they can be assumed in the ensuing investigations.

Management
1. Review the interpretation of graphs into symbolic statements and symbolic statements into graphs. Make sure that students are comfortable with the formula $f(x) = mx + b$.
2. You will want to give students rulers so that their lines will be as accurate as possible.
3. You will want to give students rulers so that their lines will be as accurate as possible.

Procedure
1. After reviewing the concepts involved in functions, graphing function rules, and translating graphs into function rules, hand out the first student sheet and rulers and go over the instructions. *Use what you know about functions and their graphs to determine the equation of each graph on your paper.*
2. Have students work together in small groups to determine the equations. When all groups have finished, hand out the second student sheet and go over the instructions. *This process is the reverse of that on the first sheet. Use the function rule to sketch the line of each.*
3. After groups have finished the second student sheet, hand out the question sheet. Close with a time of

class discussion and sharing once students have answered the questions.

Discussion

1. Which method was easier for you, to go from graphs to function rules, or from function rules to graphs? Explain.
2. What do the graph and the function rule look like when the slope is zero? [The graph is a straight horizontal line. The function rule will consist of the *b* term only.]
3. What do the graph and the function rule look like when the y-intercept is zero? [The line passes through the origin where *b* or the y-intercept is zero. The function rule will consist of the *mx* term only.]
4. What does it mean to have a slope of 2/5? [The line goes right five points for every two points it goes up.]

5. How is this different from a slope of 5/2? [The line goes right two points for every five points it goes up.]
6. What happens when the slope is negative? [The line slopes down as it moves to the right. If the slope is -5/2 it goes down five and right two.]
7. Why do we say that the x-axis is the "input," and the $f(x)$, or y-axis, is the "output"? [Traditionally in algebra the independent (input) variable goes on the x-axis, and the dependent (output) variable goes on the $f(x)$ axis.]

Extension

Have students create their own functions to graph and trade them with classmates.

* Reprinted with permission from *Principles and Standards for School Mathematics*, 2000 by the National Council of Teachers of Mathematics. All rights reserved.

Solutions

Student sheet one

1.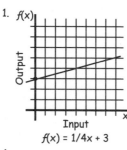
   $f(x) = x + 2$

2.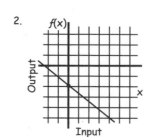
   $f(x) = 3/2x$

3.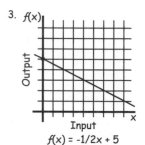
   $f(x) = -3/4x + 7$

4.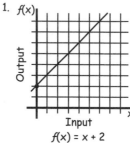
   $f(x) = -1/8x + 4$

5.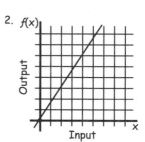
   $f(x) = -2/3x - 1$

6.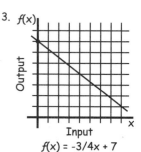
   $f(x) = 5/2x - 3$

Student sheet two

1. $f(x) = 1/4x + 3$

2. $f(x) = -3/4x - 2$

3. $f(x) = -1/2x + 5$

4. $f(x) = 2x$

5. $f(x) = 3/5x - 1$

6. $f(x) = 4$

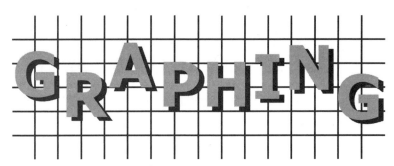

FUNCTIONS

Use what you have learned about functions and their graphs to determine the function rule of each graph shown below. The first one has been done for you as an example.

1.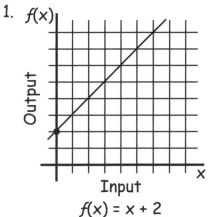

f(x) = x + 2

2.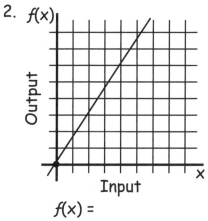

f(x) =

3.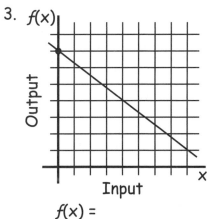

f(x) =

4.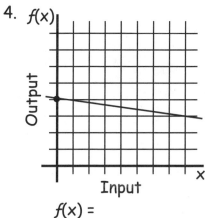

f(x) =

5.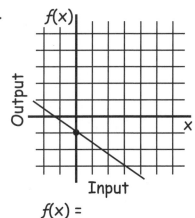

f(x) =

6.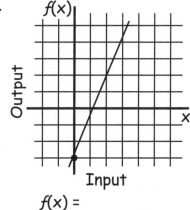

f(x) =

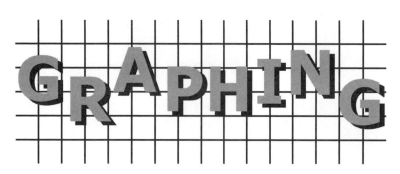

FUNCTIONS

This is the reverse of the process you did on the first sheet. Take the function rule for each graph and draw in the appropriate line.

1.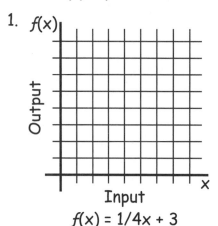

$f(x) = 1/4x + 3$

2.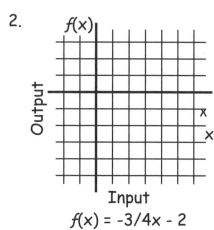

$f(x) = -3/4x - 2$

OK, now reverse the process and...

3.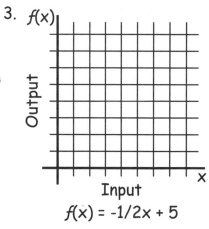

$f(x) = -1/2x + 5$

4.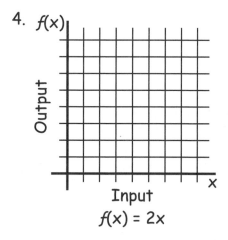

$f(x) = 2x$

5.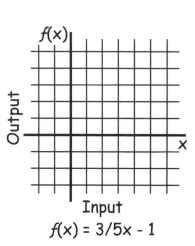

$f(x) = 3/5x - 1$

6.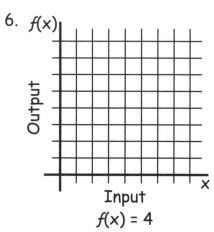

$f(x) = 4$

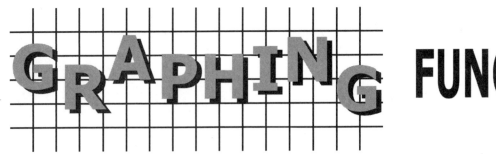

GRAPHING FUNCTIONS

Answer the following questions when you have completed both student sheets.

1. Which method was easier for you, to go from graphs to function rules, or from function rules to graphs? Why?

2. What do the graph and the function rule look like when the slope is zero?

3. What do the graph and the function rule look like when the y-intercept is zero?

4. What does it mean to have a slope of 4/3? How is that different from a slope of 3/4? How do the lines change when the values are negative?

5. Why do we say that the x-axis is the "input" and the $f(x)$, or y-axis, is the "output"?

Part Four:
Finding Linear Functions In Interesting Objects

Activities involving interesting objects frequently reveal that linear functions are imbedded. Such interesting objects are found in abundance almost everywhere in the students' world. As students discover that linear equations can model many relationships in the world around them their interest and understanding builds. *Part Four* contains a sampling of such activities.

Important algebraic concepts such as slope, y-intercept, domain, range, rule, etc. show up with regular frequency, allowing students to become immersed in all that is associated with linear functions.

It is important to remember that algebra uses its own specialized language. Therefore, special attention must be given to the development of facility in its use. These investigations provide interesting real-world contexts for employing algebraic language in the discussion of a situation, the resulting data, graph, rule, domain, range, etc.

On the Level III explores the behavior of a balance as multiple weights on one side are balanced by a single weight on the other. Students discover that when the balance is in equilibrium, the relationship between the sides can be modeled by a linear function.

Licorice whips constitute the interesting objects in *Let's Party!* Students study the rate of change that takes place as they take successive similar-sized bites from their licorice whips, thereby making connections between algebraic concepts and a real-world situation. They gather data from the very kinesthetic experience of eating licorice whips and sipping punch and then consider them in very abstract ways.

So what do linear functions have to do with ropes? In *Functioning with Knots* students study how the length of the rope gets shorter as knots are tied in it. They represent the resulting data and interpret the graph's meaning in the context; recognize the connection between the rate of change and the slope of the line; and develop a rule that relates the outcome to the variable conditions in the context.

In *Candy Combinations* students determine all of possible options for constructing a mixture of five- and seven-cent candies so that each represents at least 20% of the total number of pieces and that the total cost is $7.00. They discover an inverse relationship, construct a graph, determine the domain and range and write a function rule.

What is more natural in the real world of students than to think about money? In *Nickels and Dimes* they study the relationship between the number of nickels and dimes that add to exactly one dollar.

Mystery Mass presents students with a situation in which they are required to use indirect means for finding the unknown mass of an object. The activity is presentable at three different levels: fully-structured, semi-structured, or open-ended. In the open-ended approach, students face the challenge of developing an indirect procedure that leads to finding the mass of the object.

On the Level III

Topic
Algebra—Linear Functions

Key Question
How can the language of algebra be used to describe data collected from a simple lever?

Focus
Students will use a plastic drinking straw to construct an equal-arm balance. They will collect and analyze data to discover the linear relationship between one or more weights added at the same location on the right arm of the balance, a single weight added at a constant location to the right arm, and a single paper clip added to the left arm of the balance.

Guiding Documents
Project 2061 Benchmark
- *Symbolic equations can be used to summarize how the quantity of something changes over time or in response to other changes.*

NRC Standard
- *Mathematics is important in all aspects of scientific inquiry.*

NCTM Standards 2000*
- *Represent, analyze, and generalize a variety of patterns with tables, graphs, words, and, when possible, symbolic rules*
- *Investigate how a change in one variable relates to a change in another variable*
- *Use symbolic algebra to represent situations and to solve problems, especially those that involve linear relationships*
- *Explore relationships between symbolic expressions and graphs of lines, paying particular attention to the meaning of intercept and slope*

Math
Algebra
    linear equation of the form
       $y = mx + b, m \geq 1, b > 0$
    independent, dependent
       variable
    domain, range

Science
Physical science
    force and motion
       Law of the Lever
         torque
         lever arm (moment arm)
         equilibrium

Integrated Processes
Observing
Collecting and recording data
Inferring
Predicting
Generalizing

Materials
For each group:
    plastic 10" drinking straw
    transparent tape
    jumbo-size paper clip
    5 regular paper clips
    3" x 6" piece of cardboard
    permanent marking pen
    scissors

Background Information
Mathematics
    The general form for the equation of a straight line is
$$y = mx + b$$
where *m* is the slope and *b* the y-axis intercept of the line.

    In this activity the slope m is greater than 1, and the y-axis intercept is greater than zero. The equation for this straight line reduces to $y = mx + b$.

    The equation $y = mx + b$ is modeled by placing *m* paper clips at position *x* on the right arm of the balance, a single clip at position *b* on the right arm, and a single clip at position *y* on the left arm of the balance. In the diagram, 3 clips at position 2 and one clip at position four on the right arm of the balance are balanced by a single clip at position 10 on the left arm.

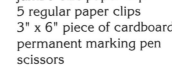

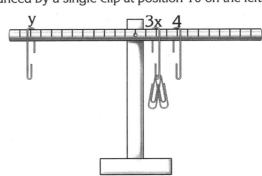

A *function* is a set of ordered pairs (x, y) in which each value of *x* is paired with exactly one value of *y*.

The first element of the ordered pair, x, is called the independent variable. The second element of the ordered pair, y, is called the dependent variable.

The *domain* of a function is the set of *x* values specified for the function; the *range* is the resulting set of *y* values.

Science: (See *The Science of the Equal-arm Balance.*)

Management

1. This activity is designed to be done in groups of three or four.
2. Pre-punch one straw per group (see *Constructing an Equal-arm Balance*].
3. It is an important component of the activity that each group construct and adjust their own equal-arm balance. If time or any other factor makes student construction impossible, construct one balance per group.

Procedure

Have students construct an equal-arm balance (see *Constructing the Equal-arm Balance*).

Collecting and Analyzing Data

1. Show students how to open one paper clip so that each end has a hook. Tell them to hang two clips on the smaller end and then hang the large end on the straw.

hang this end on straw   hang two clips on this end

2. Instruct the students to hang a single clip at position 2 on the right arm. This clip represents the constant *b* in the equation y = mx + b. Tell them they are to keep this clip in its current, constant position. The right arm of the balance is now down.
3. Tell the students to hang three clips (representing 3x) at the zero position (the end of the jumbo paper clip) and then to hang a single clip to the position on the left arm (y=2) that levels the balance and to record that position in the table.
4. Instruct the students to hang the three paper clips at the first mark (x=1) on the right arm of the balance. Tell them to hang one paper clip on the left arm of the balance and to carefully move the clip until the three clips are balanced. Have them record the position of the left-arm paper clip on the student page.
5. Instruct the students to move the right-side paper clips to the second mark (x=2) on the right-side arm of the balance. Direct them to carefully move the left paper clip until the three clips are again balanced and to then record its position in the data table.
6. Have the students repeat this process until the data table is completed for the right-arm positions x = 0, 1, 2, and 3.

7. Direct the students to graph the data, write the equation, and answer the questions on the student page.

Discussion

1. What patterns do you see in the table? [y = (x • 3) + 2]
2. How could you extend the data collection posibilities? [Connect two or more plastic straws together to make an equal-arm balance.]
3. Look at the picture of the equal-arm balance on your student sheet. Why do the paper clips on the right arm of the equal-arm balance balance with a single clip placed on the left arm? [Since the lever arm is balanced, the counterclockwise torques must equal the clockwise torques.]

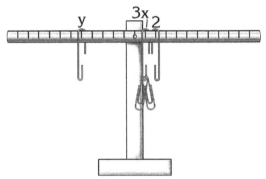

counterclockwise torques	clockwise torques
$\tau = F \times d$	$\tau = F \times d$
$\tau(1) = 1 \times 5 = 5$	$\tau(1) = 1 \times 1 = 1$
	$\tau(2) = 1 \times 1 = 1$
	$\tau(3) = 1 \times 1 = 1$
	$\tau(4) = 1 \times 2 = 2$

5 torque units = 5 torque units

Solutions

1.

x	0	1	2	3
y	2	5	8	11

2.

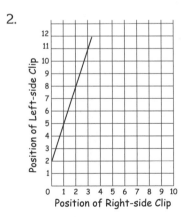

3. What is the equation of the line? [y = 3x + 2]
4. What is the slope of the line? [3]
5. What is the y-axis intercept of the line? [2]
6. What is the independent variable? [x, the position of the clip on the right arm of the balance]
7. What is dependent variable? [y, the position of the clip on the left arm of the balance]
8. What is the domain? [0, 1, 2, 3]
9. What is the range? [2–11]
10. What part of the equal-arm balance represents the independent variable? [the right arm]
11. What part of the equal-arm balance represents the dependent variable? [the left arm]
12. How is "slope" represented when using an equal-arm balance to model the equation y = x? [The coefficient of x, in this case three, represents the slope.]
13. What limits data collection? [The length of the straw used to make the equal-arm balance.]
14. On the graph, what does the line y = 3x + 2 tell you about the behavior of the equal-arm balance? [The line y = 3x + 2 represents the positions (ordered pairs) of the clips that balance the equal-arm balance.]

15. On the graph, what does the shaded region below the line y = 3x + 2 tell you about the behavior of the equal-arm balance? [The region below the line represents the positions (ordered pairs) of the clips that cause the equal-arm balance to lower the right arm.]
16. On the graph, what does the region above the line y = 3x + 2 tell you about the behavior of the equal-arm balance? [The region above the line repesents the positions (ordered pairs) of the clips that cause the equal-arm balance to lower the left arm.]

Extension

Encourage interested students to connect two or three straws together to make an equal-arm balance that will collect more data.

*   Reprinted with permission from *Principles and Standards for School Mathematics,* 2000 by the National Council of Teachers of Mathematics. All rights reserved.

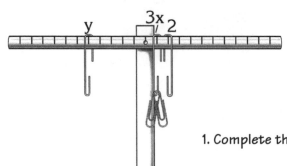

On the Level /II

1. Complete the table.

Data Table

x	0	1	2	3	4
y					

2. Draw the graph.

Graph

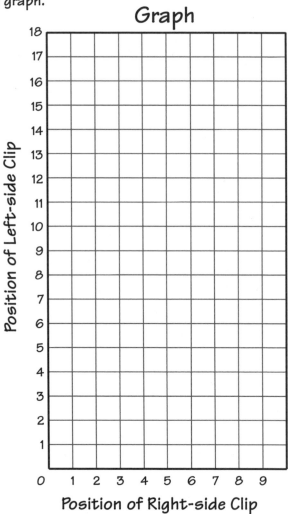

Position of Left-side Clip (vertical axis, 1–18)

Position of Right-side Clip (horizontal axis, 0–9)

one centimerter marking scale

Equation

3. Write the equation.

On the Level I/II

4. What is the slope of the line?

5. What is the y-intercept of the line?

6. What is the independent variable?

7. What is the dependent variable?

8. What is the domain?

9. What is the range?

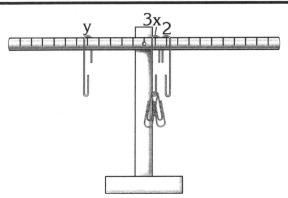

The following are questions about how the equal-arm balance models the above linear equation.

10. What piece or pieces on the balance represent the independent variable?

11. What piece or pieces on the balance represent the dependent variable?

12. How is "slope" represented when using an equal-arm balance to model the equation y = x?

13. What limits data collection?

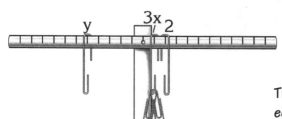

Equal-arm Balance

On the Level III

The graph shown below describes the behavior of the equal-arm balance.

14. On the graph, what does the line y = 3x tell you about the behavior of the equal-arm balance?

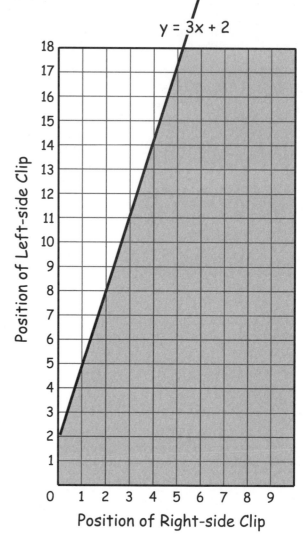

15. On the graph, what does the shaded region below the line y = 3x + 2 tell you about the behavior of the equal-arm balance?

16. On the graph, what does the region above the line y = 3x + 2 tell you about the behavior of the equal-arm balance?

On the Level Summary

An Equal-arm Balance Model for the Linear Equation, y = mx + b.

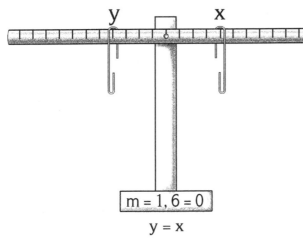

m = 1, 6 = 0

y = x

  x = position on right arm,
  m = number of clips at position x,
  y = position of balancing clip on left arm

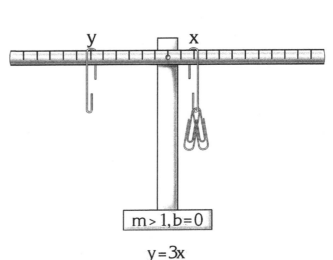

m > 1, b = 0

y = 3x

  x = position of clips on right arm,
  m = number of clips at position x, m > 1,
  y = position of balancing clip on left arm

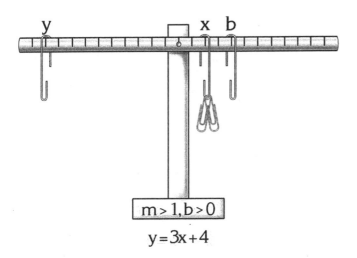

m > 1, b > 0

y = 3x + 4

  x = position on right arm,
  m = number of clips at position x, m > 1,
  y = position of balancing clip on left arm
  b = position of clip on right arm (constant)

¡LET'S PARTY!

Topic
Algebra—Linear Functions

Key Questions
How can you represent the relationship of the length of a licorice whip and the number of bites you have taken?
How can you represent the relationship of the height of punch in a glass and the number of sips you have taken?

Learning Goals
Students will:
- represent data on a graph and interpret the graph's meaning in the context;
- recognize the connection of the rate of change in numeric form as an equivalent to the slope of the line in graphic form; and
- develop an equation that relates the outcome to the rate of change and the original starting condition.

Guiding Documents
Project 2061 Benchmarks
- *Mathematical statements can be used to describe how one quantity changes when another changes. Rates of change can be computed from magnitudes and vice versa.*
- *Graphs can show a variety of possible relationships between two variables. As one variable increases uniformly, the other may do one of the following: always keep the same proportion to the first, increase or decrease steadily, increase or decrease faster and faster, get closer and closer to some limiting value, reach some intermediate maximum or minimum, alternately increase and decrease indefinitely, increase and decrease in steps, or do something different from any of these.*

NCTM Standards 2000*
- *Represent, analyze, and generalize a variety of patterns with tables, graphs, words, and, when possible, symbolic rules*
- *Relate and compare different forms of representation for a relationship*
- *Explore relationships between symbolic expressions and graphs of lines, paying particular attention to the meaning of intercept and slope*
- *Use graphs to analyze the nature of changes in quantities in linear relationships*

Math
Measuring
Rates
Graphing
   slope, intercept
Variables
Writing equations

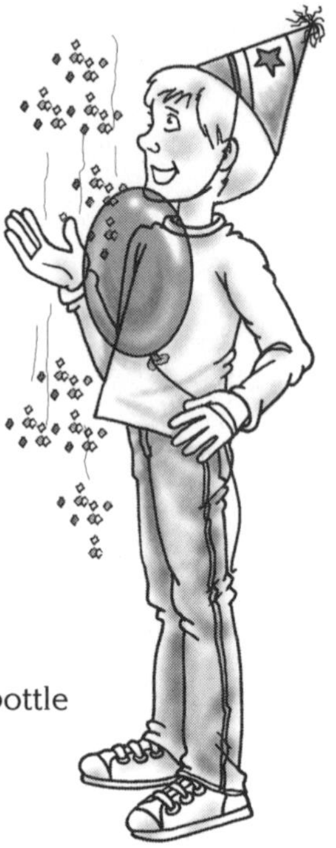

Integrated Processes
Observing
Collecting and recording data
Interpreting data
Generalizing

Materials
Red licorice whips
Centimeter ruler
Straight-sided glass or water bottle
Water or fruit punch
Drinking straws, optional

Background Information
Students have difficulty making connections between algebraic concepts and real-world situations. This investigation encourages students to gather and record data from the very kinesthetic experiences of eating licorice whips and sipping punch and consider them in very abstract ways. Displays of the data allow students to establish the relationship between the measurement of how much is left to how many bites and sips have been taken.

As the licorice whip is eaten, students place it on the graph paper and record the data. In this way a graph is constructed without generating any numbers; the experience is recorded directly in the graphic mode. By taking bites of the same size, the end point of each sequential length forms a straight line. From their experience students are quick to connect the steepness of the line to be continual shortening of the whip. They easily recognize the relationship of the steepness of the line to the size of a bite. The larger the bite the quicker the line drops. Using the graph the students can extend the line to determine how many bites they get out of a whip.

The graph can be used to answer the question "How big is a bite?" by comparing the actual changes in lengths. In order to communicate an accurate answer, students quite naturally convert the lengths and changes of lengths into numeric measurements and record them on a chart. By analyzing this numeric data, students find that they can determine a bite's size by finding the difference between two consecutive lengths. To find a typical bite size, students will compare all the consecutive differences and confirm that they are all about the same size. They then determine that a more accurate number can be gained by averaging the changes. The *average change* is the numeric description of the bite size and relates to they graph by communicating how much the line drops each bite, its negative slope.

Posing the question of "How can you determine the length of a whip after eight bites?" provides a segue into communicating symbolically. Most students will provide an answer about subtracting the typical length until eight bites have been taken. They intuitively relate the number to the context. When asked to find a quicker way, the concept of multiplication surfaces and they suggest that you can multiply the typical bite size by eight, the number of bites taken. If a typical bite size were two centimeters, the amount eaten could be determined by two times the number of bites (b) or (2b). This expression tells only how much has been eaten so it must be subtracted from how long the whip was initially. Most whips are typically 16 cm long so the generalization of how long (l) the remaining whip is might be written: l = 16 - 2b. As students observe the equation they have generated, they should be asked to recognize that the bite taken away from the whip is the factor 2 in the expression, the negative 2 slope of the graph, and the 2 cm typical bite from the numbers on the chart. The size of the bite is communicated symbolically, graphically, and numerically. Likewise the original length of the whip is communicated numerically by the length when no bites have been taken. Graphically it is where the line intersects the vertical scale, the y-axis, giving it the name "y-intercept." Symbolically it is the constant from which the change is taken away.

After this introduction to the various representations that can be used to describe the situation, the students' understanding can be applied and extended by asking more questions. The question, "After taking just five bites, how can you determine how many bites you get out of a licorice whip?" can be solved using any of the representations. Numerically, the typical bite size is subtracted from the length until it reaches zero. Graphically, it is found by extending the line until it intercepts the x-axis where a length of zero is represented. Students do not tend to answer this question symbolically but describe it as taking the original length and dividing it by the typical bite size to get the number of bites. With prompting they can describe the situation using the example numbers as:

$$16 \div 2 = b$$
$$8 = b$$

When students can work through a problem backwards in this way, they can be presented with the more formal algebraic notation. Using the symbolic equation developed in the activity, they substitute zero

for the length and solve for the number of bites (b) by working backwards.

$$
\begin{array}{rcl}
l & = & 16 - 2b \\
0 & = & 16 - 2b \\
-16 & = & -16 \\
\hline
-16 & = & -2b \\
\div(-2) & = & \div(-2) \\
\hline
8 & = & b
\end{array}
$$

The steps in the symbolic manipulations are the same as the steps in the numeric manipulations they originally suggested.

Having developed a meaningful understanding of the representations allows the students to move from one type to another. Provided with the symbolic equation of l = 15 - 1.5b for a licorice whip, they can translate it into the context that you have a 15 cm long whip and take of 1.5 cm every bite. Students can draw the graph placing a dot at (0,15) to represent the starting point, the y-intercept. Then each dot is placed on a bite line 1.5 cm lower than the preceding dot. The resulting string of dots has a slope of (-1.5). When asked to determine how many bites have been taken if the whip is 6 cm long, students will work backwards as they would if they substituted 6 in the equation for length(l) and solved for bites (b).

$$6 = 15 - 1.5b$$

First they would find the difference between 6 and 15 to determine how much was eaten.

$$
\begin{array}{rcl}
6 - 15 & = & 15 - 1.5b - 15 \\
-9 & = & -1.5b
\end{array}
$$

Then they would divide the length of what was eaten by the size of a bite to determine the number of bites.

$$
\begin{array}{rcl}
-9 \div (-1.5) & = & (-1.5)b \div (-1.5) \\
6 & = & b
\end{array}
$$

This investigation provides an excellent opportunity to show how situations can be communicated in numeric, graphic, and symbolic forms. It also provides an opportunity for an introduction to some ideas of the function concept.

Asking students to consider if the graph is just the distinct points plotted or if there are more points between those plotted causes them to consider the idea of *continuous* versus *discrete* functions. The question might be posed as: "Should the graph be drawn as a solid line, or just a dashed line to show us the pattern?" The teacher may need to explain that the continuous line shows that the pattern is true anywhere along the line, while a dashed line communicates that the pattern is true only at the plotted points. A lively discussion can follow. Some students claim that it must be a dashed line because a bite can either be taken or not taken, but only a part of a bite cannot be taken. They see it as a discrete function. Other students will claim that they can take part of a piece of pizza or half a gulp of soda, so they can take part of a bite of a licorice whip. They see it as a continuous function that demands a solid line. The consideration of the difference between discrete and continuous functions is relatively more important than the conclusion.

This experience provides an introduction to the dependence of the outcome on conditions. A function relates the effects of a situation to its causes. The length of a licorice whip (effect) depends on three things (causes): how long it was initially, how many bites have been taken, and how big a bite is. Change any one of those and the length of the whip changes. An important concept of functions is not the notation but the dependence of the outcome on the conditions inputted. $L(b) = 16 - 2b$ should be interpreted to mean: The length (L) of a whip when (b) bites are taken depends on the initial length of the whip (16), the size of the bites (2) and the number bites taken (b). Looking at functions in this simple context provides a meaningful insight to them.

Management

1. Before doing the activity make sure the graph is adequate for the materials. The graph is based on licorice whips that are generally 16-17 cm in length and 0.5 L water bottles that run 15-16 cm high. The activity can be adjusted by changing the numbers on the length axis or by cutting the whips to an appropriate length and filling the bottle to an appropriate height.

2. To get data that provide a useful model of algebraic ideas, the bites and sips should be made consistently the same size. Consistent bites can be encouraged by having students determine the approximate size of a bite and asking them to grasp the licorice whip so that they bite down to their fingers. Providing straws for students tends to give more consistent results for sips.

3. Collaborative groups of four work well for this activity. Each student records the data for his or her own whip. They can use the data of one student from their group drinking out of the glass or water bottle, but to keep peace in the classroom, plan on letting all the students have a small cup of punch.

4. In order to obtain linear data, it is important that the drink container have vertical sides. Having students bring in 0.5 liter water bottles provides the most convenient source.

5. In some situations it would be advantageous to gather the licorice data and drink data on different days. In this way, students learn from the first experience and apply their learning to the second, and the procedure is less chaotic.

Procedure

1. Tell the students that they are going to be having a party with the refreshments being licorice whips and punch. Explain to them what they will do to collect the party data: For licorice they will place the whip down along the respective bite line and mark its length at the start and after each bite.

For the punch, tell them that they will measure the height of the liquid with a ruler and record the data on the chart. Encourage the students to take consistent bites and sips (see *Management 2*).

2. After the materials are distributed, allow time for the students to collect and record the data on the graph or chart as they take each sip or bite.

3. After the students have taken five bites and sips, have them finish the whips and punch noting how many bites it took to eat the whip and sips to finish the punch.

4. Direct the students to translate the licorice whip data from the graph into numeric data on the chart, and turn the numeric data of the punch into a graph. Students might want to use a different colored pencil or ink for the punch than the one used for the licorice.

5. Have the students discuss and then determine how they could use the data in the charts to determine how many bites or sips it should have taken them until the food was gone. Encourage them to compare their calculations and the actual results.

6. Have students compare the graphic data of bites and sips and how they relate to the situation and the numeric data.

7. Have students discuss and develop an equation that tells how much food is left when the number of bites or sips has been substituted into the equations.

Discussion

Numeric Interpretation

1. How big a bite (sip) did you typically take? [answers vary but should be average of differences in heights each bite (sip)]

2. How can you determine how many bites (sips) it will take to finish the food? [original length ÷ typical bite length = number of bites]

3. How can you determine how much licorice (punch) is left if you know how many bites you have taken? [length = original length - (number of bites • typical bite length)]

Graphic Interpretation

4. What pattern is formed by the length of the whip (height of punch)? [The lengths are arranged in nearly a line.]

5. What does this line tell you about what was happening to your whip (punch)? [It was getting shorter each time.]

6. From the graph, how can you tell what a bite size was? [from the slope, how much the line went down each time a bite was taken]

7. How could you use the graph to determine how many bites (sips) would have been taken to eat all the whip (drink all the punch)? [extend the line until there was 0 cm of length]

8. What would the line look like if you had taken bigger bites (sips)? [greater negative slope, it would go down steeper or faster]

Symbolic Interpretation

9. How can you write in symbols how much licorice (punch) is left if you know how many bites (sips) you have taken? [l = original length - (number of bites • typical bite length). (If students have difficulty with this step, take them back through the number interpretation. How much shorter does the whip get with each bite? How much is the whip shortened if you take b bites? How much is left after taking b bites?)]

10. How do each of the numbers (constants) in your equation show up on the graph and in the context? [the factor with b is the slope and the typical bite, the constant from which the product is subtracted is the y-intercept and the original length]

11. How could you use your equation to determine how many bites are required to get a whip that is 4 cm long? [substitute 4 as the length and solve]

Extension

Provide partial information to students and have them work backwards through the record sheet to rebuild all the data and answer questions. For example

provide students with the following data for them to insert in the chart:

After 2 sips a student's punch was 11 cm high and after 5 sips it was 5 cm high.

- How much punch does the student drink each sip? [2 cm]
- How much punch was in the student's glass originally? [11+2+2=15 cm]
- How many sips will the student get out of the glass? [15÷2=7.5≈7 sips]
- How would you write an equation relating the height of the punch to the number of sips? [h=15-2s]
- How does the situation show up in the graph and the equation?

¡LET'S PARTY!

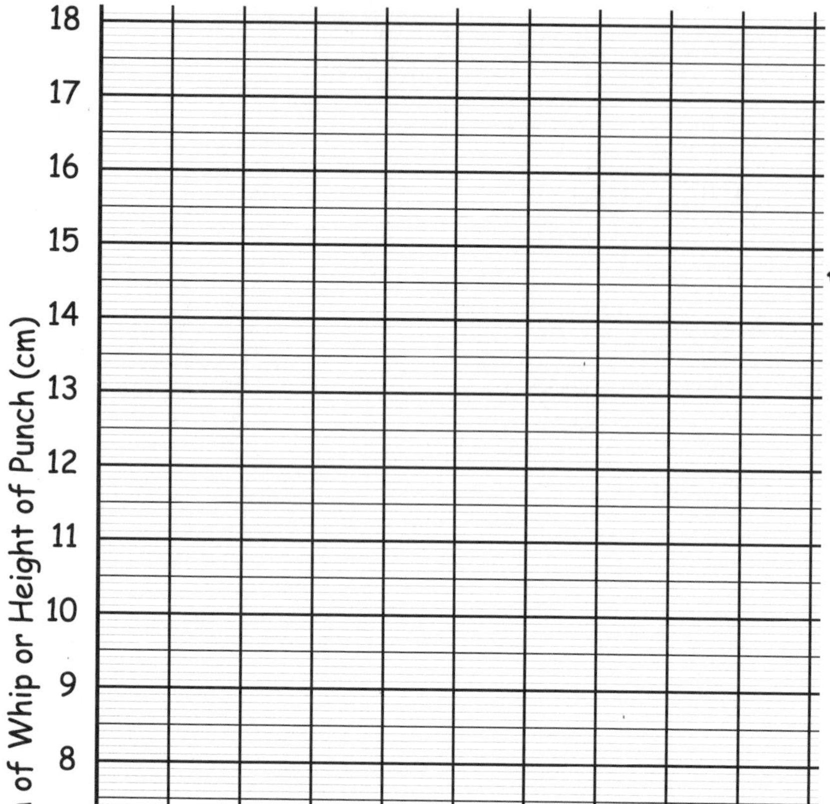

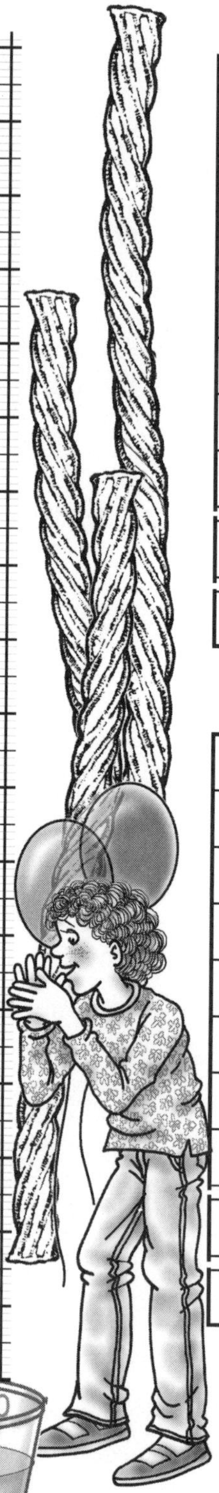

Licorice Whip

Bites	Length(cm)
0	
1	
2	
3	
4	
5	
6	
8	
b	

Fruit Punch

Sips	Height(cm)
0	
1	
2	
3	
4	
5	
6	
9	
s	

Length of Whip or Height of Punch (cm)

Bites or Sips

Functioning with Knots

Topic
Algebra—Linear Functions

Key Questions
How can a graph or an equation show that a length of rope gets shorter because of knots made in it?

How can graphs and equations for two different diameters of rope be used to determine when the two lengths of rope will be the same lengths and have the same number of knots in them?

Learning Goals
Students will:
- represent data on a graph and interpret the graph's meaning in the context;
- recognize the connection of the rate of change in numeric form as an equivalent to the slope of the line in graphic form;
- develop an equation that relates the outcome to the variable conditions in the context;
- work backwards from a limited amount of data to generate an equation and line on a graph; and
- recognize how equations can be solved simultaneously both graphically and symbolically.

Guiding Documents
Project 2061 Benchmarks
- *Mathematical statements can be used to describe how one quantity changes when another changes. Rates of change can be computed from magnitudes and vice versa.*
- *Graphs can show a variety of possible relationships between two variables. As one variable increases uniformly, the other may do one of the following: always keep the same proportion to the first, increase or decrease steadily, increase or decrease faster and faster, get closer and closer to some limiting value, reach some intermediate maximum or minimum, alternately increase and decrease indefinitely, increase and decrease in steps, or do something different from any of these.*

NCTM Standards 2000*
- *Represent, analyze, and generalize a variety of patterns with tables, graphs, words, and, when possible, symbolic rules*
- *Relate and compare different forms of representation for a relationship*
- *Explore relationships between symbolic expressions and graphs of lines, paying particular attention to the meaning of intercept and slope*

- *Use graphs to analyze the nature of changes in quantities in linear relationships*
- *Model and solve contextualized problems using various representations, such as graphs, tables, and equations*

Math
Measuring
Rates
Graphing
   slope, intercept
   interpreting
Variables
Writing equations
Simultaneous equations

Integrated Processes
Observing
Comparing and contrasting
Collecting and recording data
Interpreting data
Generalizing

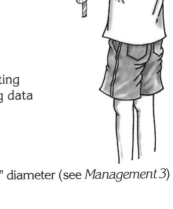

Materials
Lengths of rope, $\frac{1}{8}$", $\frac{3}{16}$", $\frac{1}{4}$" diameter (see *Management 3*)
Straight edge
Meter stick

Background Information
The length (L) of rope with knots is dependent on three variables:
- The initial length (i) of rope without any knots
- The amount the rope is shortened (s) with each knot
- The number of knots (k) in the rope.

To determine the length of the rope you multiply the number of knots by the amount the rope is shortened by each knot subtracted from the initial length of the rope without any knots. In function notation this relationship, or procedure, would be written:

$$L(i,s,k) = i - (s \bullet k)$$

Each rope has a constant initial length that is easily measured. Each diameter of rope is shortened by a constant amount per knot. For a given piece of rope, once the constants are determined the only variable is the amount of knots.

The context encourages students to write the equation in a meaningful format rather than the more traditional ($y = mx + b$) format. Using the commutative property the function can be rewritten in the more familiar slope intercept form:

$$L(i,s,k) = -sk + i$$

As the equations and graph are compared, two relationships become apparent: the initial length (i) to the y-intercept and the slope to the shortening rope(s).

The concept of the domain of a function naturally develops with rope investigations. The number of knots is limited to whole numbers because of the discrete nature of knots. The number of knots that can be tied in a length of rope is also limited by the initial length of rope. Since a knot shortens the length of a rope but still maintains a length, the rope cannot be shortened to a length of zero.

For more information regarding how students think about this and similar investigations, refer to *Background* in *Stacking Cups*.

Management

1. This series of investigations is based around the same context, the length of a rope as knots are added to it. Most teachers will find it beneficial to revisit the context several times as students' understanding becomes more sophisticated. Other teachers find a more holistic understanding develops when the series of investigations is used as a unit. Several contexts can be thoroughly explored before going on to a more abstract approach based on the intuitive understanding developed from the context. This investigation should be preceded by *Stacking Cups* which provides a more evident visual relationship between the variables and their representations and has a positive change or slope.

2. The investigations work well in collaborative groups of four students. However some teachers may prefer having the data gathered as a class. This provides more control and direction but does not allow students to practice the related skills of measurement and will not provide the first-hand experience some students require.

3. Before starting the activity the teacher will need to prepare the ropes for each group. For class discussions it is best for all the groups to have similar length ropes. At least two sets of different diameters provides enough experience for most students. Single samples of several other diameters provide material for full class investigations. Below are diameters and lengths that work well for all the investigations.

Diameter	Length
$\frac{1}{8}$"	65 cm
$\frac{3}{16}$"	75 cm
$\frac{1}{4}$"	90 cm

For diameters other than these, the teacher should experiment to determine what lengths provides data that work with the other ropes.

4. Except for *Part Four* on simultaneous equations, the diameters and lengths of the rope are not critical. For *Part Four,* the thicker rope should be longer in length. Knots on a thicker rope are larger, shortening the rope more each knot than a knot on thinner rope.

5. Synthetic fiber rope (nylon, polyester) is more flexible and more appropriate for these activities than natural fiber (cotton, hemp) rope. After the teacher has cut ropes out of synthetic fibers heat the ends with a flame to keep them from unraveling.

6. A single overhead knot should be used in this investigation. The teacher should demonstrate how to tie this knot before students begin the investigations.

7. The students' record page is produced in two formats. The one without any information in the tables is used when the teacher wants students to discuss and determine the independent and dependent variables. The following procedure is based on this format. The second form is more directed and is for students who are not experienced enough to deal with determining the category of variables and their relation to graphing.

Procedure

Part One: Relating Multiple Representations

1. Introduce the context of the activity by showing the students a length of rope in which several knots are tied. Lead the students to recognize that as knots are tied, the rope gets shorter. Have them discuss and decide what the dependent variable is by considering: Does the length of the rope depend on the number of knots? or Does the number of knots depend on the length of the rope?

2. When the class has determined that the number of knots is the independent variable and length of the rope is the dependent variable, direct them to record data under the appropriate column. If the students are not familiar with the algebraic convention of using x for the independent variable and the y as the dependent variable, provide appropriate instruction.

3. Direct the students to measure and record the length of the rope with zero knots and then after each of up to four knots. Make sure that the students are all tying single overhand knots. Tell them not to stretch the rope but simply extend it its full length.

4. Ask the students to graph their data. If students are not familiar with adjusting scales on graphs, provide instruction.

5. Have students discuss the patterns they find in the graph and how they relate to the patterns in the chart and context.

6. Encouraging the students to consider the patterns they found, have them predict how long the rope should be if five, six, and seven knots were tied. Have them check their predictions by tying the appropriate number of knots in the rope and measure.

7. Hold a class discussion as to how they made their predictions with the graph and the numbers from the chart. Have the students describe the procedure they used to predict from the numeric chart and then translate their procedure into algebraic form. If students have difficulty in converting their verbal descriptions into symbolic form, facilitate by providing guiding questions.

8. Have students discuss how the terms in the equation relate to the patterns in numbers, on the graph, and to the context.

9. Pose a situation to the students that requires them to work backwards. For example: "How can you determine how many knots to tie in a rope to make it 35 cm long?" Have the class share ways they could use their chart, the graph, and the equation to find a solution.

10. Have students discuss whether the equation will work for any number of knots. Instruct them that they are determining the domain for this function. Have them tie knots to determine how many knots can be tied with the rope length. Have them record the domain as a list ({0, 1, 2,..., maximum}).

11. If students need more practice, have them follow the procedure for different thicknesses of rope. Have the students compare the charts, graphs, and equations of the different ropes.

Discussion

1. What caused the length of the rope to get shorter? What is the independent variable? [number of knots]

2. What patterns do you see in the chart? [The numbers go down about the same amount each time.]

3. How can you determine how much shorter the rope gets with each knot? [average the change for each knot for a number of knots: find how much the length decreases for four knots, and divide the decrease by four to find out the decrease for each knot]

4. What patterns do you see on your graph? [forms a straight line, goes down about the same amount each time]

5. How can you use the graph to determine how long the rope will be after the next knot? [extend the line]

6. How could you use the graph to determine the length of the rope if you know how many knots are tied? [go vertically from number of knots until it intersects the line and then go horizontally]

7. If you know how many knots are in it, how can you use the chart to determine how long the rope is without any knots? [Extend the chart by subtracting the shortened length for each knot until you get to the correct number of knots.]

8. If you know the number of knots (k) in the rope, how would you write an expression with multiplication to tell you how much the rope is shortened? [$s \cdot k$, s = average shortening per knot]

9. If you know the number of knots tied in the rope and how long the rope is without any knots, how would you write an equation (a symbol sentence) that tells how long the rope is? [$L(k) = i - sk$, i=initial length, s=shortening per knot, k= knots; students' equations should have appropriate numbers for all variables but (k).]

10. How do the numbers in your equation relate to the graph and the rope? [factor:slope:shortening per knot; number taken away from: y-intercept: initial rope length]

11. How do differences is rope thickness and length show up in their corresponding graphs and equations? [bigger rope:bigger knot: greater slope: larger factor; longer initial length: greater y-intercept: larger number taken away from]

Procedure

Part Two: Working Backwards from Partial Information

1. Show the class two ropes that are the same diameter and length without any knots. Tie a different number of knots in each length—three knots and seven knots. Measure the length of each and tell the students the length and number of knots for each rope.

2. Distribute a record sheet and have the students use the data to generate a table and graph. Using the table or graph, direct the students to develop an equation for the situation.

3. Have the class discuss how they used the graph or table to determine the length of rope without any knots and how that length shows up in the equation. Untie the knots in one of the ropes to check if their methods worked.

4. Using their equation have students predict the length of the rope with nine, 10, an 11 knots (L(9), L(10), L(11)). As a class check the students' predictions by tying knots in the rope and measuring.

Discussion

1. What patterns do you see in the table?[shortened the same amount each knot]
2. What patterns do you see in the graph?[straight, diagonal line, goes down the same amount each knot]
3. How is the pattern in the table related to the pattern in the graph? [The length the rope shortens with each knot is the amount the graph goes down for each knot.]
4. How do you express how much the rope is shortened if you know the number of knots (k) that have been tied? [amount the rope is shortened each knot (s) • number of knots (k), sk, (Students should use the constant (s) from their graph or table.)]
5. How can you determine how long the rope is without any knots? [extend the line on the graph until it intercepts the y-axis, add the shortening length for each knot until the number of knots is down to zero]
6. Describe in words how you can determine the length of a rope if you know the number of knots in the rope. [From the length of a rope with no knots, subtract the shortening length of a knot the number of times a knot is tied.]
7. How could you write your description in algebraic symbols? [$L(i,s,k) = i - (s \cdot k)$, L = length of rope, i = initial length of rope, s = shortening length per knot, k = number of knots; students should insert constants for (i) and (s) from data]

Procedure

Part Three: Developing an Equation from Context Information

Note: Before doing this lesson the teacher should tie the maximum number of knots in a length of rope and determine how much the rope is shortened with each knot.

1. Have the students discuss their past experiences with ropes and develop the general function as a class.

    $L(i, s, k) = i - sk$

    L = length of rope in cm at a time
    i = initial length of rope without knots
    s = shortened length of rope in cm per knot
    k = number of knots tied

2. Show the class a rope on which the maximum number of knots has been tied. Have the class measure and record the length and number of knots on the rope.
3. Ask the students to recall from prior experience with this diameter of rope or tell them how much

the rope is shortened with each knot. Using the information have the students determine the initial length of rope without knots numerically, graphically, or symbolically.

4. Have them discuss their methods of determining the length of the rope and then untie the knots and measure the length to check.
5. Direct the students to complete the table, graph, and equation and discuss how each relates to the others. If appropriate, lead a discussion of what is the appropriate domain and range for this situation.

Discussion

1. What are the things you need to know to determine how long a rope will become if you tie knots in it? [initial length (i), shortened length (s), number of knots (k)]
2. Describe in words how you would determine the length of rope with knots in it. [From the length of a rope with no knots, subtract the shortening length of a knot the number of times a knot is tied.]
3. How could you write your description in algebraic symbols? [$L(i,s,k) = i - (s \cdot k)$]
4. How can you use the general equation to find the initial length of the rope? [substitute all you know, the length of the rope with knots ($L(i,s,k)$), the shortening length (s), and the number of knots (k); solve for the initial length (i) since it is the only variable]
5. How could you determine the initial length of the rope with the graph or the table? [extend the line on the graph until it intercepts the y-axis, add the shortening length for each knot until the number of knots is down to zero]

Procedure

Part Four: Simultaneous Equations

1. Prepare two lengths of ropes of different diameters which the students have studied. Make sure the thicker rope is longer than the thinner rope.
2. Show the students the two ropes and have them develop an equation for each that will predict its length as knots are tied in it.
3. Focusing student attention on their equations, have them discuss how they might predict if a knot were tied in each rope, how many knots would need to be tied to make both ropes the same length.
4. Have the students graph a line for each rope on the same graph. They may choose to construct the graph by using a table or by going directly from the equations.
5. Focus student attention on the intersection and have them discuss what the intersection says about both ropes.

6. Have the students tie a knot in each rope until the ropes are the same length. Have them measure the length of each rope and check if the length and number of knots match the graph's data.

7. Have the class discuss how the equations can be manipulated to get the same solution. (The teacher may need to direct the line of thinking that since both equations determine the length of the ropes, and since both ropes are of equal length, the expressions for both equations are equal. Putting the two expressions on opposite sides of an equal symbol shows this relationship.)

8. After showing the class the simultaneous equations, have them solve for the number of knots in the ropes and substitute the solution into one of the equations to find the lengths of the ropes. As a class have the students discuss the graphic and symbolic method of finding a solution.

9. Show a third length of rope that is a different diameter than the first two and ask them to determine when the ropes will be the same length and have the same number of knots.

10. Have the students solve the question graphically and symbolically and check their solutions with the ropes.

Discussion

1. How many knots does each rope have where the lines intersect on the graph?

2. How long is each rope where the lines intersect on the graph?

3. What does the intersection of the lines tell you on the graph? [when both ropes are the same length and have the same number of knots]

4. If the number of knots is put into the equation what does the equation tell you? [the length of the rope]

5. If the lengths for both equations are equal, what does that tell you about both expressions? [The expressions are equal.]

6. How can you symbolically write that both equations are equal? [$L_1(k) = L_2(k)$]

7. Is it easier for you to graphically or symbolically find when two ropes are equal in number of knots and length? Why?

8. Which solution, graphic or symbolic, do you think is more accurate? Why?

Extension

Have students predict the maximum number of knots that can be tied in a given length of rope. This is can be solved by looking at two functions. One the shortening of the rope considered in this activity. The second is the increase in the chain of knots remaining on the rope. When the shortened rope is simultaneously the same length as the chain of knots you have no more rope with which to tie another knot. Students will need to gather data about the length of a knot and use a graph or the manipulation of the equations to arrive at an approximate solution.

Functioning with Knots

Knots	Length(cm)
0	
1	
2	
3	
4	
5	
6	
9	
k	

Knots	Length(cm)
0	
1	
2	
3	
4	
5	
6	
9	
k	

Length of Rope

Number of Knots

Y							
X							

Y						
X						

Functioning with Knots

Candy Combinations

Topic
Algebra—Linear Functions

Key Question
What are all of the options in constructing a mixture of five and seven cent candies so that each represents at least 20% of the total number of pieces?

Learning Goals
Students will:
- build a data table for an inverse relationship;
- construct a graph of the data;
- determine the domain and range; and
- write a function rule that fits the data.

Guiding Documents
Project 2061 Benchmarks
- *Mathematical ideas can be represented concretely, graphically, and symbolically.*
- *Tables and graphs can show how values of one quantity are related to values of another.*
- *Organize information in simple tables and graphs and identify relationships they reveal.*

NCTM Standards 2000*
- *Represent, analyze, and generalize a variety of patterns with tables, graphs, words, and, when possible, symbolic rules*
- *Investigate how a change in one variable relates to a change in another variable*
- *Use symbolic algebra to represent situations and to solve problems, especially those that involve linear relationships*
- *Explore relationships between symbolic expressions and graphs of lines, paying particular attention to the meaning of intercept and slope*

Math
Building a data table
Graphing discrete quantities
Investigating inverse relationships
Writing a linear equation

Integrated Processes
Observing
Collecting and recording data
Comparing and contrasting
Interpreting data
Generalizing

Materials
Student sheets

Background Information
This investigation involves graphing discrete data. While points representing possible candy combinations lie on the same straight line and the function is linear, no other points on this line represent possible solutions. Solutions are indicated as solid dots and the line on which the solutions are located is dashed to indicate that points in the intervals between dots are not solutions. Furthermore, the domain is restricted by the conditions in the situation.

Management
1. Students must understand the concepts of function, domain, range, continuous data, and discreet data in order to complete this activity.
2. Students should work together in small groups of three or four.

Procedure
1. If necessary, discuss the concepts that are used in the activity to clarify any questions students may have.
2. Hand out the student pages and go over the instructions.
3. Have students work in their groups to construct a data table, graph the data, and answer the questions.
4. Close with a time of class discussion and sharing after all groups have finished.

Discussion
1. What process did you go through to create a data table showing all of the options? [discovering that only multiples of five Toasties need to be considered and building a table for all such multiples from 0-100]
2. How did you transfer this information onto the graph?
3. Describe (write a description of) the domain. [The domain consists of the multiples of five Toasties from 30 to 80.]
4. Describe (write a description of) the range. [The range consists of the multiples of seven Munchies from 28 to 98.]
5. Is the number of Munchies a function of the number of Toasties? [Yes.] Why? [The data have a linear relationship; as the number of Toasties increases by five the number of Munchies decreases by seven.]
6. Write a rule that fits the data. [M = (-7/5)T + 140.]

7. Is this data continuous or discrete? [discrete] How do you know? [You cannot have partial pieces of candy and you must use the entire $7.00 budget. These restrictions limit the possibilities to only the points marked on the graph, and do not include the points on the line in between.]

Solutions

Students will arrive at solution combinations in various ways. They will discover that only multiples of 5 Toasties constitute possible solutions. This greatly reduces the number of cases that need to be examined.

When all possible solutions are graphed, an additional restriction is imposed by the fact that the numbers of pieces of each type of candy must constitute at least 20% of the mixture. This restricts the domain, and hence the range, as shown in the graph.

Questions on the student page are designed for discussion. Therefore, they are included in the *Discussion* section.

Toasties	0	1	2	3	4	5	6	7	8	9	10
Cost	0	.07	.14	.21	.28	.35	.42	.49	.56	.63	.70
Munchies	140	?	?	?	?	133	?	?	?	?	126
Cost	7.00	?	?	?	?	6.65	?	?	?	?	6.30

Toasties	0	5	10	15	20	25	30	35	40	45	50
Cost	0	.35	.70	1.05	1.40	1.75	2.10	2.45	2.80	3.15	3.50
Munchies	140	133	126	119	112	105	98	91	84	77	70
Cost	7.00	6.65	6.30	5.95	5.60	5.25	4.90	4.55	4.20	3.85	3.50

Toasties	55	60	65	70	75	80	85	90	95	100
Cost	3.85	4.20	4.55	4.90	5.25	5.60	5.95	6.30	6.65	7.00
Munchies	63	56	49	42	35	28	21	14	7	0
Cost	3.15	2.80	2.45	2.10	1.75	1.40	1.05	.70	.35	0

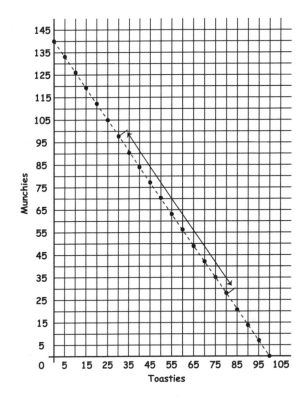

Candy Combinations

As chairperson of the refreshment committee at school, you have been assigned responsibility for preparing a candy mixture for an upcoming party. You have been instructed to spend your entire budget of $7.00. Your committee has selected Toasties and Munchies as the candies for the mixture. The local candy store sells Toasties for $.07 each, and Munchies for $.05 each. Your committee is to submit a description of all possible options to the teacher.

Include the following in your report:
- • a data table showing all options
- • a description of the domain and range
- • a graph of the data
- • a rule that fits the data

1. Use the back of this page for building a data table showing all possible options.
2. Use the grid on the next page for graphing the data.
3. Write a description of the:
   a. domain

   b. range

4. Is the number of Munchies a function of the number of Toasties? Why or why not?

5. Write a rule that fits the data.

6. Is the data discrete or continuous? Please explain.

7. If you faced a similar problem in the future, what did you learn that would be helpful in attacking the problem?

Candy Combinations

Use the grid below to graph your data. Label each axis with the appropriate candy and number the lines.

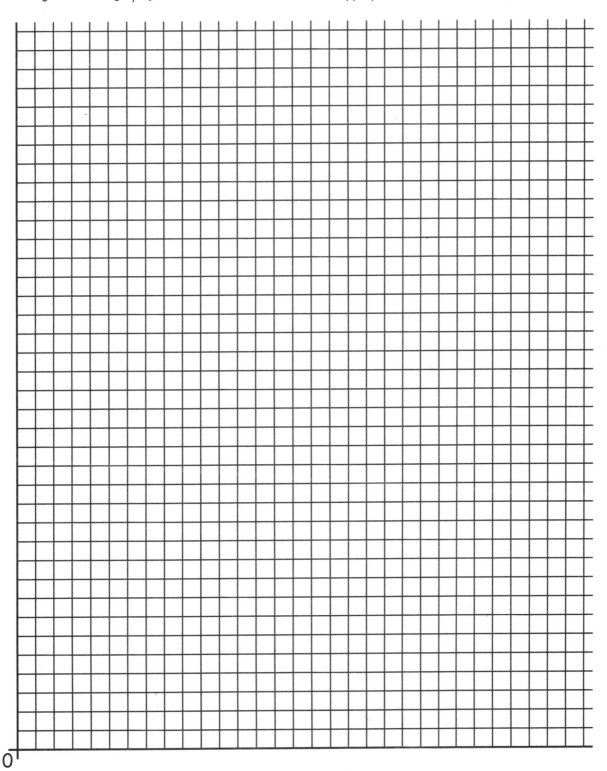

0

Nickels and Dimes

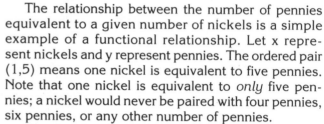

Topic
Algebra—Linear Functions

Key Question
How can the language of algebra be used to describe the relationship between the number of nickels and dimes that add to exactly one dollar.

Learning Goals
Students will:
- construct a table, draw a graph, and write an algebraic rule for the number of nickels and dimes that add to exactly one dollar; and
- apply the domain and range concepts to a real-world situation.

Guiding Documents
Project 2061 Benchmark
- *Symbolic equations can be used to summarize how the quantity of something changes over time or in response to other changes.*

NCTM Standards 2000*
- *Represent, analyze, and generalize a variety of patterns with tables, graphs, words, and, when possible, symbolic rules*
- *Investigate how a change in one variable relates to a change in another variable*
- *Use symbolic algebra to represent situations and to solve problems, especially those that involve linear relationships*
- *Explore relationships between symbolic expressions and graphs of lines, paying particular attention to the meaning of intercept and slope*

Math
Algebra
    function
        domain, range

Integrated Processes
Observing
Communicating
Generalizing

Materials
Rulers (for drawing lines)

Background Information
One definition for *function* states that a function is a set of ordered pairs (x, y) in which each value of x is paired with exactly one value of y. Students learn to graph ordered pairs very early in the math curriculum.

The relationship between the number of pennies equivalent to a given number of nickels is a simple example of a functional relationship. Let x represent nickels and y represent pennies. The ordered pair (1,5) means one nickel is equivalent to five pennies. Note that one nickel is equivalent to *only* five pennies; a nickel would never be paired with four pennies, six pennies, or any other number of pennies.

Knowing that there are five pennies in every nickel, a table relating the number of pennies in a given number of nickels can be constructed.

A function can therefore be thought of as a *rule* that assigns exactly one value to a variable *y* for every given value of a variable *x*. The given variable x is called the *independent variable* and y, the variable to which values are assigned by the rule, is called the *dependent* variable.

The fact that the are five pennies in every nickel is essentially a rule. The rule can be compactly expressed by the equation y = 5x where y is the number of pennies in x nickels.

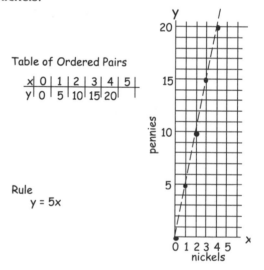

Table of Ordered Pairs

x	0	1	2	3	4	5
y	0	5	10	15	20	

Rule
    y = 5x

The *domain* of a function is the set of x values specified for the function; the range is the set of values assigned by the rule to the y variable. In the example, the domain is nickels and the range is pennies.

The slope-intercept form of a linear function is written as y = mx + b where *m* is the slope and *b* the y-intercept.

The *slope* is defined as *rise*, the vertical change between two points, divided by the *run*, the horizontal change between two points. In the above graph, the rise equals five and the run equals one. Therefore, m, the slope, equals 5/1 or 5.

The y-intercept is defined as the point where the function intercepts the y-axis. In the graph, the y-intercept equals zero.

The slope-intercept form, $y = mx + b$, can now be written as $y = 5x + 0$ or simply $y = 5x$.

The fact that one nickel equals five cents is combined with the fact that one dime equals ten cents to pose the Key Question for this activity. All of the above definitions can now be applied, in the same manner, to this more challenging problem.

If x represents nickels and y represents dimes, then $5x + 10y = 100$ is the equation for the rule.

The equation for the rule that relates the number of nickels and dimes that add to one dollar is a member of the Addition Family of linear algebraic equations.

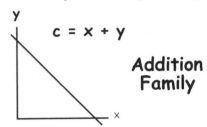

c = x + y

Addition Family

Management

1. To facilitate student involvement, group the students in pairs. This can be especially helpful when students are asked to find the rule for the function.

Procedure

1. Teach or review the *Background Information* with the students and clarify the meaning of all terminology.
2. Tell the students that they are to imagine they have a dollar's worth of nickels and a dollar's worth of dimes. Instruct them to find the different ways nickels and dimes can be grouped so that their sum equals exactly one dollar. As an example, ask them how many dimes would be grouped with eight nickels to make one dollar? [Eight nickels equals forty cents so six dimes grouped with eight nickels equals one dollar.]
3. Distribute the *Nickels and Dimes* student page.
4. Instruct students to build the table.
5. Distribute rulers and tell the students to draw the graph using a dashed line.
6. Tell the students to write the rule. Allow student pairs to discuss strategies for finding the rule.
7. Have the students record the domain and range of the function.

Discussion

1. What observations can you make from the data table? Why are their no dimes paired with odd numbers of nickels?
2. Explain what the graph illustrates.
3. Choose a point on the graph and apply the rule to that point.

Solutions

1.

Number of Nickels (n)	0	1	2	3	4	5	6	7	8	9	10
Number of Dimes (n)	10		9		8		7		6		5

(continued)

	11	12	13	14	15	16	17	18	19	20
		4		3		2		1		0

2.

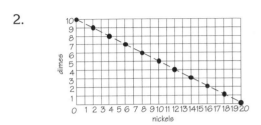

3.
$$d = -1/2n + 10$$
$$\text{or } f(n) = -1/2n + 10$$

4. **Domain** = [0, 2, 4, 6, 8, 10, 12, 14, 16, 18, 20]
   Range = [0, 1, 2, 3, 4, 5, 6, 7, 8, 9, 10]

Extensions

If you would like students to practice and extend the skills exercised with the *Nickels and Dimes*, the first student page, distribute the second student page, *Dimes and Nickels*. The table, graph, rule, domain, and range for *Dimes and Nickels* are shown below.

Number of Dimes (n)	0	1	2	3	4	5	6	7	8	9	10
Number of Nickels (n)	20	18	16	14	12	10	8	6	4	2	0

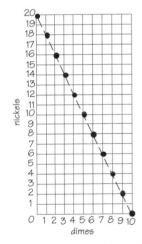

$$n = -2d + 20$$
$$\text{or } f(n) = -2d + 20$$

Domain = [0, 1, 2, 3, 4, 5, 6, 7, 8, 9, 10]
Range = [0, 2, 4, 6, 8, 10, 12, 14, 16, 18, 20]

Nickels and Dimes

Only certain numbers of nickels and dimes add up to exactly $1

Let n, the independent variable, represent nickels.
Let d, the dependent variable, represent dimes.

1. Build the table.

n	0	1	2	3	4	5	6	7	8	9	10	11	12	13	14	15	16	17	18	19	20
d	10																				

2. Draw the graph.

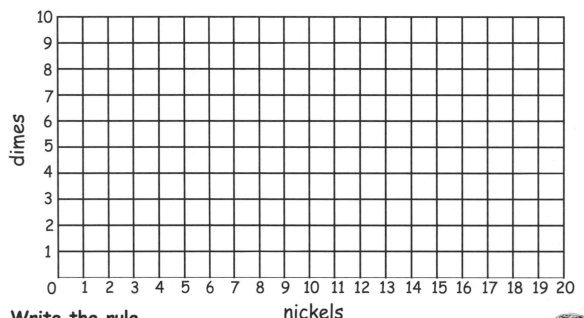

3. Write the rule.
4. What is the domain?

What is the range?

144

Dimes and Nickels

Only certain numbers of nickels and dimes add up to exactly $1

Let d, the independent variable, represent dimes.
Let n, the dependent variable, represent nickels.

1. Build the table.

d	0	1	2	3	4	5	6	7	8	9	10
n	20										

2. Draw the graph.

3. Write the rule.

4. What is the domain?

   What is the range?

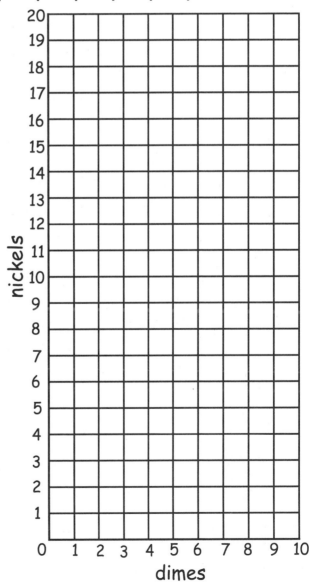

Mystery Mass
How Wendy, Chan, and Carlos Addressed the Challenge

This imaginary discussion among three students illustrates the desired ideal for the way that students should address the challenge presented by activities such as *Mystery Mass*. To reach this level of discussion requires constant thoughtful guidance and nurturing by the teacher along with much patience. Dr. Polya advised teachers to ask students enough questions to keep them moving forward but not so many as to leave nothing for them to do. Because this investigation calls for an unusual approach in order to find the solution, it presents a unique opportunity for students to engage in strategy discussions.

The investigation is introduced by Miss Brooks, the teacher of Wendy, Chan, and Carlos.

"It is important to learn to solve problems in more than one way. Dr. George Polya was a world-renowned mathematician who loved to tell his students that 'it is better to solve one problem five ways than five problems one way.' The purpose of studying mathematics is not so much to solve a large number of problems as to find multiple ways of solving a smaller number of problems.

"Why couldn't we just find the mass of the object in the usual way?" Phil complains. "That is a lot easier."

"Certainly it would be easier but that would miss the whole point. The purpose is to prepare you to cope with those real-world situations where an indirect means of making measurements will be required.

"Remember, too, that it is important to learn to solve problems in more then one way. Dr. George Polya was a world-renowned mathematician who loved to tell his students that 'it is better to solve one problem five ways than five problems one way.' The purpose of studying mathematics is not so much to solve a large number of problems as to find multiple ways of solving a smaller number of problems.

"Today you have the opportunity to follow his advice. I will be interested to see how many ways of solving this problem you come up with. After we finish, we will report and compare our methods. That should be interesting to all of us."

Wendy, Chan, and Carlos set to work planning their strategy.

"What do we have? A two-pan balance, the object with an unknown mass, and five- and ten-gram pieces," Chan points out. "Somehow, the clue for solving the problem with linear functions lies hidden in one of these."

The long pause that follows is finally broken by Wendy.

"The only use for the balance is to bring the two quantities into equilibration. There is no clue there. I don't think we'll find the clue in the mystery mass either. That leaves the two sets of masses."

"I think I've got an idea," Carlos offers. "It's obvious we have to put the unknown mass on the balance so let's put it in the left pan. That leaves us with the decision about what to do with the two types of pieces."

"If we want to create a regular pattern required by linear functions, it's clear we can't mix the two types of pieces," Chan opines. "That suggests we should put them on opposite sides of the balance."

"I think I've got it!" Wendy exults. "The mystery mass brought the left side down. The only way for the right side to catch up is to place ten-gram pieces on it."

" But we can't just put masses on the right till it balances because that would be using direct measurement," Carlos objects. "So, why don't we place five-gram pieces on the left as we place ten-gram pieces on the right?"

"That brings us face to face with linear functions," Wendy reminds her colleagues. "If we take your suggestion we can create patterns by adding ten-gram pieces one by one to the right matched by adding five-gram pieces to the left."

"I like that!" Chan says admiringly. "I see that it would create two different conditions. On the left we have a mixture of an unknown mass *plus* five-gram pieces and on the right we would have only ten-gram pieces."

"That suggests two different linear functions, one for the left and the other for the right, doesn't it?" Wendy queries.

"I think you're right," Chan responds. "I've been thinking about the right side because it's clean since it has only ten-gram pieces. We start with zero mass, then add ten-gram pieces one by one. To me that looks like the first type of linear function in our chart."

"Aha!" Carlos observes. "It has to be. It's a linear function that passes through the origin because we start with zero mass and zero pieces! Each time we add a piece the total goes up ten grams. That'll graph as a straight line passing through the origin. The ordered pairs (total mass, number of pieces) give us the slope. Since we have a point and a slope we can sketch the graph right now!"

"You're convincing!" Wendy confesses. "But the left side is a different story because it starts with the mystery object on the pan. This gives the linear function a y-intercept other than zero. The value for b in the rule has to be positive."

"You know what? The value of the y-intercept is the mass of the mystery object!" Chan explains.

"That's mighty interesting," Carlos responds. "I always get a charge out of seeing something in the real world that corresponds with something in the linear function rule. Here is another example! However, we won't know the y-intercept until we find the unknown mass of the object."

"One thing we can get is the slope," Wendy continues, "it is rise over run, in this case total mass over number of pieces. But we have no point to anchor this line so we can't graph it. Somehow, we have to get a point for this second line."

"It looks like we're stuck," Carlos complains. "Where do we go from here?"

Silence settles over their conversation as they ponder their dilemma.

"Look! When the two sides balance, both lines share a common point," Chan observes excitedly. "What we have to do is find the point where the two sides balance! It is the balancing act that ties the two linear functions together."

"Bravo!" Carlos enthuses. "We'll find that point as we gather the data. I'm ready to go to work building the data table and graphing the data. I'm eager to see where we will get a balance. What data do we need?"

"I can think of four things," Wendy responds, "the total mass in the left pan, the total mass in the right pan, the number of pieces added, and which way the balance tilts. I think that's all we need."

Chan sketches the table.

"I can see how we get the total mass on the right but what do we do with the left? It has an object with an unknown mass." Carlos remarks with puzzlement.

"Let's just assign x as the mass of the object," Wendy suggests. "That's how we use x. It stands for the unknown. If we do that then the total mass on the left starts with x and continues with $x + 5$, $x + 10$, etc."

They begin, adding five-gram masses to the left side matched by ten-gram masses on the right. With each successive addition they note the tilt of the pan.

Mass in Left Pan	x	x + 5	x + 10	x + 15	x + 20	x + 25	x + 30	x + 35	x + 40	x + 45
Mass in Right Pan	0	10	20	30	40	50	60	70	80	90
Number of Pieces	0	1	2	3	4	5	6	7	8	9
Side Tilting down	Left	Left	Left	Left	Left	Left	Left	Right	Right	Right

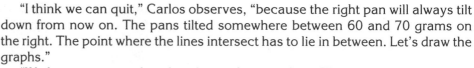

"I think we can quit," Carlos observes, "because the right pan will always tilt down from now on. The pans tilted somewhere between 60 and 70 grams on the right. The point where the lines intersect has to lie in between. Let's draw the graphs."

"We have to remember that this is discrete data. That means we will have discrete points instead of a line in our graph," Chan adds.

Wendy has already begun to plot the points and soon the graph of the function for the right side is completed.

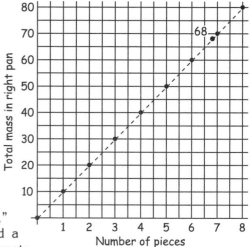

"One down and one to go," Chan exults with satisfaction.

"Watching the balance, I noticed that it went down very slowly when we added the seventh ten-gram piece," Wendy notes. "That suggests the actual balance point is much closer to 70 grams than to 60 grams on this right side. I am going to estimate 68 grams."

"That looks about right to me," Carlos concurs. "I think we need a dashed line to help us locate our estimate even though these are discrete data," he adds as he sketches the dashed line.

"This intersection gives us a point to anchor the graph of the second function," Chan suggests.

"We know that the slope is five because the mass increased five grams with the addition of each new piece. That means we have a point and a slope so we can sketch a similar dashed line through this point with a slope of 5. It will help us locate the other points that belong to the graph of this second function," Wendy informs her colleagues.

The dashed line and the points representing the second function are quickly graphed.

The second linear function is quickly graphed.

"Look! The y-intercept is about at 34. That means the mystery object has to have a mass of about 34 grams," Chan concludes.

"That was an interesting path!" Wendy observes as she proceeds to summarize their procedure. "First, we graphed the linear function for the right side, next we thought of associating the point where the two sides balance with the point of intersection of the two lines, and then we graphed the second line beginning at that point of intersection. That is an indirect method if I've ever seen one!"

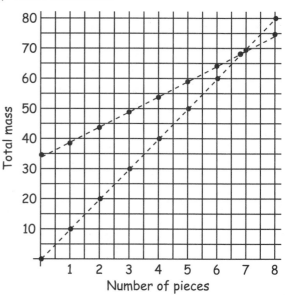

"Now that we have found the mystery mass by an indirect method, I think we ought to check it by direct measurement," Carlos suggests.

"Obviously!" Chan says, seconding the idea.

Using direct measurement, they find the object has a mass of 33 grams.

"We can check this result by comparing it with the point where the two sides balance," Carlos suggests. "The change in tilt occurred after we had added seven pieces to each side. Each time we added matched pairs, the mass on the right increased five grams more than on the left. After seven additions, the increase is 35 grams. Thirty-five added grams on the right outbalances the 33 grams mass of the object so the right tilts down. That confirms 33 grams as the mass of the mystery object."

"Isn't it interesting to see how the linear function rule models what happens in the real world?" Wendy summarizes. "In the rule, b turns out to be the mystery mass and the key point that ties the two functions together is where the sides balance! Algebra doesn't get any more real than that!"

"We now have all the data we need to write the rule for each side," Chan concludes. "Using n for the number of pieces, the rule for the contents on the left side is $f(n) = 5n + 34$. If we want it to apply to the initial mass of any object, the more general form would be $f(n) = 5n + O$ where O is the mass of the object. The rule for the contents on the right side is simply $f(n) = 20n$. That ought to wrap it up."

MYSTERY MASS

Topic
Algebra—Linear Functions

Key Question
How can linear functions be used to find the unknown mass of an object by indirect means?

Learning Goals
Students will:
- discover the relationship of linear functions to a real-world situation,
- use linear functions to find the mass of an object by indirect means,
- collect and graph discrete data, and
- write linear function rules for the situations.

Guiding Documents
Project 2061 Benchmarks
- *Mathematically ideas can be represented concretely, graphically, and symbolically.*
- *Tables and graphs can show how values of one quantity are related to values of another.*
- *Organize information in simple tables and graphs and identify relationships they reveal.*

NCTM Standards 2000*
- *Represent, analyze, and generalize a variety of patterns with tables, graphs, words, and, when possible, symbolic rules*
- *Investigate how a change in one variable relates to a change in another variable*
- *Use symbolic algebra to represent situations and to solve problems, especially those that involve linear relationships*
- *Explore relationships between symbolic expressions and graphs of lines, paying particular attention to the meaning of intercept and slope*

Math
Discerning linear functions in a situation
Identifying independent and dependent variables
Designing and using a data table
Graphing discrete quantities
Formulating linear equations
Estimation

Integrated Processes
Observing
Collecting and recording data
Comparing and contrasting
Interpreting data
Generalizing

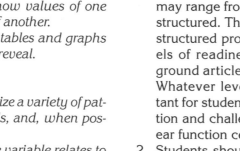

Materials
For each group:
two-pan balance
supply of 5-gram and 10-gram pieces
object with an unknown mass (between 25 and 50 grams)

For each student:
ruler
student sheets

Background Information
Please see the article entitled *Linear Functions in Review* for the background on this activity.

Management
1. The challenge in *Mystery Mass* is for students to find the mass of an object by indirect means utilizing linear function concepts. The investigation may range from fully structured to completely unstructured. The student sheets provide for a semi-structured procedure. For students at other levels of readiness, modify as needed. The background article utilizes an unstructured approach. Whatever level of structure is used, it is important for students to be fully briefed about the situation and challenged to maximally incorporate linear function concepts.
2. Students should work together in groups of three or four. Each group will need an object with an unknown mass. The mass should be somewhere between 25 and 50 grams. The objects may be the same for each group, or different.
3. It is important to distinguish between discrete and continuous data in every application. In this activity students are dealing with discrete data, and should use dashed lines to connect the points on their graphs.
4. The graph for the first function representing the right side of the balance is that of a proportional relationship (one which goes through the origin). The graph for the second function which represents the left side of the balance is not proportional (one which does not go through the origin).
5. The key to being able to graph the second function lies in the point of intersection of the two graphs. This point is where the two sides are in balance. Depending on the mass of the unknown object, this point will likely require students to make an estimate that lies between two 10-gram pieces.

Procedure

1. Have students get into groups and distribute the materials.
2. Hand out the first student sheet and go over the procedure as a class. Be sure students understand that the goal is not to find the mass of the object using direct measurement, but to determine the mass *indirectly*.
3. As students work to complete the table, move from group to group, giving assistance as needed.
4. Once all groups have completed the table, hand out the remaining student sheets and help students construct their graphs. They will need to correctly label and number each axis based on the data they collected in the first part of the activity. Remind students that they should be using dashed lines to connect the points because the data is discreet.
5. When all groups have determined the approximate mass of the mystery object, have students check their estimates using direct measurement. If any of the values are highly discrepant, have students explore where the error may have occurred.
5. After they have completed their graphs and directly measured their objects, have students work individually to complete the questions, then close with a time of class discussion and sharing.

Discussion

1. Describe the method you used to determine the mass of the object.
2. When you used direct measurement, did this value agree with your estimate? Why or why not? What are some possible reasons for any discrepancies?
3. What did your graph look like? Why?
4. How were you able to determine which variable to put on each axis?
5. What is the approximate mass of your object? How do you know?
6. What is the independent variable in the left pan? ...the right pan? [The number of pieces is the independent variable for both pans.]
7. What is the dependent variable in the left pan? ...the right pan? [The mass in that pan is the dependent variable for each pan.]
8. How were you able to graph both lines?

9. Are both of the lines the same? [No] Why or why not? [The left pan (mystery object) has non-proportional data, while the right pan has proportional data. Only the proportional line goes through the origin.]

Extension

Use gram units other than five and ten and see how this changes the results and the processes.

Solutions

Solutions will vary depending on the mass of the unknown object. See the article entitled *Linear Functions in Review* for sample tables and graphs from this activity.

One group of students found the mass of a mystery object indirectly by using the following prœdure. They placed the mystery object with an unknown mass in the left pan of a balance. They added one 5-gram piece to the left pan each time they added a 10-gram piece to the right pan.

Duplicate their procedure to find the mass of your mystery object. Record your data in the table below.

Mass in Left Pan (g)									
Mass in Right Pan (g)									
Number of Pieces									
Side Tilting Down									

Answer these questions after you have completed the following two pages.

1. Describe the sequence of steps you followed to find the mass of the mystery object.

2. What is the approximate mass of your mystery object? How do you know?

3. What meaning do you attach to the intersection of the two graphs?

MYSTERY MASS

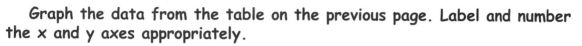

Graph the data from the table on the previous page. Label and number the x and y axes appropriately.

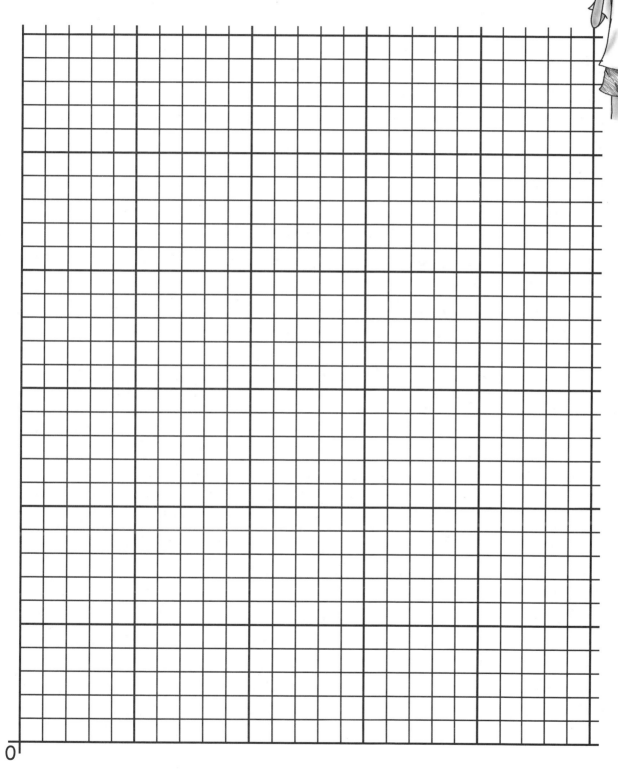

0

MYSTERY MASS

Identify and/or describe the following:

Left Pan

a. Independent variable:

b. Dependent variable:

c. Slope:

d. Relationship of the dependent variable to the independent variable:

e. Let "I" represent the independent or input variable and "O" the dependent or output variable. Write an expression relating I and O:

f. Is the output proportional to the input? Please explain.

Right Pan

a. Independent variable:

b. Dependent variable:

c. Slope:

d. Relationship of the dependent variable to the independent variable:

e. Let "I" represents the independent or input variable and "O" the dependent or output variable. Write an expression relating I and O:

f. Is the output proportional to the input? Please explain.

Part Five:
More Interesting Objects And Linear Functions

The activities in *Part Five* continue the study of interesting, everyday objects in which relationships can be modeled by linear functions. There is continued emphasis on the development of facility in using the language and processes of algebra.

In *Stacking Cups* students collect data relating the number of paper cups to the height of their stack. Measurement is done directly on the graph and then translated into numeric form. Connections between the abstract and concrete are built as the meaning of the graph, including its slope and y-intercept, is interpreted in this real-world context.

The Thick of Things has students collect data from stacking objects of uniform thickness, such as pattern blocks or tiles, directly on a graph. Based on the resulting numeric data, they examine the relationship between the number of pieces and the thickness of the pile and write a function rule to describe it.

In *Pattern Block Functions* students study the relationship between perimeters and the number of tiles in various pattern block sequences. While gathering data they are forced to focus sharply on the concept of perimeter. They make the interesting discovery that the graphs for all the different pattern blocks sequences have the same y-intercept and ponder the question, "Why?"

Rising Towers focuses on the concepts of surface area and volume. Uniform cubes are stacked to create towers and the relationships of height to volume and height to surface area are analyzed to determine whether they are proportional. Students are required to defend their conclusions.

Rectangle Jamboree is an investigation of the relationship among rectangles with the same perimeter. In constructing the graph all of the rectangles are placed in the first quadrant with one vertex at the origin. An interesting relationship between the results and the addition table is discovered.

In *Books upon Books* students determine at what point a stack of thin books placed on, for example, a telephone directory, will equal the height of a stack of the same number of thicker books placed directly on the desk. They formulate and graph linear equations for each stack and use them to determine the answer.

A Winter Holiday Adventure is the one activity in this publication drawn from life science. Students explore the rate of growth of an amaryllis or similar plant and discover that the growth in length is a linear function of the time. Curve-fitting concepts are an important aspect of this investigation. Hopefully, this activity will pique the curiosity of students to want to explore the growth rates of a broad range of plants and turn this into a major long-term project.

Topic
Algebra—Linear Functions

Key Questions
How can the height of a stack of cups be shown on a graph or in an equation?
How can graphs and equations for two different types of cups be used to determine when the two stacks of the cups will be the same height and have the same amount of cups in them?

Learning Goals
Students will:
- represent data on a graph and interpret the graph's meaning in the context,
- recognize the connection of the rate of change in numeric form as an equivalent to the slope of the line in graphic form,
- develop an equation that relates the outcome to the variable conditions in the context,
- work backwards from a limited amount of data to generate an equation and line on a graph, and
- recognize how equations can be solved simultaneously both graphically and symbolically.

Guiding Documents
Project 2061 Benchmarks
- *Mathematical statements can be used to describe how one quantity changes when another changes. Rates of change can be computed from magnitudes and vice versa.*
- *Graphs can show a variety of possible relationships between two variables. As one variable increases uniformly, the other may do one of the following: always keep the same proportion to the first, increase or decrease steadily, increase or decrease faster and faster, get closer and closer to some limiting value, reach some intermediate maximum or minimum, alternately increase and decrease indefinitely, increase and decrease in steps, or do something different from any of these.*

NCTM Standards 2000*
- *Represent, analyze, and generalize a variety of patterns with tables, graphs, words, and, when possible, symbolic rules*
- *Relate and compare different forms of representation for a relationship*
- *Explore relationships between symbolic expressions and graphs of lines, paying particular attention to the meaning of intercept and slope*

- *Use graphs to analyze the nature of changes in quantities in linear relationships*
- *Model and solve contextualized problems using various representations, such as graphs, tables, and equations*

Math
Rates
Graphing
   slope, intercept
   interpreting
Variables
Writing equations
Simultaneous equations
Measuring

Integrated Processes
Observing
Comparing and contrasting
Collecting and recording data
Interpreting data
Generalizing

Materials
Disposable cups (see *Management 3*)
Straight edge
Meter stick

Background Information
In one sample of cups, a stack of six Styrofoam coffee cups was the same height as a stack of six paper cups even though each paper cup was 2.5 cm taller than each Styrofoam cup. The height of the stack depends on more than the height of each cup. The height of the stack of cups depends on three things.
- The number of cups (c) in the stack clearly helps determine the height of the stack.
- As the cups are stacked it becomes evident that each cup adds only a short part of the top (called the rim in the future) of its total height to the stack's height.
- The third component of the stack's height is the part of the cup that remains after the rim is taken away.

As students study the data generated by a stack of cups, they recognize how these components can be seen in the numeric, graphic, and symbolic representations as well as in the cup itself.

Given a set of Styrofoam cups, students can lay a stack of a known amount of cups on the vertical line representing that amount of cups and then mark the height of the stack on the line with a dot. As stacks of one, two, three, and four cups are marked on the graph, the students will recognize that the dots form a line. Extending this line on the graph will allow the heights of stacks with a greater number of cups to be predicted.

With the graph directly constructed from the cups, students will relate the rise between adjacent dots to the height of the rim of each cup. On Styrofoam cups this rim is very evident. To confirm the rise in the graphed line is equivalent to the rim of the cup, the rim can be placed on the graph. As students transfer the graphed data to the numeric chart, they will see that the height increases by about the same amount each time. The average increase is the same as the typical rise (slope), which can be confirmed by measuring the cup's rim with a ruler. If the rim of a Styrofoam cup measures 1.2 cm, the increase in the height of a stack of could be expressed as (1.2 • c).

This expression does not tell height of the stack as is quickly shown by substituting the number of cups from the data and not getting the measured height. As students consider a stack they will see that the height is not all rims, but includes the part of the first cup that is not the rim. Students will suggest measuring the height of this part (8.3 cm for the sample Styrofoam cup) and adding it to the product of the expression. Their suggestion can be written algebraically as:

$$H(c) = 1.2c + 8.3$$

The factor with c in the equation is the slope of the line and the rim of the cup. The remaining part of the cup is added to the expression in the equation and shows up where the line on the graph intersects the vertical axis, the y-intercept. This experience provides a very concrete model of the slope-intercept form of an equation and how it relates to a graph and a situation.

This experience also provides understanding for the concepts of function. Students need to determine that the height of the stack is dependent on the number of cups. So the height of the stack is a function of the number of cups. The stack is made out of individual cups so it is graphed as distinct dots with a dashed line representing the pattern. The number of cups must be a whole number so the domain for the function is whole numbers.

The y-intercept on the graph provides an interesting point of discussion. When there are zero cups, the stack must have no height. The y-intercept would suggest that the sample has a height of 8.3 cm when there are no cups. The linear pattern of the graph and its equivalent equation are true when the number of cups is a whole number greater than zero. The domain of numbers we are allowed to use is limited.

When students are provided with only limited data, they need to use algebraic thinking to construct what is missing. Students were shown a stack of four hot cups 14.1 cm high and a stack of seven hot cups 16.2 cm high. Then they were asked to determine the height of one cup and develop an equation relating the height of the stack to the number of cups in the stack. Students chose one of two ways to proceed.

Some preferred the graphic format in which they plotted two points on the graph representing the two stacks and then drew a line connecting the two points,

explaining that the stack would increase at a consistent rate. Using the graph they determined the height of one cup and generated numeric data to complete a table. From the numbers they determined the typical rim height ($\approx$0.6-0.7 cm), the slope. They determined the y-intercept ($\approx$11 cm) by looking at the graph. Using what they knew of the context, they reasoned that the height of the stack was the product of the rim height and number of rims plus the height of the first cup without its rim:

$$H(c) \approx 0.6c + 11.$$

Because of precision in graphing, this is an approximation.

More precise equations were developed by the other students that chose the numeric format. By finding the difference in cups and heights, these students reasoned that it took three rims to increase the height of the stack by 2.1 cm. By dividing the change between the three cups, they found each rim had a height of 0.7 cm. Working backwards by subtracting four (0.7 • 4 = 2.8 cm) typical rims from the height of four cups (14.1 cm), they determined the height of one cup without the rim (14.1 - 2.8 = 11.3 cm). The equation generated by this line of thinking was:

$$H(c) = 0.7c + 11.3.$$

When all students were shown a large stack of 25 cups and challenged to use their equations to predict the height, they found their predictions differed by over 2 cm. When the stack was measured, the students saw that the numerically-generated equation was more precise.

As students have experience with a variety of cups, they will come to generalize that the height of a stack depends on or is a function of three variables, the rim height (r), the part of the cup remaining when the rim is ignored (l) and the number of cups (c). This function can be written in algebraic form:

$$H(r,c,l) = rc + l,$$

equivalent to the more familiar

$$y = mx + b.$$

Given one cup students can generate an equation for that type of cup by measuring. The (r) is the rim height, which on a paper cup is the recessed lip on the bottom of the cup. The (l) is what remains of the cup ignoring the rim. The equation is graphed by placing a point on the y-axis the height of (l), the y-intercept. A second point is graphed by moving one cup to the right and up the (r) rim height. Connecting and extending the line between these two points, graphs the pattern of change made by stacking the cups. The precision of the equation and graph can be checked against stacks of the cup.

If students were to graph the data from the Styrofoam and paper cups used in the first two examples on the same graph, they would discover the lines would intersect at the point of six cups and 15.5 cm of height. When asked about the significance of the intersection, many students will have little idea. When asked to make a stack of six cups of both types, they will be quick to recognize they are the same height—15.5 cm. Now they will say that the intersection tells them that both stacks are equal in height and number of cups at the same time, or simultaneously. They see the relationship graphically and in the context. Seeing it in symbolic form is more difficult. Have students reconsider the two equations:

$$H_1(c) = 1.2c + 8.3$$
$$H_2(c) = 0.7c + 11.3$$

Since both equations determine the height of a stack, and since both stacks are of equal height, the expressions for both equations are equal. Putting the two expressions on opposite sides of an equal symbol shows this relationship.

$$H_1(c) = H_2(c)$$
or
$$1.2c + 8.3 = 0.7c + 11.3$$

Using this equation the students can solve for (c).

$$
\begin{array}{r}
1.2c + 8.3 = 0.7c + 11.3 \\
\underline{-0.7c = -0.7c} \\
0.5c + 8.3 = 11.3 \\
\underline{-8.3 = -8.3} \\
0.5c = 3 \\
\underline{\div 0.5 = \div 0.5} \\
c = 6
\end{array}
$$

Substituting 6 into either equation for the number of cups will generate a height of 15.5 cm.

Provided with a meaningful model students can reason through the situation numerically and graphically to develop an understanding to the more abstract symbolic representation.

Management

1. This series of investigations is based around the same context, stacks of cups. Most teachers will find it most profitable to revisit the context several times as students' understanding becomes more sophisticated. Other teachers find a more holistic understanding develops when the series of investigations is used as a unit. Several contexts can be thoroughly explored before going on to a more abstract approach based on the intuitive understanding developed from the context.

2. These investigations work well in collaborative groups of two to four students. However some teachers may prefer having the data gathered as a class. This provides more control and direction but does not allow students to practice the related skills of measurement and will not provide the first-hand experience some students require.

3. The investigations are based on three different types of disposable cups: Styrofoam coffee cups, paper hot drink cups, and paper cold drink cups. Each group will need a set of four to five cups each and a combined class sample of 20 to 30 cups. An appropriate selection is available at restaurant supply stores. Check local fast food restaurants to see if the required cups might be donated to your class.

4. Except for *Part Four* on simultaneous equations, the height of the cups is not critical except that the cups should vary in body height and rim height. For *Part Four*, it is critical that the shorter height cup have a larger rim height than the taller cup. This will allow the stack of shorter cups to equal the stack of taller cups as more cups are added.

Procedure

Part One: Relating Multiple Representations

1. Explain to the students that they are going to consider how rapidly a stack of cups grows in height as more cups are added to the stack.

2. Distribute five cups to each group and a record sheet to each student. Explain the measuring and recording procedure of laying the stack of cups down along the respective cup line and marking the stack's height with a dot. (There is a slight discrepancy between the height of the stack and this diagonal length, but it is minimal and can be ignored.) Use stacks of one to five cups to generate a series of dots.

3. Have the students measure and record the stack height directly on the graph and discuss the patterns formed.

4. Direct them to translate the data from the graph to numeric data on the chart.

5. Discuss what patterns are found in the chart and then encourage the students to use the patterns to predict the heights of stacks of six, seven, and 15 cups. As a class, have them check the accuracy of their predictions.

6. Discuss how the patterns in the chart show up on the graph and in the context of the stacks of cups.

7. Encourage the students to consider the numeric patterns in the chart and have them describe a procedure of how to determine the height for a specified number of cups and then translate their procedure into an equation.

8. Discuss the similarities and relationships among the equation, graph and chart.

9. Have the students repeat the procedure for another type of cup and make comparisons among the tables, graphs, and equations generated by each type of cup.

Discussion

1. What patterns do you see in the heights of cup stacks on your graph? [form a straight line, go up about the same amount each time]

2. How could you use the graph to determine how high the next stack will be? [extend the line]

3. How could you use the graph to determine the height of a stack if you knew the number of cups? [go vertically from number of cups until it intersects line and then go horizontally]

4. What does the graph tell you about how the stack grows? [each cup makes the line go up about the same amount]

5. How can you determine the typical amount the stack grows with each cup? [average the change for each

cup for a number of cup additions; find how much it increases for three cups and divide the increase by three to find out the increase for one cup]

6. Where do you see this increase in the stack of cups? [in the stack of rims]

7. How would you write an expression to tell you how much of the stack is made of rims if you know the number of cups(c) in the stack [i • c, i = average increase]

8. What is missing from the height of the stack if you know the part of the stack's height the rims contribute? [the part of the first cup that is not the rim]

9. How would you write an equation (a symbol sentence) that tells how to find the height of a stack of cups if you know the number of cups in the stack? [H(c) = ic + r, i = increase of rim, c = number of cups, r = remainder without rims, students' equations should have appropriate numbers for all variables but (c).]

10. How do the numbers in your equation relate to the graph and the cups in the stack? [factor:slope:rim, number added: y-intercept: cup without rim]

11. How do differences in cup types show up in their corresponding graphs and equations? [bigger rim: greater slope: larger factor, bigger cup without rim: greater y-intercept: larger number added]

Procedure
Part Two: Working Backwards from Partial Information

1. Show the class a stack of four cups and stack of seven cups. As a class, determine the heights of each stack.

2. Ask the students to determine the height of a stack of 15 cups while completing the chart and graph for the stack.

3. Have the students share their methods of finding the solution.

4. Direct the students to use the graphic and numeric data to develop an equation relating the height to the number of cups.

5. Hold a discussion as to how the students generated the equation by relating the factor to the slope or average rim height, and the added height to the y-intercept and a cup height less the rim.

6. Allow time for the students to use their equations to predict the heights of various stacks and check their results by measuring the stacks.

Discussion

1. How can you determine the height of a stack of 15 cups using your graph? [plot known points, assume a linear relationship so connect and extend line to 15 cups]

2. How can you determine the height of a stack of 15 cups using your table? [find average difference, multiply average difference by the number of cups needed (8) and add to the height of 7 cups]

3. How can you use your graph to develop an equation for the stack? [the y-intercept is the number to which the product is added, the slope is the factor with (c)]

4. How can you use your table to develop an equation for the stack? [height of one cup minus rim height is the number to which the product is added, the average increase or rim height is the factor with (c)]

5. How accurate were the predictions your equation outputted? How could you adjust your equation to get better predictions?

Procedure
Part Three: Measuring the Cup to Understand the Function

1. After each group has been given one cup as a sample, hold a class discussion about what parts of the cup determine how high a stack will be.

2. Direct the students to measure the required parts and use the measurements to develop a chart predicting the height of the stack with different numbers of cups.

3. Using the data from their charts, have the students make a graph.

4. By referring to their charts and graphs, direct students to develop an equation relating stack height (H) to number of cups (c).

5. Have them apply their equations to predict the height of stacks with various amounts of cups, and then direct them to measure the stacks to check the equation's accuracy.

6. Pose a problem to the students in which the height of a stack is measured and they use their equations to work backwards to determine the number of cups in the stack. Have the students check the accuracy of their predictions by allowing them to measure the actual stack.

Discussion

1. What parts of a cup determine how tall a stack of them will be? [rim, remaining cup without rim]

2. How did you develop a chart of data after you measured the two parts of the cup that determine the stack's height? [one cup is known, keep adding rim height to get height for other amounts of cups]

3. How do the dimensions of the parts show up in the graph? [rim: slope; remaining cup without rim: y-intercept]

4. How do the dimensions of the parts show up in the equation? [rim: factor with variable; remaining cup without rim: starting value to which product is added]

5. How do you use your equation to determine how many cups are in a stack of known height? [substitute height for (H) and solve for cups (c), subtract starting height from present height (H) to find how much height was gained with rims, divide

the height of all the rims by the height of each rim to find the number of rims or cups in the stack]

Procedure

Part Four: Simultaneous Equations

1. Give the students, or have them recall, the equations for the Styrofoam cups and paper cups that are larger than but closest to the same size as the Styrofoam cups. Ask them to consider how tall both stacks would have to be if they had the same number of cups and were equal in height.

2. Have the students graph a line for each stack on the same graph. They may choose to construct the graph by using a table or by going directly from the equations.

3. Focus student attention on the intersection and have them discuss what the intersection says about both stacks.

4. Have the students make a stack of each type of cup using the amount of cups suggested by the graph to confirm that the stacks are of equal height.

5. Have the class discuss how the equations can be manipulated to get the same solution. (The teacher may need to direct the line of thinking that since both equations determine the height of a stack, and since both stacks are of equal height, the expressions for both equations are equal. Putting the two expressions on opposite sides of an equal symbol shows this relationship.)

6. After showing the class the simultaneous equations, have them solve for the number of cups and substitute the solution into one of the equations to find the height of the stack. As a class, make two stacks of cups using the number predicted for each type. Measure and check to see if the same number of cups in each stack makes equal heights as predicted.

7. Give the students or have them recall the equation of a third cup and ask them to determine when it and the Styrofoam cup will have stacks of equal height and number of cups.

8. Have the students solve the question graphically and symbolically and check their solutions against stacks of the cups.

Discussion

1. How many cups does each stack have where the lines intersect on the graph?

2. How high is each stack where the lines intersect on the graph?

3. What does the intersection of the lines tell you on the graph? [The stacks are equal in number of cups and height.]

4. When the number of cups is substituted into both equations, what will the solutions tell us? [the height of the stack]

5. If the heights for both equations are equal, what does that tell you about both expressions? [The expressions are equal.]

6. How can you symbolically write that both equations are equal? [ex: $1.2c + 8.3 = 0.7c + 11.3$]

7. Explain if it is easier for you to graphically or symbolically find when two stacks are equal in number of cups and height.

8. Which solution, graphic or symbolic, do you think is more accurate? Why?

* Reprinted with permission from *Principles and Standards for School Mathematics*, 2000 by the National Council of Teachers of Mathematics. All rights reserved.

STACKING CUPS

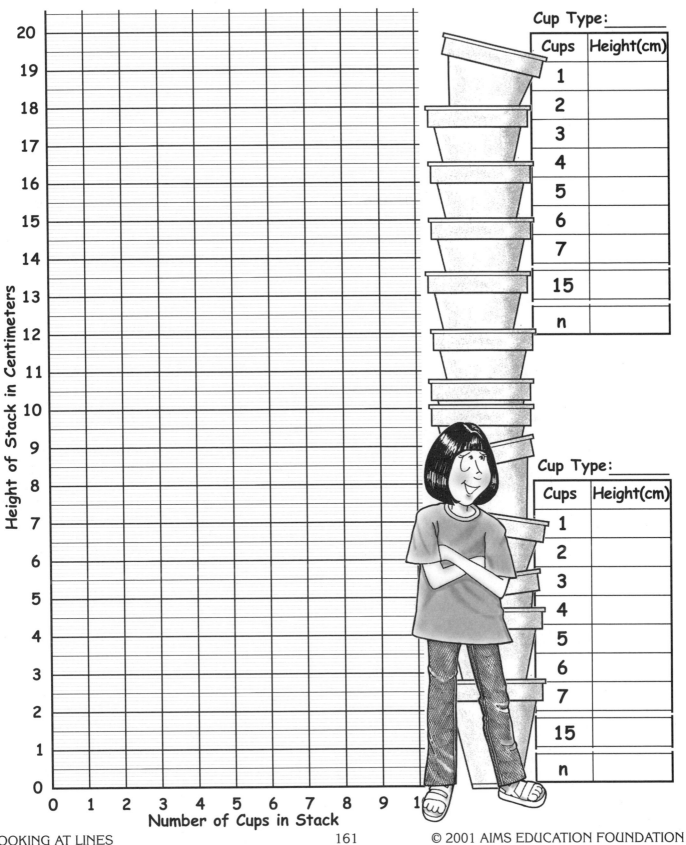

Cup Type: _____

Cups	Height(cm)
1	
2	
3	
4	
5	
6	
7	
15	
n	

Cup Type: _____

Cups	Height(cm)
1	
2	
3	
4	
5	
6	
7	
15	
n	

Height of Stack in Centimeters

Number of Cups in Stack

The THICK of Things

Topic
Algebra—Linear Functions

Key Questions
How can you make a graph show how thick a pile of things will get as you add more objects?

How can you write a number sentence (equation) to determine how thick a pile of things is if you know how many objects are in the pile?

Learning Goals
Students will:
- represent data on a graph and interpret the graph's meaning in the context;
- recognize the connection of the rate of change in numeric form as an equivalent to the slope of the line in graphic form; and
- develop an equation that relates the outcome to the rate of change and the original starting condition.

Guiding Documents
Project 2061 Benchmarks
- *Mathematical statements can be used to describe how one quantity changes when another changes. Rates of change can be computed from magnitudes and vice versa.*
- *Graphs can show a variety of possible relationships between two variables. As one variable increases uniformly, the other may do one of the following: always keep the same proportion to the first, increase or decrease steadily, increase or decrease faster and faster, get closer and closer to some limiting value, reach some intermediate maximum or minimum, alternately increase and decrease indefinitely, increase and decrease in steps, or do something different from any of these.*

NCTM Standards 2000*
- *Represent, analyze, and generalize a variety of patterns with tables, graphs, words, and, when possible, symbolic rules*
- *Relate and compare different forms of representation for a relationship*
- *Explore relationships between symbolic expressions and graphs of lines, paying particular attention to the meaning of intercept and slope*
- *Use graphs to analyze the nature of changes in quantities in linear relationships*

Math
Measuring
Rates
Graphing
    slope, intercept
    interpreting
Variables
Writing equations

Integrated Processes
Observing
Comparing and contrasting
Collecting and recording data
Interpreting data
Generalizing

Materials
Objects of uniform thickness (pattern blocks, tiles, lumber)
Block of wood
Rulers

Background Information
Students need experiences that relate numeric data to graphic and symbolic displays. The consistent increase in the height or thickness of a pile of uniformly thick objects, such as tiles or pattern blocks, produces such an experience.

Students can make a graph directly from the tiles by laying one tile on its side on the vertical line representing one tile and marking its thickness. If a pile of two, three, four, and five tiles are each placed on their respective lines and their thickness is marked, a linear pattern begins to emerge. The increase in the height of the line on the graph represents the thickness of a tile and the number representing this length is called the slope of the line. An equation can symbolically show the relationship of the height of pile to the number of tiles in the pile. If each tile is 2 cm thick the equation could be written as H(t) = 2t , where H is the height of the pile and (t) is the number of tiles. The connection of the 2 cm thickness of the tile, to the 2 cm rise on the graph for each additional tile, to the 2 as factor of (t) in the equation is easily grasped by the students.

As students follow a similar procedure with different thicknesses of tiles, some interesting observations will be made. All the lines on the graph intersect at the same point where no tiles have no height (0,0). The thicker tiles have steeper lines and greater factors to multiply with the number of tiles.

Ask students to develop graphs and equations and then to use them to predict what will happen with piles beyond their experience. The students should extend their graphs to extrapolate answers for larger piles, and substitute the number of tiles into the equation to predict the height of larger number of tiles. Because the context is convenient, the student's predictions can be tested.

If the pile of tiles is built on a block of wood and the pile including the wood is studied the students will see a shift in the data. The slopes of the lines on the graph are parallel to the corresponding lines made by the same tiles without the block. All the lines have been slid up the block's thickness on the graph. To compensate for a 4.5 cm thick block, each point on the line will rise 4.5 cm. In the equation this increase must be added changing the equation to: $H(t) = 2t + 4.5$. Again the students have a situation where they can relate the graphic and symbolic representations to the context. On the graph the line starts at the thickness of the block on the line representing zero tiles. The thickness of the block is the y-intercept. In the equation the thickness of the block, or the y-intercept, is combined with the thickness generated by the number of tiles and their thickness.

The concrete nature of this situation allows students to think through numeric solutions to questions that force them to work backwards. The experience of considering how to solve such problems prepares them for dealing with it in the more symbolic form of algebra. Consider the comments made by students and the algebraic equivalents when the following question was posed to students using the example equation.

"How many tiles were used if the pile with the block were 28.5 cm thick?"

"First we need to get rid of the block's thickness so we'll take away 4.5 cm."

$$H(c) = 2t + 4.5$$
$$28.5 = 2t + 4.5$$
$$24 = 2t$$

"Then I divided the thickness by 2 because each tile is two centimeters thick and I got 12 tiles."

$$12 = t$$

Management
1. Students can work individually to construct their own graph if there are enough materials.
2. Before the activity the teacher must gather an adequate supply (five per student group) of a material that is consistent in one dimension. Tiles or pattern blocks are appropriate and are often found in a math classroom. Paper clips, pencils, pennies, or pieces of finished lumber are alternatives.
3. Each student group will need a block of wood for *Part Two* of the activity. For class discussion it is convenient if these blocks are all the same. An alternative is the binding of a textbook.

Procedure
Part One
1. Have the students discuss the first *Key Question*.
2. Explain to the students how they will collect the data by laying the pile of tiles on its side along the vertical line representing that number of tiles and marking its thickness.
3. Distribute the materials and have students mark the heights of one-, two-, three-, four-, and five-tile high piles on the graph.
4. Have students convert the graphic data to the numeric form on the chart.
5. Hold a class discussion about what patterns the students find in the table and graph, and how these patterns relate to each other. Direct the students to use the patterns to complete the numeric values in the chart.
6. Have the class discuss how they could use the patterns to find the thickness of any number of tiles and describe the process in words.
7. As a class develop the algebraic equation that is equivalent to the class's verbal description.
8. Have the students check their procedures by using their graphs, charts, and equations to predict the thicknesses of piles of different numbers of tiles. Then let them check their predictions with a ruler and tiles.
9. For more practice, have the students repeat the procedure with a different thickness tile. Discuss how the graphs and charts differ for different thicknesses of tiles.

Part Two
1. Invite the students to discuss how they think the numbers and graph will change if a block of wood is included in the pile of tiles.
2. Distribute a block of wood to each group and tell them to make a graph of piles of up to five tiles including the block in the thickness of the pile.
3. Have the students change the graphic data to numeric data on the chart.
4. Hold a class discussion concerning the patterns the students see in the graph and chart and how this graph and chart are different than those of the pile without the block.
5. Encourage them to discuss how they think the block will change the equation and then have the students modify the equation and check that it works for the data they have collected.
6. Have students discuss how the graph, chart, and equation represent the thickness of the tile and block differently.
7. Direct them to use their graph, chart, and equation to predict the thicknesses of piles of

different numbers of tiles with a block. Then let the students check their predictions with a ruler and tiles.

8. Have the students repeat the procedure with a block of a different thickness. Discuss how this block changes the graph, chart, and equation.

Discussion

1. What patterns do you see in the graph? [The height marks form a line.]
2. What does the pattern tell you about the tiles? [They are the same thickness.]
3. How does this pattern show up in the chart of numbers? [The thickness gets greater by the same amount each tile.]
4. How could you tell the height of a pile if you know the number of tiles in it? [Take the thickness of a tile times the number of tiles.]
5. How could you write this process as a number sentence (equation)?
6. How does the graph change if you make a pile with a thicker tile? [steeper line]

7. Compare and contrast the graphs of a pile with and without the block. [parallel, raised the height of the block]
8. Compare and contrast the chart of a pile with and without the block. [Every number has increased by the thickness of the block.]
9. What do you need to change about your number sentence (equation) when you add the block to the pile? [add the thickness of the block to the equation]
10. How does the graph change when you use a thicker (thinner) block? [greater (lesser) y-intercept]

Extension

Pose questions to the class as suggested in *Background Information* and have students work backwards to determine the solutions. Have the students discuss the thinking and processes they used to determine their solutions before checking the correctness of their solutions with a pile and a ruler.

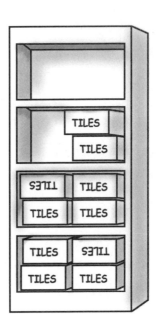

The THICK of Things

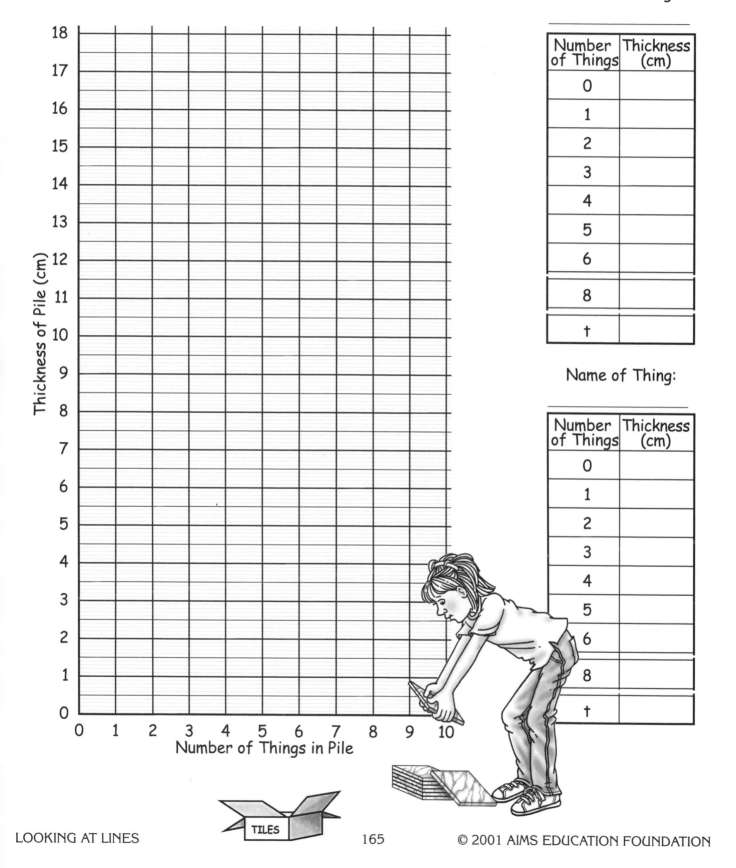

Name of Thing: _____

Number of Things	Thickness (cm)
0	
1	
2	
3	
4	
5	
6	
8	
†	

Name of Thing: _____

Number of Things	Thickness (cm)
0	
1	
2	
3	
4	
5	
6	
8	
†	

TILES

Pattern Block Functions

Topic
Algebra—Linear Functions

Key Question
How are the perimeters related to the number of tiles in a pattern block sequence?

Learning Goals
Students will:
- explore, identify, and describe the relationship between perimeters and number of tiles in a pattern block sequence;
- graph the (number of tiles, perimeter) ordered pairs for triangle-, square-, trapezoid-, and hexagon-shaped pattern blocks arranged in a sequence;
- write a rule for each relationship; and
- explain why the y-intercept for all four shapes is 2.

Guiding Documents
Project 2061 Benchmarks
- *Mathematical ideas can be represented concretely, graphically, and symbolically.*
- *Tables and graphs can show how values of one quantity are related to values of another.*
- *Organize information in simple tables and graphs and identify relationships they reveal.*

NCTM Standards 2000*
- *Represent, analyze, and generalize a variety of patterns with tables, graphs, words, and when possible, symbolic rules*
- *Model problem situations with objects and use representations such as graphs, tables, and equations to draw conclusions*
- *Investigate how change in one variable relates to a change in a second variable*
- *Explore what happens to measurements of a two-dimensional shape such as its perimeter when the shape is changed in some way*
- *Represent data using tables and graphs such as line plots, bar graphs, and line graphs*

Math
Building a data table
Graphing discrete quantities
Exploring relationships
Writing linear equations
Limit

Integrated Processes
Observing
Collecting and recording data
Comparing and contrasting
Interpreting data
Generalizing
Inferring

Materials
Colored pencils
Rulers
Student sheets
Pattern blocks, optional

Background Information
The relationships between perimeters and the number of tiles differ slightly for the triangle, square, trapezoid, and hexagon chains. The functions are, respectively, $p(s) = 3s + 2$, $p(s) = 4s + 2$, $p(s) = 5s + 2$, and $p(s) = 6s + 2$. In each case the coefficient of s equals the number of sides in a single tile. The data are discrete because the chains are built using whole tiles; therefore, the lines connecting the graphed points are dashed rather than solid.

It needs to be emphasized that these relationships are not proportional. In a proportional relationship the y-intercept would be zero and any two sets of ordered pairs for a given block would be proportional. Neither is true in this instance.

It is interesting to observe that the y-intercept for all four sequences is two and that each of the generalizations contains the term +2. If students are deemed ready for introduction to the concept of limits, they should be challenged to ponder this coincidence and seek an explanation. Hopefully, some students will notice these roles for two on their own and want an explanation.

The explanation involves the concept of limit, a very important notion in mathematics. It has reasonable explanations and in this case can be modeled as shown on the last student page.

A study of the sequences shows that parts of the perimeter are constant and parts vary. The combined length of the two ends remains constant but the lengths of top and bottom sides vary. The combined length of the two ends is two units. The combined length of the top and bottom sides varies depending on how much of the strip is visible. *Suppose we disregard the discrete nature of the data* and permit the top and bottom lengths to shrink. (Notice that opposite ends need to be parallel for this approach to work):

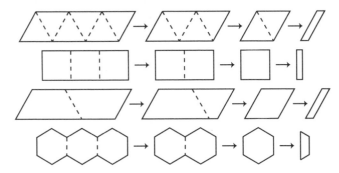

Note that the perimeter shrinks as the length shrinks while the lengths of the two ends remain the same. From this we can conclude that *the perimeter of the strip approaches two as the visible length of the strip approaches zero*. Just before the strip disappears the perimeter is very close to two since the length of the strip is almost zero. At the theoretical limit the length is zero and the perimeter is two. This verifies that the y-intercept on the graph is two when the length is zero and justifies the term of two in the rule when $n = 0$.

Management

1. Students may work on this activity individually or in small groups.
2. Students will need colored pencils in four different colors to make their graphs and distinguish between the different lines.

3. The use of pattern blocks with this activity is optional. You may wish to have some available to students so that they can extend the patterns shown on the first student sheet.

Procedure

1. Distribute the materials to students and go over the instructions as a class.
2. Have students work individually or in small groups to collect their data and generalize the patterns to the *n*th term, if they are able.
3. Be sure students understand that they are graphing the data from each shape in a different color. Have students extend the lines all the way to the y-axis so that they can identify the y-intercept. Remind students that they should be using dashed lines because of the discrete nature of the data.
4. Have a time of class discussion and sharing, and if appropriate for your students, use the extension sheet to examine the concept of limits.

Discussion

1. Why did you use a dashed line to connect the points on your graph? [The data are discreet.]
2. What is the y-intercept for the triangles? ...the squares? ...the trapezoids? ...the hexagons? [The y-intercept for all four shapes is two.]
3. Why is the y-intercept the same for all of the shapes? [As the length of the strip approaches zero, the perimeter approaches two.]
4. What generalizations were you able to develop for the perimeters of the different shapes when there are *n* tiles? (See *Solutions*.)

Extension

For advanced students who are able to deal with the concept of limit, use the sheet *Model for Showing the Concept of Limit* to help explain why the y-intercept for each graph is at 2.

* Reprinted with permission from *Principles and Standards for School Mathematics*, 2000 by the National Council of Teachers of Mathematics. All rights reserved.

Solutions

The table from the first student sheet and the graph from the second student sheet are shown below as they should be completed.

	Number of Tiles						
	1	2	3	4	5	10	n
Triangle Tiles	3	4	5	6	7	12	$n + 2$
Square Tiles	4	6	8	10	12	22	$2n + 2$
Trapezoid Tiles	5	8	11	14	17	32	$3n + 2$
Hexagon Tiles	6	10	14	18	22	42	$4n + 2$

(Perimeter)

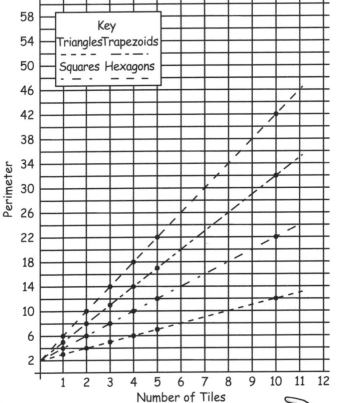

Pattern Block Functions

Shown are pattern block sequences using four different tiles. If you have pattern blocks available, use them to extend the sequences. For each, find the outside perimeter in relation to the number of tiles. Consider the side of the square to have a measure of one unit. Record the data in the table at the bottom of the page. If the sequence forms a pattern, write the rule.

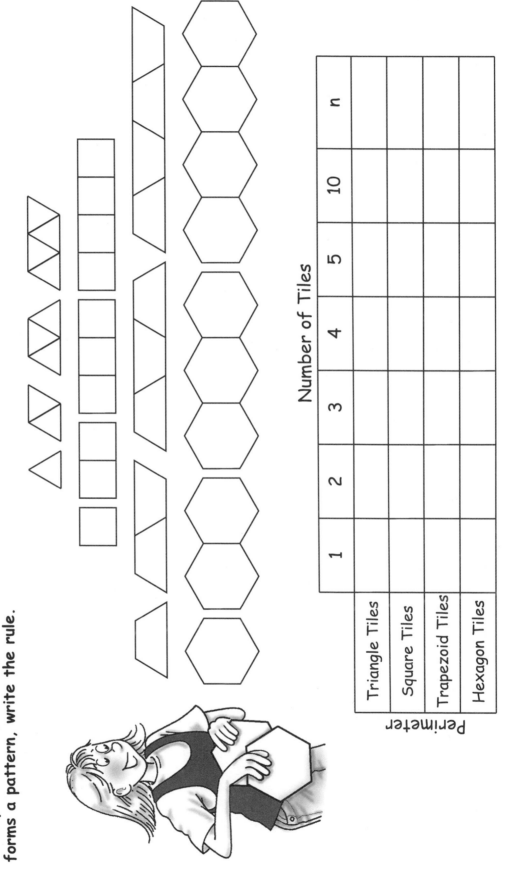

	1	2	3	4	5	10	n
Triangle Tiles							
Square Tiles							
Trapezoid Tiles							
Hexagon Tiles							

Number of Tiles

Perimeter

Pattern Block Functions

Using the data from the previous page, graph the ordered pairs (number of tiles, perimeter). Since the data are discrete, connect the points with dashed lines. Use a different color for each line and identify which pattern block is graphed by each line.

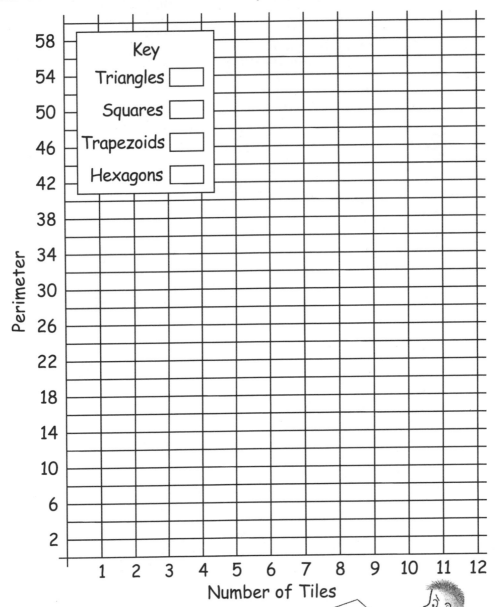

Key

Triangles ☐

Squares ☐

Trapezoids ☐

Hexagons ☐

Perimeter (y-axis): 2, 6, 10, 14, 18, 22, 26, 30, 34, 38, 42, 46, 50, 54, 58

Number of Tiles (x-axis): 1, 2, 3, 4, 5, 6, 7, 8, 9, 10, 11, 12

Connect the graphed points for each type of tile with a broken line extending to the y-axis.

1. What do you observe at the y-axis?

2. What is your explanation for this result?

Pattern Block Functions

Model for Showing the Concept of Limit

Extension

1. Copy this sheet onto cardstock.
2. Cut out the rectangular strip on the bottom half of the paper.
3. Use a blade or the edge of your scissors to cut the slit on the top half of the paper. Try to cut it exactly the length it is drawn.
4. Insert the rectangular strip into the slit so that about 10 centimeters of the strip shows. Slowly pull the strip to the left so the length of the strip shrinks. As the length approaches zero, you can see the perimeter approach two (twice the width of the strip).

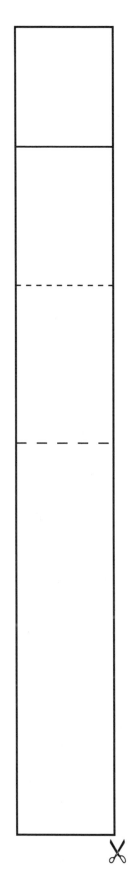

RISING TOWER

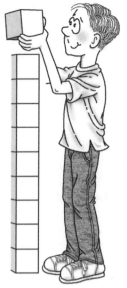

Topic
Algebra—Linear Functions

Challenge
Defend your conclusion as to whether or not the surface areas and volumes are proportional to the height of the towers in this activity.

Learning Goals
Students will:
- determine the surface area-to-height and volume-to-height ratios for stages one to four and *n*;
- determine that the surface area-to-height ratio is not proportional;
- determine that the volume-to-height ratio is proportional; and,
- defend their conclusion using arguments based on both table and graphs.

Guiding Documents
Project 2061 Benchmarks
- *Graphical display of numbers may make it possible to spot patterns that are not otherwise obvious, such as comparative size and trends.*
- *Mathematical ideas can be represented concretely, graphically, and symbolically.*
- *Organize information in simple tables and graphs and identify relationships they reveal.*

NCTM Standards 2000*
- *Describe, extend, and make generalizations about geometric and numeric patterns*
- *Model and solve contextualized problems using various representations such as graphs, tables, and equations*
- *Use graphs to analyze the nature of changes in quantities in linear relationships*
- *Identify functions as linear or nonlinear and contrast their properties from tables, words, or equations*
- *Explore relationships between symbolic expressions and graphs of lines, paying particular attention to the meaning of intercept and slope*

Math
Measurement
    height
    surface area
    volume

Function
Ratio and proportion

Integrated Processes
Observing
Collecting and recording data
Graphing data
Comparing and contrasting
Interpreting data
Generalizing

Materials
Student sheets
Interlocking cubes, 10 per student
Rulers

Background Information
Rising Tower deals with two linear functions: surface area as a function of the height and volume as a function of the height. The graph of the former is a straight line that does not pass through the origin and the relationship is not proportional. The graph of the latter is a straight line that passes through the origin, confirming that the relationship is proportional. Students will test for proportionality based on both the respective ratios and the graphs. Both graphs are continuous since we consider that the tower is increasing in height from zero to *n* even though measurements are made at intervals.

Management
1. Students will need 10 cubes each to make models of the first four stages of the Rising Tower. Centicubes, Unifix Cubes, or other similar cubes work well because they lock together as they stack. If you do not have enough cubes for each student, groups may share.
2. If students have not yet been exposed to the concepts of surface area and volume and how to calculate them, you will need to do a quick lesson before introducing this activity.
3. If your students have not had much experience generalizing to the *n*th term, you may wish to eliminate that requirement on the first student sheet or do the generalization together as a class.

Procedure
1. Hand out the student sheets and cubes and go over the instructions. *Determine the height, volume,*

surface area, volume-to-height ratio, and surface area-to-height ratio for stages one to four of the Rising Tower. Generalize each value to the nth term. Graph the volume as a function of the height and the surface area as a function of the height.

2. When students have finished graphing their results, be sure that they each write down their defense for whether or not the volume and surface area are proportional to the height.

3. Close with a time of class discussion where students share their conclusions and defend them.

Discussion

1. What would be the height of the Rising Tower at stage seven? [7] ...the volume? [7] ...the surface area? [30] ...the volume-to-height ratio? [7/7] ...the surface area-to-height ratio? [30/7] ...at stage 10? [10, 10, 42, 10/10, 42/10]

2. What generalizations were you able to develop for the different values? [Height: n, Volume: n, Surface Area: $4n + 2$, Height/Volume: n/n, Surface Area/Height: $(4n + 2)/n$]

3. What methods did you use to determine the generalizations?

4. Is the volume proportional to the height of the tower? [Yes.] How do you know? [The graph forms a straight line that goes through the origin.]

5. Is the surface area proportional to the height of the tower? [No.] How do you know? [The ratios are not equivalent, and although the graph forms a straight line, the line does not pass through the origin.]

Extension

Make towers that begin with different numbers of cubes and compare the height and surface area values. One possibility is shown below.

*   Reprinted with permission from *Principles and Standards for School Mathematics,* 2000 by the National Council of Teachers of Mathematics. All rights reserved.

Solutions

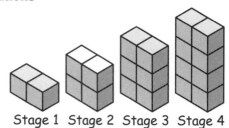

Stage 1 Stage 2 Stage 3 Stage 4

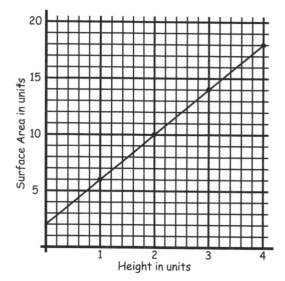

Stage	1	2	3	4	n
Height	1	2	3	4	n
Volume	1	2	3	4	n
Surface Area	6	10	14	18	4n + 2
Volume / Height	1/1	2/2	3/3	4/4	n/n
Surface Area / Height	6/1	10/2	14/3	18/4	(4n+2)/n

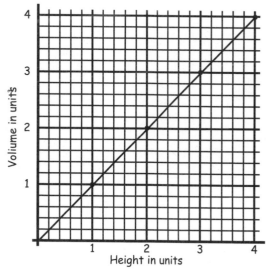

RISING TOWER

Use the cubes your teacher gives you to build models of each stage of the Rising Tower as shown below. Assume that each cube has edges measuring one unit in length. At each stage determine the tower's height, volume, and total surface area (including the bottom). Then find the volume-to-height ratio and the surface area-to-height ratio. Remember that the height is measured in units while the volume is measured in cubic units, and the surface area in square units.

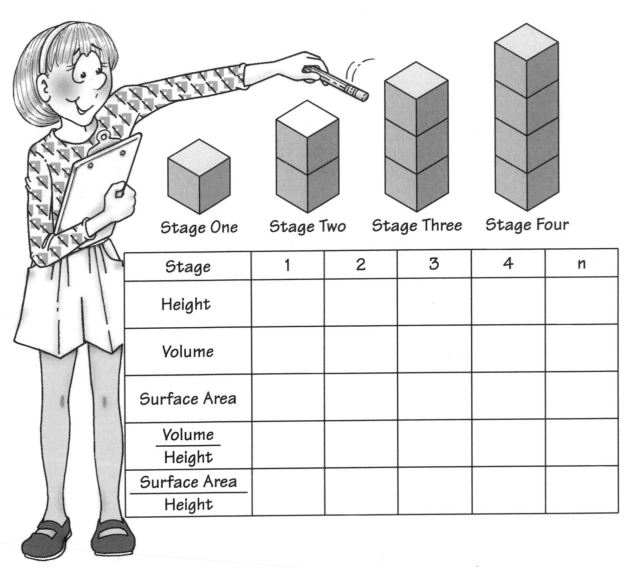

Stage One   Stage Two   Stage Three   Stage Four

Stage	1	2	3	4	n
Height					
Volume					
Surface Area					
Volume / Height					
Surface Area / Height					

What would the height, volume, surface area, volume-to-height ratio, and surface area-to-height ratio be for a stage seven tower? ...a stage 10 tower? Show your work below.

RISING TOWER

Graph the volume as a function of the height.

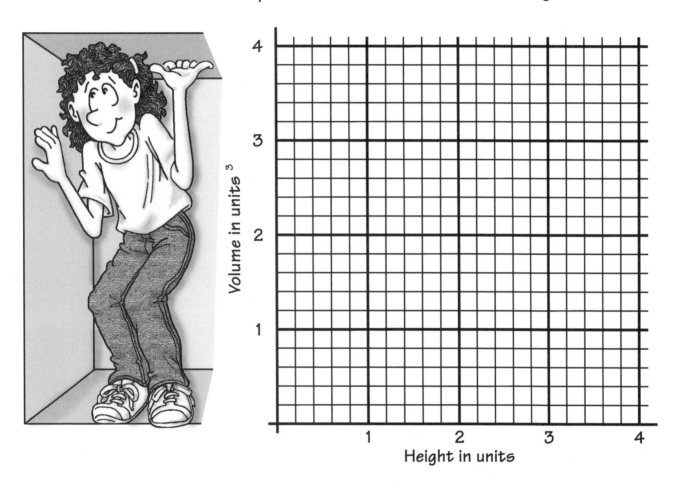

Is the volume proportional to the height of the tower?
Defend your conclusion.

RISING TOWER

Graph the surface area as a function of the height.

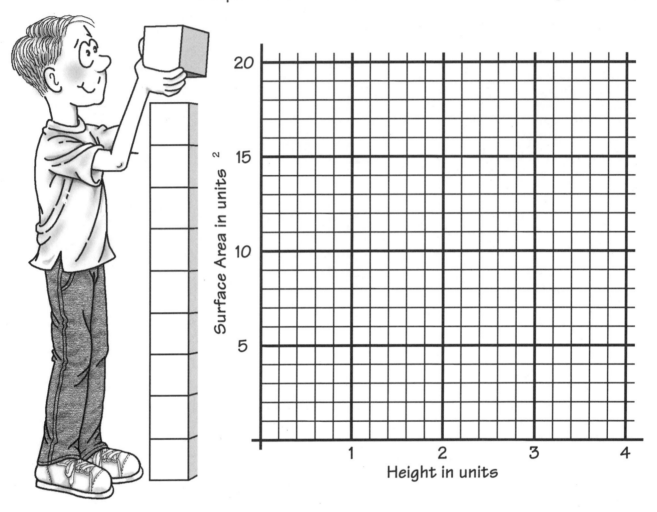

Is the surface area proportional to the height of the tower?
Defend your conclusion.

RECTANGLE JAMBOREE

Topic
Algebra—Linear Functions

Key Question
How are rectangles with the same perimeter and one vertex at the origin related to linear functions?

Learning Goals
Students will:
- use their knowledge of perimeters find all rectangles with constant perimeters and one vertex at the origin;
- discover that the vertices opposite the origin lie in a straight line; and
- determine the range, domain, slope, y-intercept, and rule of this line.

Guiding Documents
Project 2061 Benchmarks
- *The graphic display of numbers may help to show patterns such as trends, varying rates of change, gaps, or clusters. Such patterns sometimes can be used to make predictions about the phenomena being graphed.*
- *Graphs can show a variety of relationships between two variables. As one variable increases uniformly, the other may do one of the following: always keeps the same proportion to the first, increase or decrease steadily, increase or decrease faster and faster, get closer and closer to some limiting value, reach some intermediate maximum or minimum, alternately increase and decrease indefinitely, increase and decrease in steps or do something different from any of these.*
- *Mathematical ideas can be represented concretely, graphically, and symbolically.*
- *Organize information in tables and graphs and identify relationships they reveal.*

NCTM Standards 2000*
- *Represent, analyze, and generalize a variety of patterns with tables, graphs, words, and, when possible, symbolic rules*
- *Explore what happens to measurements of a two-dimensional shape such as its perimeter and area when the shape is changed in some way.*
- *Investigate how a change in one variable relates to a change in a second variable*
- *Make and use coordinate systems to specify locations and to describe paths*

- *Explore relationships between symbolic expressions and graphs of lines, paying particular attention to the meaning of intercept and slope*
- *Use graphs to analyze the nature of changes in quantities in linear relationships*

Math
Perimeters of rectangles
Graphs
Linear functions
    domain
    range
    slope
    y-intercept
    rule

Integrated Processes
Observing
Collecting and recording data
Organizing data
Interpreting data
Comparing and contrasting
Generalizing

Materials
Rulers
Student sheets
Colored pencils, optional

Background Information
This activity incorporates many of the major aspects of linear functions in a readily understood situation, making it suitable for students new to these concepts. Extensive practice in finding rectangles with a given perimeter is provided.

Since all action takes place in the first quadrant, we are considering real rectangles. This opens the door to several important ideas. The vertices of rectangles with a given perimeter and one vertex at the origin are points of the same straight line. At the outset, the activity limits consideration to rectangles which can be formed along grid lines. As that restriction is lifted, an infinite number of rectangles meet the specifications. All of their vertices opposite the origin are points of the same straight line. The length and width are related inversely: as the length increases, the width decreases at the same rate.

The domain ranges from zero to one-half of the indicated perimeter. Correspondingly, the range is from one-half the indicated perimeter to zero. At either zero the rectangle escapes the realm of the real. The y-intercept is at one-half the indicated perimeter.

Management

1. You may wish to give students colored pencils so that they can draw the rectangles with different dimensions/perimeters in different colors.
2. Students are asked to identify the slope, y-intercept, rule, domain, and range of a line and should be familiar with these terms before they begin the activity.

Procedure

1. Distribute the materials and go over the instructions as a class.
2. Have students work individually or in small groups to complete both grids and answer the questions.
3. Direct students in a time of class discussion where they can share their discoveries and observations.

Discussion

1. What did you observe about the vertices opposite the origin on the first student sheet? [They all fall on a straight line.]
2. Can you draw other rectangles with a perimeter of 20 if you don't have to follow the grid lines? Explain. [Yes. An infinite number of rectangles are possible with sides that are not whole units. All of these rectangles have vertices that fall on the same line as those with whole-unit sides.]
3. What can you say about any point on the line that connects the vertices? [Any rectangle with one vertex at the origin and the opposite vertex on the line will have a perimeter of 20 units.]
4. What is the slope of the line? [⁻1] ...the y-intercept? [10] ...the rule? [$f(x) = ⁻1x + 10$] ...the domain? [zero to 10] ...the range? [10 to zero]
5. What do you observe when you look at the second grid? [All of the numbers fall on diagonals; the diagonals are parallel; the smaller the perimeter, the closer the diagonal is to the vertex; etc.]
6. What can you say about the grid when it is filled with numbers that identify the perimeters of all possible whole-unit rectangles? [It is an addition table for the even numbers from two to 12. See *Solutions* for completed table.]

* Reprinted with permission from *Principles and Standards for School Mathematics*, 2000 by the National Council of Teachers of Mathematics. All rights reserved.

Solutions

The grids for both student sheets are given below as they should be completed.

Student Sheet One

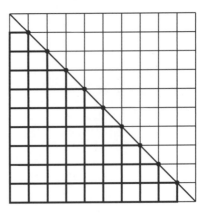

Student Sheet Two

26	28	30	32	34	36	38	40	42	44	46	48
24	26	28	30	32	34	36	38	40	42	44	46
22	24	26	28	30	32	34	36	38	40	42	44
20	22	24	26	28	30	32	34	36	38	40	42
18	20	22	24	26	28	30	32	34	36	38	40
16	18	20	22	24	26	28	30	32	34	36	38
14	16	18	20	22	24	26	28	30	32	34	36
12	14	16	18	20	22	24	26	28	30	32	34
10	12	14	16	18	20	22	24	26	28	30	32
8	10	12	14	16	18	20	22	24	26	28	30
6	8	10	12	14	16	18	20	22	24	26	28
4	6	8	10	12	14	16	18	20	22	24	26

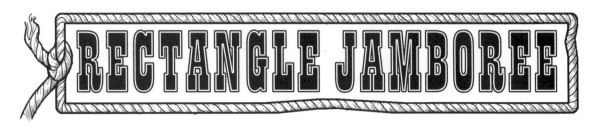

RECTANGLE JAMBOREE

On the grid below, the distance from one intersection to the next is one unit. Your challenge is to discover all rectangles that have a perimeter of 20 units and one vertex at the origin. Sides of the rectangles must be along grid lines. Outline each possible rectangle.

1. Mark the vertices opposite the origin with a heavy dot. What do you observe?

2. Can you draw other rectangles to the same specifications if you need not follow grid lines? Please explain.

3. Connect vertices opposite the origin with a line. What can you say about any point on this line?

4. Identify the following for this line:
   a. slope
   d. domain
   b. y-intercept
   e. range
   c. rule

RECTANGLE JAMBOREE

On this grid, draw the top side of each rectangle with a perimeter of 20 units and one vertex at the origin. From each vertex draw downward one unit of the right side. This creates a stepped design. Write 20 for the perimeter in the upper right-hand corner of each rectangle.

Repeat the process for perimeters of 10, 14, 18, and 24 units.

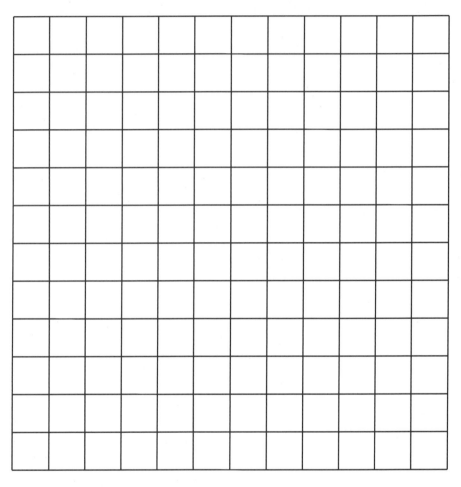

1. What do you observe?

2. If you were assigned to write a number in the upper right-hand corner of every square in the grid, what would make your task easier?

3. Fill the grid with such numbers. What can you say about the completed grid as a table of numbers?

BOOKS upon BOOKS

Topic
Algebra—Linear Functions

Key Question
At what point will a stack of thin books placed on a telephone directory be equal in height to a stack of the same number of thick books placed directly on the desk?

Learning Goals
Students will:
- collect and graph discrete data;
- identify independent and dependent variables, slopes, and proportional relationships;
- write linear function rules for each stack of books; and
- use linear equations to determine when the stacks will be at the same height.

Guiding Documents
Project 2061 Benchmarks
- *Mathematical ideas can be represented concretely, graphically, and symbolically.*
- *Tables and graphs can show how values of one quantity are related to values of another.*
- *Organize information in simple tables and graphs and identify relationships they reveal.*

NCTM Standards 2000*
- *Represent, analyze, and generalize a variety of patterns with tables, graphs, words, and, when possible, symbolic rules*
- *Investigate how a change in one variable relates to a change in another variable*
- *Use symbolic algebra to represent situations and to solve problems, especially those that involve linear relationships*
- *Explore relationships between symbolic expressions and graphs of lines, paying particular attention to the meaning of intercept and slope*

Math
Discerning linear functions in a
  situation
Identifying independent and
  dependent variables
Designing and using a data table
Graphing discrete quantities
Formulating linear equations
Estimation
Measurement

Integrated Processes
Observing
Collecting and recording data
Comparing and contrasting
Interpreting data
Generalizing

Materials
For each group:
  four thinner books with identical thickness
  four thicker books with identical thickness
  telephone directory or similar book
  metric ruler

For each student:
  colored pencils
  student sheets

Background Information
This activity builds on understandings acquired in previous experiences such as *Mystery Mass* and *Candy Combinations*.

There are two ways in which the linear equations in this activity can be represented. In the first, I represents the input (number of books added); O represents the output (height of the stack in centimeters), m represents the thickness of each book, and b represents the thickness of the telephone directory. The value of I is the same in both equations because the number of books in the stack at each stage is always kept the same. The linear equations are $O_1 = m_1 I + b_1$ and $O_2 = m_2 I + b_2$. The second way these equations can be represented is using the standard forms: $f(n_1) = m_1 n + b_1$ and $f(n_2) = m_2 n + b_2$.

These equations are useful for finding the answers to the two questions posed on the first student sheet: *When will the two stacks be the same height?* and *When will the stack of thicker books be twice as high as the stack of thinner books?* When the two stacks are the same height, the two functions are equal. Therefore, $m_1 n + b_1 = m_2 n + b_2$. The second stack is twice as high as the first when $2(m_1 n + b_1) = m_2 n + b_2$. In the second stack, $b_2 = 0$ since there is no telephone book and that stack rests directly on the table. The values of m and b are determined in the investigation, leaving n as the sole unknown. It is highly probable that n will not be a whole number because the two stacks will likely never be the same height due to the discrete nature of the book thicknesses. Students are expected to conclude that the point of equality lies somewhere between two discrete numbers of books, for example, "between eight and nine books in each stack."

If this type of an approach to solving the problem is new to students, it will be important to guide them through the process to establish an initial understanding. In any event, the process and the discrete nature of the data should be thoroughly discussed.

Management
1. As described in the *Background Information*, there are two ways in which the linear equations can be represented. Select the option that is most appropriate for your students.
2. Students should work together in groups of three or four. Each group will need two sets of four identical books and a telephone directory. The two sets of books need to be of different thicknesses. Each group does not need to have the same thicknesses of books, but it is nice if they do so that the data collected can be compared.

Procedure
1. Have students get into groups and distribute the materials.
2. Go over the procedure for the activity as a class, being sure that all students are clear on what they are to do.
3. As students stack their books and collect the data, move from group to group, giving assistance where needed.
4. If necessary, assist students in determining the generalization for each equation.
5. Once all of the data is collected, have students graph the data and answer the questions.
6. Close with a time of class discussion and sharing.

Discussion
1. What is the independent variable for the two functions? [the number of books added to the stack]
2. What is the dependent variable for the two functions? [the height of the stack]
3. What is the slope of the line for the thinner books? ...the thicker books?
4. What is the y-intercept for the thinner books? ...the thicker books? [0]
5. Are the data discreet or continuous? [Discreet] How do you know? [The height of the stack and the number of books are specific values. The points on the lines are the only values possible using the given variables.]
6. Describe the relationship between the inputs and outputs. [The relationship is linear in both cases. As each book is added, the heights of the respective stacks increase by constant increments.]

7. What formula did you develop for each stack?
8. Is the relationship between the independent and dependent variables proportional for the thin books? [No] ...the thick books? [Yes] Please explain. [In order for a relationship to be proportional the graph of the line must pass through the origin. Because the thin books are stacked on top of a telephone book, their line does not pass through the origin, while the line for the thick books does.]
9. When will the two stacks of books be the same height? How do you know?
10. When will the stack of thicker books be twice the height of the thinner books? How do you know?

Extension
Have students experiment with variations on the original problem such as stacking two thin books for every thick book, or starting with large stacks and removing books rather than adding them.

Solutions

Solutions will vary greatly depending on the thicknesses of the books used by each group. One sample set of solutions is given below.

| | Measure | | | | | Predict | | | Generalize |
Number of Books	1	2	3	4	5	6	10	20	n
Height of Thinner Books in cm	5.9	6.9	7.9	8.9	9.9	10.9	14.9	24.9	n + 4.9
Height of Thicker Books in cm	2.3	4.6	6.9	9.2	11.5	13.8	23	46	2.3n

Thin Books
Slope: 1
y-intercept: 4.9
Equation: $f(n) = n + 4.9$

The two stacks of books will be the same height—somewhere between three and four books, but closer to four.

$2.3n = x + 4.9$
$1.3n = 4.9$
$n \approx 3.8$ books

Thick Books
Slope: 2.3
y-intercept: 0
Equation: $f(n) = 2.3n$

The stack of thick books will be twice as as high as the stack of thin books—somewhere between 32 and 33 books, but closer to 33.

$2.3n = 2(n + 4.9)$
$2.3n = 2n + 9.8$
$.3n = 9.8$
$n \approx 32.7$ books

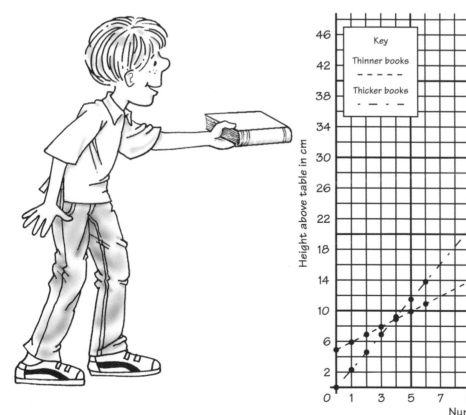

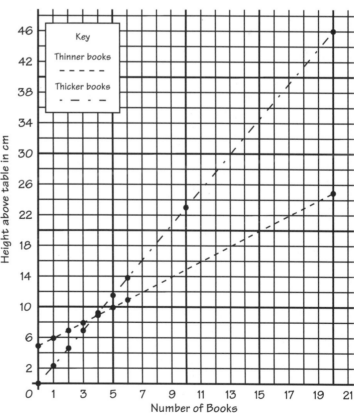

Key

Thinner books
– – – – –

Thicker books
– ∙ – ∙ –

Height above table in cm

Number of Books

BOOKS upon BOOKS

For this investigation, use two sets of four identical books and a telephone directory. One set must contain thicker books than the other.

Place the thinner books onto the telephone directory one by one. Place the thicker books directly onto the desk one by one. In both stacks measure the distance from the desktop to the top of the last book after each placement.

Associate a linear function with the growth of each stack. Use the function to predict the height of each stack for five, six, 10 and 20 books. Finally, generalize to the nth term.

	Measure				Predict				Generalize
Number of Books	1	2	3	4	5	6	10	20	n
Height of Thinner Books in cm									
Height of Thicker Books in cm									

Answer the following questions after you have completed the remainder of the student sheets.

1. When will the two stacks be the same height? Explain your reasoning.

2. When will the stack of thicker books be twice as high as the stack of thinner books? Explain your reasoning.

BOOKS upon BOOKS

Graph the line for each stack of books below. Use a different color for each line.

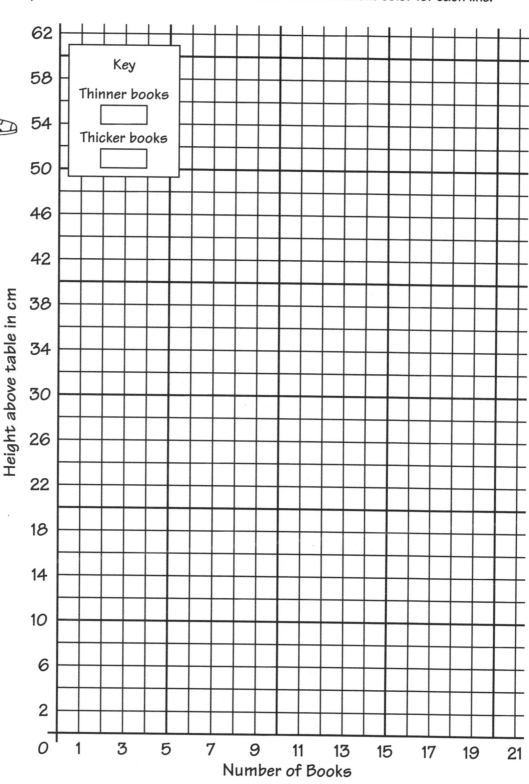

Key

Thinner books

Thicker books

Height above table in cm

Number of Books

BBOOKS upon BOOKS

Define/respond to the following:

Stack of Thinner Books

1. Independent variable:

2. Dependent variable:

3. Slope:

4. Y-Intercept:

5. Is the data discrete or continuous? How do you know?

6. Write a description relating inputs and outputs.

7. Write an expression in the form of $f(n) = mn + b$ for this stack.

8. Is the relationship between the independent and dependent variables proportional? Please explain.

Stack of Thicker Books

1. Independent variable:

2. Dependent variable:

3. Slope:

4. Y-Intercept:

5. Is the data discrete or continuous? How do you know?

6. Write a description relating inputs and outputs.

7. Write an expression in the form of $f(n) = mn + b$ for this stack.

8. Is the relationship between the independent and dependent variables proportional? Please explain.

A Winter Holiday Adventure

Topic
Algebra—Linear Functions

Key Question
How can algebra be used to describe the growth of a plant such as an amaryllis?

Learning Goals
Students will:
- take measurements of a growing plant;
- make and interpret graphs of the data they collect;
- make predictions based on patterns of growth they see;
- create a function that connects time and growth; and
- do some simple curve fitting.

Guiding Document
NCTM Standards 2000*
- *Understand both metric and customary systems of measurement*
- *Select and apply techniques and tools to accurately find length, area, volume, and angle measures to appropriate levels of precision*
- *Solve simple problems involving rates and derived measurements for such attributes as velocity*
- *Represent, analyze, and generalize a variety of patterns with tables, graphs, words, and, when possible, symbolic rules*
- *Relate and compare different forms of representation for a relationship*
- *Identify functions as linear or nonlinear and contrast their properties from tables, graphs, or equations*
- *Explore relationships between symbolic expressions and graphs of lines, paying particular attention to the meaning of intercept and slope*
- *Use symbolic algebra to represent situations and to solve problems, especially those that involve linear relationships*
- *Model and solve contextualized problems using various representations, such as graphs, tables, and equations*
- *Use graphs to analyze the nature of changes in quantities in linear relationships*

Math
Algebra
    linear equations
Graphing
Measurement

Science
Life science
    plants
        growth rate

Integrated Processes
Observing
Collecting and recording data
Interpreting data
Predicting

Materials
Fast growing flower bulbs such as amaryllis
Soil
Water
Measuring tapes or meter sticks
Graphing calculator, encouraged
Chart paper, optional

Background Information
Some flowering bulbs, particularly the amaryllis sold in many stores near the winter holiday season, grow at an incredible rate. The study of the growth of the amaryllis and similar plants is particularly appropriate during this time.

Because large bulbs like the amaryllis are essentially food storage units for the plant, these flowers grow at a very steady rate. In contrast, smaller seeded plants that have little food stored will grow slowly until they have some leaf surface area to collect light energy to convert food. The growth rate of these bulbs is essentially a linear function of time. What this means is that after a few days of measurements, students can begin to predict how tall the flower shoot will be on any given day with reasonable accuracy. This information can then be graphed, and a line of best fit can be determined.

The mathematics involved in this curve fitting will be relatively simple. Since the bloom will start out at an assigned height of zero units, the y-intercept for the function will be zero. This eliminates half of the usual computations a mathematician makes to fit the data with a line of best fit. If you choose to use a graphing calculator to do some of the work for you, you may find that it delivers a slightly different answer than you and your students will come to agreement on.

Due to the fact that these bulbs are live plants, they don't follow a perfect growth pattern. The point here is that while one day's growth may vary from another's, over the length of the plant's bloom growth period it will average out. This messiness in the data should not be ignored and set aside. Instead, it should be used to generate discussion about desirable levels of precision and accuracy as well as variations common in nature. For instance, is measuring to the nearest centimeter close enough or should we measure to the nearest millimeter?

Look at the sample table recording the height of one plant over a five day period:

Day	Height in cm
1	2.5
2	5.2
3	7.6
4	10
5	12.6

It is clear that the recorded heights do not show the exact same growth for every day. But it can be said that on average this plant grew 2.5 cm each day. This is precisely the type of generalization students should be encouraged to make. It is also the goal of all curve-fitting techniques. The intent is to smooth out the rough edges that sometimes come with real-world data, thus making a model that is useful within acceptable tolerances.

In this activity students will not be using any complicated techniques to find the line that fits the data best. In fact, they will only be computing several slopes and finding the averages of the slopes. If the slopes between each of the five days in the table above are calculated and averaged, it can be seen that the average is 2.5 cm per day. This should be compared with a second approach in which the number of growing days divides the total amount of growth.

Management

1. You will need to purchase at least one flower bulb for the class. As previously indicated, amaryllis bulbs are in abundance around the winter holiday season. This activity can be done with one bulb for the whole class, or extended to use more than one for a comparative study. Bulbs such as the amaryllis usually come potted, in soil and in a box designed to keep them in the dark. They range in cost from as little as $3.00 to as much as $10.00 at a nursery.

2. If you find an amaryllis or similar bulb in a box, you can simply follow the growth instructions given. If you have to purchase a bulb, some soil, and a small pot separately, the bulb should be planted with just a small portion sticking out from the top of the soil.

3. When you are ready to begin the activity, bring the bulb out of its box and, if possible, put the pot and bulb in a window. The light serves as a trigger for the plant to begin its growth cycle. If you do this while the temperature outside is still cold, be careful not to place the plant too near the window or it will grow more slowly.

4. A few tablespoons of water each day is all the bulb will need to begin its growth cycle. Once the shoot is well established you can water the plant only when it appears stressed or is visibly wilting.

5. The calculations for the second section of this activity can be done manually or with a graphing calculator. It is highly recommended that you have students use graphing calculators.

Procedure

Part One

1. Distribute the student page on the first day that a green shoot appears at the top of the bulb.

2. On that day either stick a meter stick into the soil of the pot, or attach it to the outside of the pot itself. Do this so that every day students will have the same zero point when they measure.

3. Each day after that, *at the same time every day*, have two groups of students take separate readings, compare them, and report to the class.

4. Record the agreed on measurements in the right column of the table and the day number in the left column. (Don't use the calendar date, but number the days starting with one on the day the first measurement is taken.)

5. After the students have recorded the measurements in the table, have them also plot them on graph paper. *Do not connect the points with a broken line.* If students want to do this, explain that since the measurement represented by those connections can't be verified, it is not yet appropriate to draw in the lines.

6. After the students have measured, recorded, and plotted the data for several days, ask them to predict how tall the shoot will be the next day at the same time. Have them record their predictions. Assure them that an incorrect prediction will not affect their grade.

7. Continue to measure the plant each day for seven to ten days. Each time you come to a weekend, predict how much the plant will have grown by Monday.

8. After about ten days, the bulb (if it is an amaryllis) will go into a different part of its growth cycle, slowing its vertical growth to begin putting more energy into its bloom. Once this occurs, stop taking height measurements and concentrate on the curve-fitting portion of the assignment.

Part Two

1. Once students have collected at least seven days worth of growth data, a day can be spent doing the line-fitting portion. Have the students examine their graphs and describe what the points look like. Some may say that they line up, others may say they see a jagged line, still others may see a curve. Since the students have had experience

with lines already, guide them into a discussion about the slope between any two consecutive or non-consecutive days.

2. Have each student calculate the slope between every pair of consecutive days. Be sure to discuss what to do if some days' measurements are missing. Have the students compare and check their work with each other.

3. The data from a typical bulb will produce slopes that are approximately equal. This suggests that there is a line that would best fit the data points. One simple method for finding an approximation of that line is to find the average of all the slopes by hand. Once that has been done you should again have a discussion about the y-intercept for the line. Then have students graph that line on their graph. The student sheet asks them to make some predictions based on the graph and the equation.

Graphing Calculator Option
1. Instead of having students compute the slope by hand, have them enter the data into the statistical lists available on all graphing calculators. It is customary, though not required, that the first list be used as the independent variable—in this case the number of the day—and the second list as the dependent variable— the height of the shoot on that day).

2. Have students use the calculator's statistical plotter to see a graph of the data. Guide them through a discussion that leads to the linear connection.

3. Challenge students to calculate the slopes directly off the calculator and enter them into a third list. This list can then be averaged (i.e., have its mean calculated).

4. Since the graph has an intercept of zero and an average slope has been calculated, the average line can now be graphed by students.

5. You might want to have the students experiment with the graphing calculator and have it do a linear regression or a med-med line calculation. These will most likely be different from the average line you calculated earlier. The linear regression model is actually the line that best fits your data and is found by using a "Least Squares" technique. (Your students don't need to know this technique until they take a statistics course later in life.)

6. Once a line has been fit to the data, lead the class in a question time. The questions should seek to have the students make predictions using their equation and/ or their graph. For instance: "If the bulb had continued to grow at this rate, how tall would it be in *x* days?" or "Do you see how we missed the measurements on the fifth and sixth days because of the weekend? What do you think the plant's height was on each of those days?"

Discussion
1. What will the bulb's height be tomorrow? Explain.
2. What will the height be in four days? Explain.
3. Were your predictions from yesterday correct? Why or why not?
4. What is the intercept of the line of best fit?
5. What does the slope of our best fit line mean in terms of our investigation?
6. How tall was the plant 12 hours ago? (This question is only appropriate if you have been faithful about measuring the plant at the same time every day.)

Extensions
1. Use more than one bulb to control for a variety of variables. Keep data on each bulb and compare growth rates.
   - Light: Place one bulb directly in front of a window and place another across the room.
   - Water: Carefully measure the amount of water each bulb receives. Give one bulb two to three times more water than the other.
   - Fertilizer: Dissolve liquid fertilizer into the water that one bulb gets while withholding it from another.

2. Explore the concepts of *Extrapolation* (to predict beyond a set of data) and *Interpolation* (filling in the data points between other measurements). Point out to students how they have already been using these concepts with the data. How else can these two concepts be used with the data given? What can you extrapolate about what the height of the plant will be in a week? How can you interpolate what the height of the plant was on Saturday or Sunday?

Curriculum Correlation
Life Sciences
   Turn one of the extensions into a complete science lesson studying the growth and structure of plants, food requirements, ideal growth environment, etc.

A Winter Holiday Adventure

Use this table to record the height of your plant every day during the investigation. In the Prediction column, record your prediction of how tall the plant will be on the following day. In the Difference column, record the difference between your prediction and the actual height of the plant on that day.

Day	Plant Height in cm	Prediction in cm	Difference
1			
2			

Every day, plot the height of your plant on the graph. Write in the appropriate values on the axes. Do not connect the points at this time.

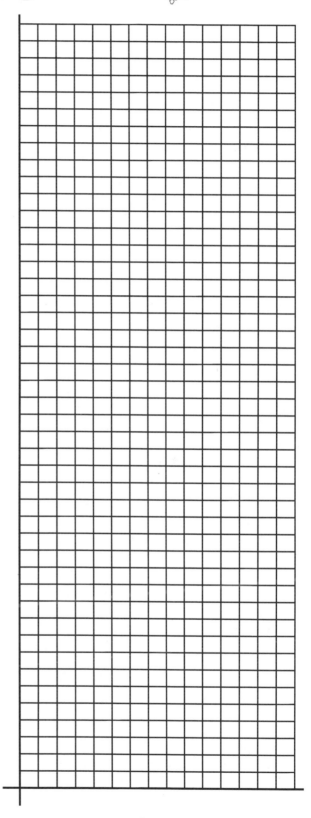

Height in cm

Day

191

A Winter Holiday Adventure

On this page you will calculate the slopes of an imaginary line connecting one day's measurements with the next day's. Before you begin, think about the slopes and answer these questions.

- What will the denominator (number at the bottom of the fraction) be in most of these slopes? Why?

- Will all the slopes you calculate have the number given above as the denominator? Why or why not?

Fill in the table below using the data you collected. In the *Height 2* column, write the height of the plant each time you recorded it, starting with the second day. In the *Height 1* column, write the height of the plant each time you recorded it on the previous day. This means the first row should compare entries two and one, the second row entries three and two, the third row entries four and three, and so on. When you have filled in all of the data, calculate the average of all of the slopes and enter it at the bottom of the table.

Height 2	Height 1	Height 2 – Height 1	Slope between points
		Average of all slopes	

You will be using the average slope calculation throughout this activity. Check with your classmates to verify that everyone has the same answer based on the data. Clarify any differences that may exist.

A Winter Holiday Adventure

Since the plant had no height at the time the activity started, the point (0,0) can be used on the graph. Plot this point on the graph. This point is the y-intercept of the line that is known as the *Best-Fit Line*. Using the average slope you calculated on the previous page and the intercept you just plotted, graph this line. Best-fit lines will not necessarily touch every data point plotted. In fact, they may touch very few.

1. Calculate the slope between the first day and the very last day you took measurements.

2. How does it compare with the average slope you calculated? Are the values nearly the same or are they very different? Why?

3. How would you express the slope as a rate of growth? Why would it be considered a growth rate? What units would be appropriate?

4. Write the equation of the best-fit line below.

5. Assuming the growth rate you calculated will remain constant, how tall will the plant be on the 15th day? ...the 100th day?

6. On what day will the plant be 100 cm tall?

7. On what day will the plant be 3m tall?

8. How tall was the plant on day 3.5?

9. On what day was the plant 22.4 cm tall?

Part Six:
Equalities and Inequalities

The concept of inequality is an important one in mathematics as well as in real-world applications. Simply stated, an inequality consists of two unequal terms or sets of terms.

Inequalities require the existence of an equality against which they can be measured. Anything less than or more than the equality is an inequality. The equality serves as a standard. The concept of inequality broadens and enriches perspectives.

The standard divides conditions in a situation into three categories: that in which elements are less than the standard, that in which they are equal, and that in which they more than the standard. For example, in a cotton classing laboratory, it is necessary to maintain a constant temperature to avoid obtaining false results. That temperature represents an equality. Anything less than the desired temperature is too cold and anything more is too warm. Both of these represent inequalities.

This threefold division is enriched through graphs. To illustrate, the graph (A) shows the line $x + y = 10$. x and y can take on an infinite number of values such as (3, 7), (2.9, 7.1), and (-4.12, 14.12).

The line itself represents pairs of numbers whose sum is 10; the region below the line represents pairs whose sum is less than 10, and the region above the line represents pairs whose sum is greater than 10. Each region contains an infinite number of pairs and every point in each region is the graph of a unique pair.

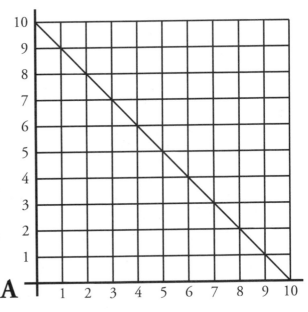

Inequalities, just like equations, can be expressed symbolically. The (x, y) pairs graphed below the line have a sum less than 10. This is written as $(x + y) < 10$. Those graphed above the line have a sum greater than 10 and this is written as $(x + y) > 10$.

Sometimes the three parts are reduced to two by statements such as "equal to or less than" or "equal to or greater than." Using the above situation, the expression "x + y is equal to or less than 10" is written as $(x + y) \leq 10$. Similarly, the expression "x + y is equal to or greater than 10" is written as $(x + y) \geq 10$.

Sometimes we want to refer to a situation in which a number has a restricted range of values such as greater than 5 but less than 12. Using x, this is written as $5 < x < 12$. Or, we have a situation in which x is equal to or greater than 7 and equal to or less than 10. Here we use the notation $7 \leq x \leq 10$.

There are numerous situations in which the combined study of equalities and inequalities provides additional insight and depth of understanding. The graphing of fractions (B) is an illustration. For this purpose, fractions are thought of and graphed as (denominator, numerator) ordered

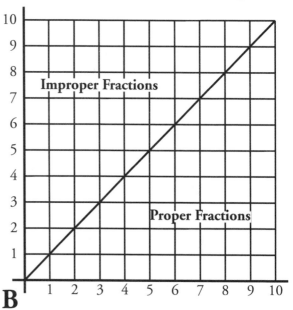

pairs. The standard is provided by fractions equal to one. The equation is $n/d = 1$. Sample ordered pairs belonging to this standard are (1, 1,), (7, 7), (2.3, 2.3), etc. Notice that the graph is a line that passes through the origin and makes a 45-degree angle with both axes. We will refer to it as the 1-line.

All points above the 1-line are graphs of improper fractions expressed by ordered pairs in which the denominator is less than the numerator. A line from the origin through any such point makes an angle with the horizontal axis whose measure is greater than 45 degrees.

All points below the 1-line are graphs of proper fractions expressed by ordered pairs in which the denominator is greater than the numerator. A line from the origin through any one of these points will make an angle with the horizontal axis whose measure is less than 45 degrees.

The n/d ratio has other meanings in other contexts. In some instances it is referred to as the ratio of "rise/run." In other instances, it denotes the slope. Lines drawn from graphed points to the origin have the rise/run ratio as their slope.

A right triangle is formed when lines are drawn from any point to the origin and to the horizontal axis. In this application (C), the ratio is that of the opposite side/adjacent side, or the tangent of the angle at the origin. All points above the 1-line treated in this way create triangles whose angle at the origin have tangents that are greater than one and those below the 1-line have tangents that are less than one.

The graphing of inequalities is similar in difficulty to that of graphing equations. First, graph the equation which serves as the standard. Next, designate all points above the equation graph as greater than the standard and all points below the equation graph as less than the standard.

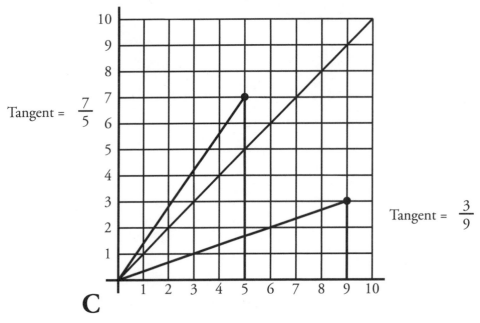

Tangent = $\dfrac{7}{5}$

Tangent = $\dfrac{3}{9}$

C

Sales Calls provides an introductory experience to working with inequalities and using standard inequality notation. Customers are assigned to three sales persons based on the traveling distances from the firm's office to the customers location. The graph consists of a map laid out in the first quadrant. It is required to divide the quadrant into three regions by using two equalities.

Calling Long Distance has students determine the most cost effective of three available services based on the average number of minutes used per month. By graphing the linear equations representing the relationship of cost to time for each service, students can quickly determine which service to recommend as the most cost effective for a given amount of usage.

Triangles of Squares involves graphing an equality represented by the Pythagorean Theorem: $(a^2 + b^2) = c^2$. This is graphed as the ordered pair $(c^2, a^2 + b^2)$ where c^2 is measured on the horizontal axis as the independent variable and $a^2 + b^2$ is measured on the vertical axis as the dependent variable. The graph of $(a^2 + b^2) = c^2$ is a straight line with a slope of 1. Where $(a^2 + b^2) > c^2$ the triangle is acute; where $(a^2 + b^2) = c^2$ the triangle is a right triangle; and where $(a^2 + b^2) < c^2$ the triangle is obtuse. By using squares with sides a, b, and c units in length, the mental image of the Pythagorean Theorem is reinforced.

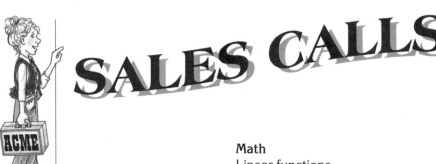

Topic
Algebra—Linear Functions and Inequalities

Key Question
How are linear functions involving inequalities used in real-world situations?

Learning Goals
Students will:
- interpret and graph inequalities from written statements; and
- use standard notation to formulate inequality statements.

Guiding Documents
Project 2061 Benchmarks
- *Mathematical ideas can be represented concretely, graphically, and symbolically.*
- *The graphic display of numbers may help to show patterns such as trends, varying rates of change, gaps, or clusters. Such patterns can sometimes be used to make predictions about the phenomena being graphed.*
- *Graphs can show a variety of possible relationships between two variables. As one variable increases uniformly, the other may do one of the following: always keep the same proportion to the first, increase or decrease steadily, increase or decrease faster and faster, get closer and closer to some limiting value, reach some intermediate maximum or minimum, alternately increase and decrease indefinitely, increase and decrease in steps, or do something different from any of these.*
- *Organize information in tables and graphs and identify relationships they reveal.*

NCTM Standards 2000*
- *Model and solve contextualized problems using various representations such as graphs, tables, and equations*
- *Relate and compare different forms of representation for a relationship*
- *Identify functions as linear or nonlinear and contrast their properties from tables, graphs, and equations*

Math
Linear functions
Equations and inequalities
Graphing
Writing equality/inequality expressions

Integrated Processes
Observing
Collecting and recording data
Organizing data
Interpreting data
Generalizing

Materials
Colored pencils
Rulers
Student sheet

Background Information
This is an introductory experience with inequaliuties, including the use of standard inequality notation. For background, read the introduction to *Part Six*.

Management
1. If students are not familiar with the notation of equalities and inequalities ($<$, $>$, $=$, $\leq$, $\geq$), you will need to go over the symbols and their meanings before you begin the activity.
2. Students will need colored pencils in three different colors for this activity. They should also have rulers so that they can draw the boundaries of each person's territory accurately.
3. According to the student sheet, travel distance is determined by finding the shortest route between the ACME office and the customer by following a road. Students should also understand, however, that there is a multitude of possible "invisible" routes between the roads which can also be used. For example, in addition to traveling two miles north and three miles east, Roxanne could travel 4.2 miles north and 1.6 miles east, or 2.3 miles east and 1.1 miles north, etc. The boundary of each person's territory is not only defined by the whole-number ordered pairs that sum six, or 12, but also by the infinite number of decimal ordered pairs that sum six or 12.

Procedure
1. Hand out the student sheet and the materials to each student and go over the instructions. If necessary,

give a few examples of how to find the travel distance to a given point.

2. Allow students to work together in small groups or individually to complete the grid and answer the questions.

3. When students are finished, have them compare their solutions with other groups/classmates and discuss what they discovered.

Discussion

1. Describe how you determined the territory assigned to each sales person.

2. What does the sales territory for Roxanne look like? (See *Solutions*.)

3. How does this territory compare to Juan's territory? ...to Terry's territory? (See *Solutions*.)

4. What shape do the boundaries between the sales territories take? [They are straight lines.] Why? [The boundaries are defined by the ordered pairs that sum six and 12, respectively. On a graph, ordered pairs with the same sum fall on a straight line.]

5. How would this information help you if the assignment distances changed? [To define the boundaries of a new territory all you need to do is plot the points that fall on each axis and connect them with a straight line.]

6. How were you able to use the notation of equalities and inequalities to describe the sales territory for each person? (See *Solutions*.)

Extension

Change the travel distances that define each person's boundaries and compare the two graphs.

Solutions

The graph from the student sheet and the inequalities that define it are shown below.

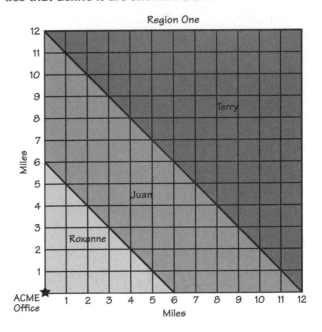

Roxanne: $R \leq 6$
Juan: $6 < J \leq 12$
Terry: $T > 12$

SALES CALLS

The ACME Corporation has assigned territories to its three sales people in Region One, which is shown below.

- Roxanne calls on all customers 6 travel miles or less from the ACME office.
- Juan is responsible for those between 6 and 12 travel miles from the office.
- Terry services customers farther than 12 travel miles from the office.

Customers are located all throughout Region One, and can be reached by the roads shown on the map below. Travel miles are determined by finding the *shortest route* that can be taken from the ACME office to the customer by following a road.

Shade the territory serviced by each sales person in a different color. Mark the outer edge of each territory with a solid line and label each territory with the appropriate person's name.

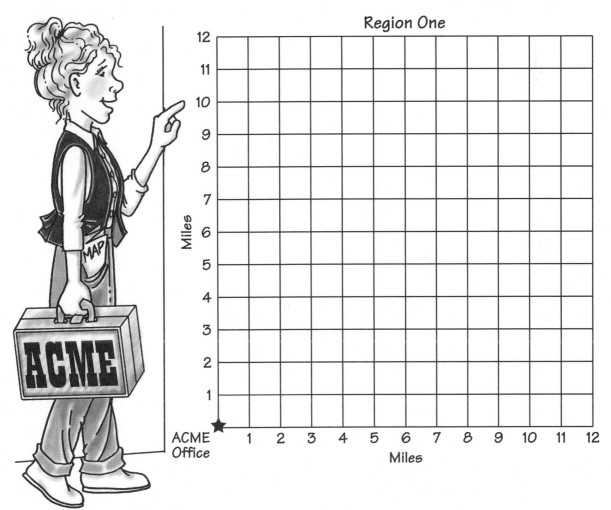

Write your answers on the back of your paper.

1. Describe how you determined the territories assigned to each sales person.
2. What did you discover that would make it easier to draw a new map if assignment distances changed?
3. Using <, =, >, ≤, and ≥ notation, write a description for each person's territory.

Topic
Algebra—Linear Functions

Key Question
How can you use tables, graphs, and rules to analyze long-distance calling rates?

Learning Goals
Students will:
- build a cost table (in dollars) detailing the charges for long-distance calling;
- graph the data;
- determine the linear function rules; and
- find the point of intersection of pairs of lines from their linear function rules.

Guiding Document
NCTM Standards 2000*
- *Model and solve contextualized problems using various representations such as graphs, tables, and equations*
- *Represent, anlayze and generalize a variety of patterns with tables, graphs, words, and, when possible, symbolic rules*
- *Identify functions as linear or nonlinear and contrast their properties from tables, words, or equations*
- *Explore relationships between symbolic expressions and graphs of lines, paying particular attention to the meaning of intercept and slope*

Math
Linear equations
Data tables and graphs
Rules
Simultaneous equations

Integrated Processes
Observing
Collecting and recording data
Comparing and contrasting
Interpreting data
Generalizing

Materials
Rulers
Colored pencils
Student sheets

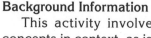

Background Information
This activity involves numerous high priority concepts in context, as is evident from the standards referenced. It is, therefore, important to allocate adequate time to each so that student understanding is nourished. How students might ultimately learn to think about these concepts is illustrated in the article that accompanies this activity. It should be studied carefully in preparation before using this activity.

These understandings develop over time through repeated experiences and thorough discussions. As students meet the concepts over and over again, their facility to use them will grow and their understanding deepen. It is the intent of the activities in this series to provide such meaningful and varied applications of linear function concepts.

It is important to study and understand the information that is provided by the article accompanying this activity. *It is important to stress that all terms in the rules must be in terms of dollars.* Students might mistakenly write the coefficient of t in cents and the basic fee in dollars. Such confusion, of course, leads to a meaningless answer.

Management
1. In order to successfully complete this activity, students must be familiar with how to determine the y-intercept and slope of a line from a graph and/or data table. They must also know how to write the rule for these equations and then use the rule to determine where a pair of lines intersects. In this activity the equation $f(x) = mx + b$ takes the form $c(t) = mt + b$ where c is the cost in dollars, t is the total number of minutes spent on long distance, and b the basic fee.
2. Because students will be comparing three different plans that are plotted on the same graph, they should have colored pencils in three different colors so that they can visually distinguish between the plans.

Procedure
1. Hand out the student sheets, colored pencils, and rulers and go over the instructions for each step.
2. Have students work together in groups to complete the student sheets. Be sure to remind students to convert all data into dollars per minute rather than leaving it in cents per minute. Students should also be told the form of the equation: $c(t) = mt + b$ and the meaning of each symbol.

3. When all groups have finished, close with a time of class discussion and sharing. Review, especially, the concepts of the y-intercept (*b*) and slope (*m*) and how they manifest themselves in the rate structure and equations.

Discussion

1. How were you able to determine the cost for different amounts of time for each plan? [Multiply the cost (in dollars per minute) by the number of minutes and add the basic fee (if applicable).]
2. For what type of customer is Telstar best suited? [Those who spend 148 minutes or less on long distance each month.]
3. For what type of customer is Gotel best suited? [Those who spend between 148 minutes and 250 minutes on long distance each month.] …Telcom? [Those who spend more than 250 minutes a month on long distance.]
4. How were you able to determine the y-intercepts? … slopes? … rules?
5. What is the y-intercept, slope, and rule for Telstar? … for Gotel? … for Telcom? (See *Solutions*)
6. Where do the lines for the different companies intersect on the graph? (See *Solutions*)

Solutions

The solutions for each section of the student page are given below, followed by the graph as students should have constructed it.

1.

Cost Table

Minutes	0	60	120	180	240	300	360
Telstar	$0	$7.14	$14.28	$21.42	$28.56	$35.70	$42.84
Gotel	$4.00	$9.52	$15.04	$20.56	$26.08	$31.60	$37.12
Telcom	$10.00	$14.08	$18.16	$22.24	$26.32	$30.40	$34.48

2. Customers who spend 148 minutes or less on long distance each month will be best served by the Telstar company. Customers who spend between 148 minutes and 250 minutes will be best served by the Gotel company. Customers who spend more than 250 minutes a month on long distance will find that Telcom is their cheapest option.
3. Notice that the cost in cents for each plan has been converted into cost in dollars so that the values will match those plotted on the graph when the intercepts are determined.

	Y-intercept	Slope of line	Rule
Telstar	0	11.9	$c(t) = .119t$
Gotel	4	9.2	$c(t) = .092t + 4$
Telcom	10	6.8	$c(t) = .068t + 10$

4. The Telstar and Gotel lines intersect at approximately 148 minutes.

$$.119t = .092t + 4$$
$$.027t = 4$$
$$t = 148 \text{ (approximately)}$$

The Telstar and Telcom lines intersect at approximately 196 minutes.

$$.119t = .068t + 10$$
$$.051t = 10$$
$$t = 196 \text{ (approximately)}$$

The Gotel and Telcom lines intersect at 250 minutes.

$$.092t + 4 = .068t + 10$$
$$.024t = 6$$
$$t = 250$$

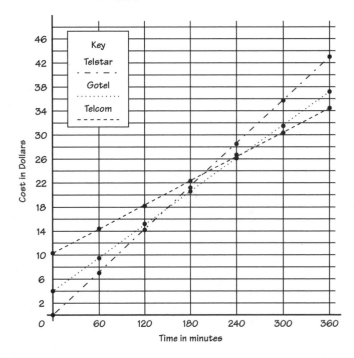

Your role is to analyze three long-distance services that are available in your community and to advise your clients regarding the option that meets their needs at lowest cost. Your clients vary greatly in how much time they spend calling long distance. You need to be prepared to respond promptly to each of them when they call for advice.

The three services and their charges are:

Telstar: no basic monthly fee; 11.9 cents per minute

Gotel: a $4.00 basic monthly fee plus 9.2 cents per minute

Telcom: a $10.00 basic monthly fee plus 6.8 cents per minute

Your assignment is to analyze the services using the following reference sheet.

1. Complete this table.

Cost Table

Minutes	0	60	120	180	240	300	360
Telstar							
Gotel							
Telcom							

2. Graph the data on the next page. Use a different color to plot the line of each company. Describe which service is best for which type of customer.

3. From your graph and/or table complete the following:

	Y-intercept	Slope of line	Rule
Telstar			
Gotel			
Telcom			

4. From the rules, determine where each pair of lines intersect. (Be sure that all of your variables are in Dollars per minute, not Cents per minute.)

Calling Long Distance

Graph the data from the table on the previous page.

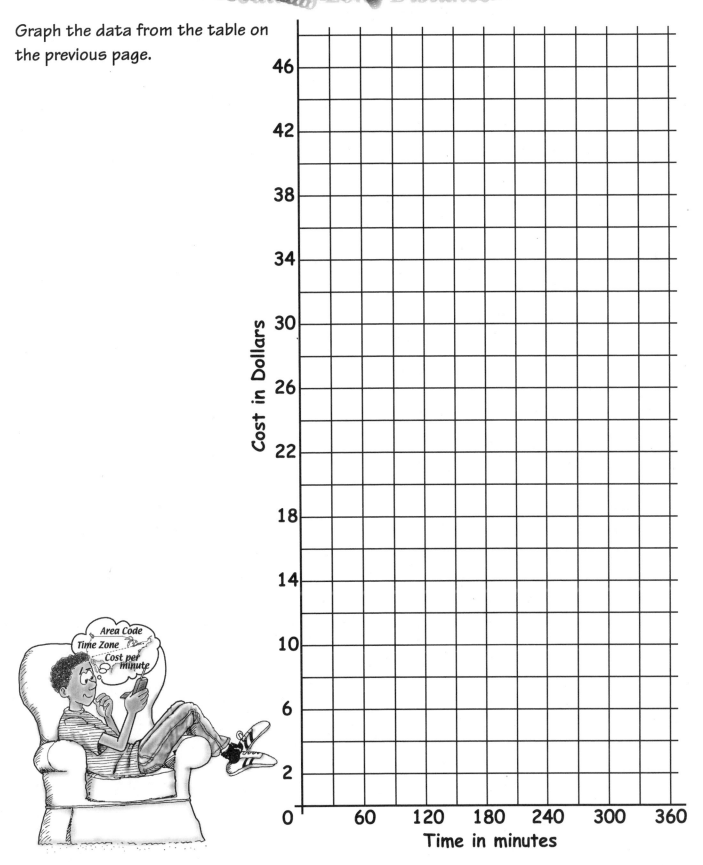

Cost in Dollars

2 · 6 · 10 · 14 · 18 · 22 · 26 · 30 · 34 · 38 · 42 · 46

0 · 60 · 120 · 180 · 240 · 300 · 360

Time in minutes

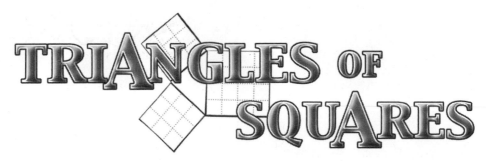

TRIANGLES OF SQUARES

Topic
Algebra, Geometry—Pythagorean Theorem

Key Questions
1. If you know the lengths of the three sides of a triangle, how can you determine if the triangle is equilateral, isosceles, or scalene?
2. If you know the lengths of the three sides of a triangle, how can you determine if the triangle is acute, right, or obtuse?

Learning Goals
Students will:
- learn to sort triangles by angles and sides, and
- recognize the equality and inequalities between the sum of the areas of the squares on the short legs of a triangle compared to the area of the square on the longest side

Guiding Documents
Project 2061 Benchmarks
- *Some shapes have special properties: Triangular shapes tend to make structures rigid, and round shapes give the least possible boundary for a given amount of interior area. Shapes can match exactly or have the same shape in different sizes.*
- *Mathematicians often represent things with abstract ideas, such as numbers or perfectly straight lines, and then work with those ideas alone. The "things" from which they abstract can be ideas themselves (for example, a proposition about "all equal-sided triangles" or "all odd numbers").*
- *Graphs can show a variety of possible relationships between two variables. As one variable increases uniformly, the other may do one of the following: always keep the same proportion to the first, increase or decrease steadily, increase or decrease faster and faster, get closer and closer to some limiting value, reach some intermediate maximum or minimum, alternately increase and decrease indefinitely, increase and decrease in steps, or do something different from any of these.*

NCTM Standards 2000*
- *Understand relationships among the angles, side lengths, perimeters, areas, and volumes of similar objects*

- *Use geometric models to represent and explain numerical and algebraic relationships*
- *Use symbolic algebra to represent situations and to solve problems, especially those that involve linear relationships*
- *Use graphs to analyze the nature of changes in quantities in linear relationships*
- *Create and critique inductive and deductive arguments concerning geometric ideas and relationships, such as congruence, similarity, and the Pythagorean relationship*

Math
Geometry
    categories of triangles
    Pythagorean Theorem
Algebra
    graphing
    equalities/inequalities

Integrated Processes
Observing
Comparing and contrasting
Generalizing

Materials
Option One:
    cardstock
    scissors
Option Two:
    AIMS Algebra Tiles
    2 cm squares

Background Information
Finding all the possible triangular regions that can be surrounded from a limited variety of discrete size squares can provide a rich understanding of triangles.

Initially students will discover that not all combinations of three squares work. In order to form a triangle, the combined edges of two shorter squares must be greater than the length of the edge of the largest square. With the four different size squares of 2, 3, 4, and 5 centimeters, 20 different combinations can be made. Three of these, however, will not form triangles (2,2,4; 2,2,5; 2,3,5).

Constructing 17 different triangles provides an excellent opportunity to reinforce the understanding of types of triangles. When sorting by sides, students will find four equilateral, three scalene, and ten isosceles triangles. When sorting by angles, students will be able to find one right, four obtuse, and 12 acute triangles.

Having students consider the sum of the areas of squares made on the two shorter legs of a triangle ($a^2 + b^2$) compared to the area of the square formed on the longest leg (c^2) develops a full concept of the Pythagorean Theorem ($a^2 + b^2 = c^2$). Placing these measurements alongside the types of triangles by angles quickly shows the following:

when $a^2 + b^2 > c^2$, it is an acute triangle,
when $a^2 + b^2 = c^2$, it is a right triangle,
when $a^2 + b^2 < c^2$, it is an obtuse triangle.

Discovering these equalities and inequalities helps students understand that the Pythagorean Theorem is true only for right triangles. It also provides a way to interpret the broader relationship of ($a^2 + b^2$) to (c^2).

By graphing the measurements, the relationship is reinforced. As students plot each triangle's point with ($a^2 + b^2$) being the vertical axis and (c^2) being the horizontal axis, they will discover that only the right triangle falls on the line with a slope of one. The acute triangles all plot above the one line and the obtuse triangles below the line. This accentuates the special relationship of the right triangle while providing a very pertinent use of graphing inequalities.

Management

1. Before the lesson, determine what materials will be used for squares. *Option One*: The blackline master may be copied onto cardstock and students may cut out the squares when they are needed. *Option Two*: AIMS Algebra Tiles, which provide a more kinesthetic appeal for students, may be used; however, the teacher will need to cut 2 cm square pieces before beginning the lesson.

2. Students should be familiar with the types of triangles by sides (equilateral, isosceles, scalene) and angle (acute, right, obtuse) before beginning this investigation. If they are not, some instruction should be done to familiarize them with all the types.

3. Emphasize to the students that they need to be careful when forming the triangles. The corners of the squares must touch each other to form a vertex. Several of the acute and obtuse triangles will be mistakenly classified as right triangles if they are not constructed accurately. A corner from a piece a paper will help students check right angles.

4. Partners work very well for this activity. One student can construct while the second records.

Procedure

1. Distribute the materials and allow students time to cut out the squares if necessary. If the materials

are not labeled for length and area have the students examine and compare the pieces to recognize the sizes are 2, 3, 4, and 5 centimeters.

2. Using the squares have students determine how many different-sized triangles can be made from these four sizes of squares.

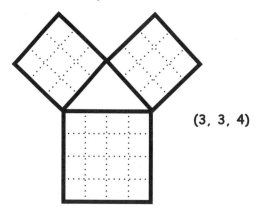

(3, 3, 4)

Although many students will begin by randomly developing combinations, encourage them to develop an ordered listing to assure they have found all the possible combinations. They should discover that three combinations of squares do not form triangles (2,2,4; 2,2,5; 2,3,5).

3. When students have confirmed that a combination of squares forms a triangle, direct them to record the lengths on the chart.

4. Encourage the students to carefully form the triangles so the corners of the squares touch exactly. Have them determine and record the type of triangle that is formed. (A corner of a paper can be used to determine right angles.)

5. Optional: Have students cut squares of paper and glue them to make permanent records of all possible triangles.

6. Direct the students to calculate the area of the square on each edge of the triangle. Have them record the sum of the areas of the squares of the two shorter legs in one column of the chart and the area of the square on the longest leg in another column of the chart.

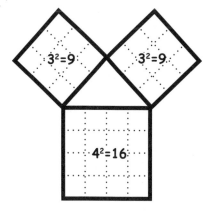

7. Tell them to choose the equality/inequality sign that makes the number sentence true.
8. Hold a discussion in which students share observations they make about the relationships of number sentences and types of triangles.
9. Have them make a graph of the data by plotting the areas of the squares on the sides of a triangle.
10. Have them observe and record the relationship of the position where each triangle is represented on the graph and the type of triangle it is. Direct them to record the algebraic equation that represents the line that is drawn on the graph [$a^2 + b^2 = c^2$ or $= 1$] and inequalities describing the regions above [$a^2 + b^2 > c^2$ or > 1] and below [$a^2 + b^2 < c^2$ or < 1] the line.

Discussion

1. How can you tell if a combination of squares will make a triangle before assembling them? [To make a triangle, the combination of the lengths of the two shorter sides must be greater than the length of the longest side ($a + b > c$).]
2. How can you look at the lengths of the sides of a triangle and determine what type of triangle it is by sides?

3. What relationship do you see in squares on the sides of a triangle and the type of triangle it is by angles? [$a^2 + b^2 > c^2$: acute; $a^2 + b^2 = c^2$: right; $a^2 + b^2 < c^2$: obtuse]
4. What is the relationship of the position of a triangle's point on the graph and the type of triangle it is by angle? [right on the one line, acute above the one line, obtuse below the one line]
5. If you know the lengths of the edges of a triangle, how can you determine what type of a triangle it is by angles? [Find the squares on all three sides. If the sum of the squares on the shortest two sides equals the square on the longest side, it is a right triangle. If the sum is greater, it is an acute triangle. If the sum is less, it is an obtuse triangle.]

Extension

Measure triangles found in the classroom and use the algebraic sentences to determine their types. Confirm that it is correct.

* Reprinted with permission from *Principles and Standards for School Mathematics*, 2000 by the National Council of Teachers of Mathematics. All rights reserved.

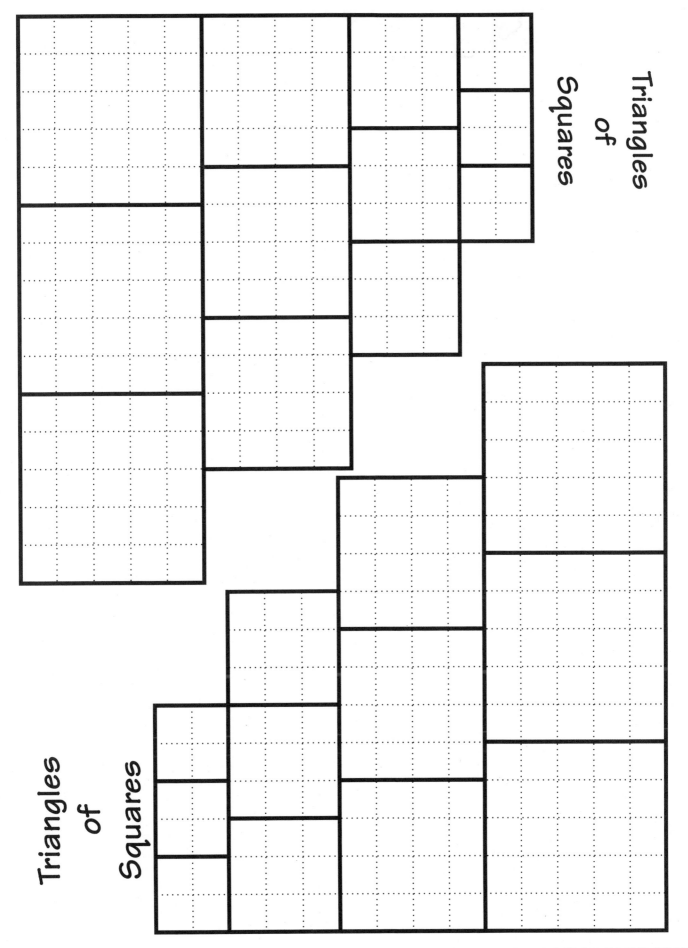

Triangles
of
Squares

TRIANGLES OF SQUARES

Make all the possible different size triangles you can out of 2, 3, 4, and 5 cm squares. Record the dimensions and complete the chart.

Length of Sides			Squares on Sides			Type of Triangle	
Shortest Side a	Mid-length Side b	Longest Side c	Sum of squares on shorter sides a^2+b^2	< > =	Area of square on longest side c^2	By Angles Acute Right Obtuse	By Sides Equilateral Isosceles Scalene

TRIANGLES OF SQUARES

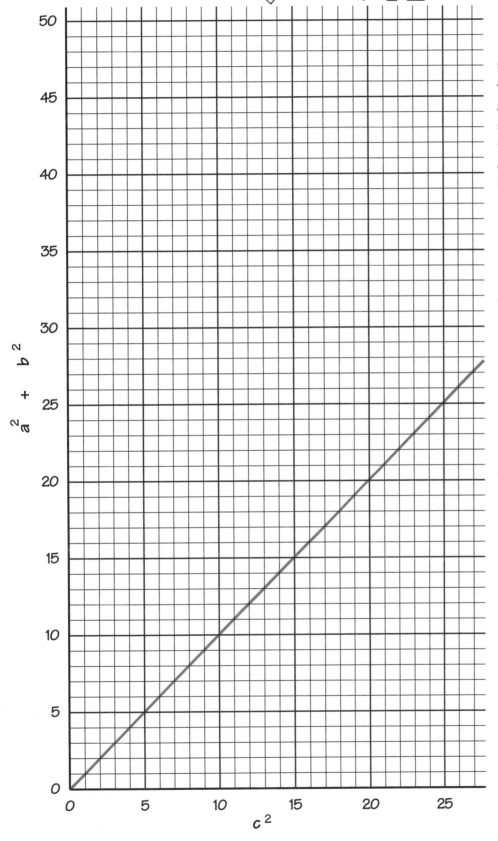

Plot a point for each triangle so it records the area of sum of the squares on the two smaller sides and the area of the square on the longest side.

a. What type of triangles get plotted above the gray line?

b. What type of triangles get plotted on the gray line?

c. What type of triangles get plotted below the gray line?

y-axis label: $a^2 + b^2$

x-axis label: c^2

The AIMS Program

AIMS is the acronym for "**A**ctivities **I**ntegrating **M**athematics and **S**cience." Such integration enriches learning and makes it meaningful and holistic. AIMS began as a project of Fresno Pacific University to integrate the study of mathematics and science in grades K-9, but has since expanded to include language arts, social studies, and other disciplines.

AIMS is a continuing program of the non-profit AIMS Education Foundation. It had its inception in a National Science Foundation funded program whose purpose was to explore the effectiveness of integrating mathematics and science. The project directors in cooperation with 80 elementary classroom teachers devoted two years to a thorough field-testing of the results and implications of integration.

The approach met with such positive results that the decision was made to launch a program to create instructional materials incorporating this concept. Despite the fact that thoughtful educators have long recommended an integrative approach, very little appropriate material was available in 1981 when the project began. A series of writing projects have ensued and today the AIMS Education Foundation is committed to continue the creation of new integrated activities on a permanent basis.

The AIMS program is funded through the sale of this developing series of books and proceeds from the Foundation's endowment. All net income from program and products flows into a trust fund administered by the AIMS Education Foundation. Use of these funds is restricted to support of research, development, and publication of new materials. Writers donate all their rights to the Foundation to support its on-going program. No royalties are paid to the writers.

The rationale for integration lies in the fact that science, mathematics, language arts, social studies, etc., are integrally interwoven in the real world from which it follows that they should be similarly treated in the classroom where we are preparing students to live in that world. Teachers who use the AIMS program give enthusiastic endorsement to the effectiveness of this approach.

Science encompasses the art of questioning, investigating, hypothesizing, discovering, and communicating. Mathematics is a language that provides clarity, objectivity, and understanding. The language arts provide us powerful tools of communication. Many of the major contemporary societal issues stem from advancements in science and must be studied in the context of the social sciences. Therefore, it is timely that all of us take seriously a more holistic mode of educating our students. This goal motivates all who are associated with the AIMS Program. We invite you to join us in this effort.

Meaningful integration of knowledge is a major recommendation coming from the nation's professional science and mathematics associations. The American Association for the Advancement of Science in *Science for All Americans* strongly recommends the integration of mathematics, science, and technology. The National Council of Teachers of Mathematics places strong emphasis on applications of mathematics such as are found in science investigations. AIMS is fully aligned with these recommendations.

Extensive field testing of AIMS investigations confirms these beneficial results.

1. Mathematics becomes more meaningful, hence more useful, when it is applied to situations that interest students.
2. The extent to which science is studied and understood is increased, with a significant economy of time, when mathematics and science are integrated.
3. There is improved quality of learning and retention, supporting the thesis that learning which is meaningful and relevant is more effective.
4. Motivation and involvement are increased dramatically as students investigate real-world situations and participate actively in the process.

We invite you to become part of this classroom teacher movement by using an integrated approach to learning and sharing any suggestions you may have. The AIMS Program welcomes you!

AIMS Education Foundation Programs

A Day with AIMS®

Intensive one-day workshops are offered to introduce educators to the philosophy and rationale of AIMS. Participants will discuss the methodology of AIMS and the strategies by which AIMS principles may be incorporated into curriculum. Each participant will take part in a variety of hands-on AIMS investigations to gain an understanding of such aspects as the scientific/mathematical content, classroom management, and connections with other curricular areas. *A Day with AIMS®* workshops may be offered anywhere in the United States. Necessary supplies and take-home materials are usually included in the enrollment fee.

A Week with AIMS®

Throughout the nation, AIMS offers many one-week workshops each year, usually in the summer. Each workshop lasts five days and includes at least 30 hours of AIMS hands-on instruction. Participants are grouped according to the grade level(s) in which they are interested. Instructors are members of the AIMS Instructional Leadership Network. Supplies for the activities and a generous supply of take-home materials are included in the enrollment fee. Sites are selected on the basis of applications submitted by educational organizations. If chosen to host a workshop, the host agency agrees to provide specified facilities and cooperate in the promotion of the workshop. The AIMS Education Foundation supplies workshop materials as well as the travel, housing, and meals for instructors.

AIMS One-Week Perspectives Workshops

Each summer, Fresno Pacific University offers AIMS one-week workshops on its campus in Fresno, California. AIMS Program Directors and highly qualified members of the AIMS National Leadership Network serve as instructors.

The AIMS Instructional Leadership Program

This is an AIMS staff-development program seeking to prepare facilitators for leadership roles in science/math education in their home districts or regions. Upon successful completion of the program, trained facilitators may become members of the AIMS Instructional Leadership Network, qualified to conduct AIMS workshops, teach AIMS in-service courses for college credit, and serve as AIMS consultants. Intensive training is provided in mathematics, science, process and thinking skills, workshop management, and other relevant topics.

College Credit and Grants

Those who participate in workshops may often qualify for college credit. If the workshop takes place on the campus of Fresno Pacific University, that institution may grant appropriate credit. If the workshop takes place off-campus, arrangements can sometimes be made for credit to be granted by another institution. In addition, the applicant's home school district is often willing to grant in-service or professional-development credit. Many educators who participate in AIMS workshops are recipients of various types of educational grants, either local or national. Nationally known foundations and funding agencies have long recognized the value of AIMS mathematics and science workshops to educators. The AIMS Education Foundation encourages educators interested in attending or hosting workshops to explore the pos-sibilities suggested above. Although the Foundation strongly supports such interest, it reminds applicants that they have the primary responsibility for fulfilling *current* requirements.

For current information regarding the programs described above, please complete the following:

Information Request

Please send current information on the items checked:

____ *Basic Information Packet* on AIMS materials   ____ *A Week with AIMS®* workshops
____ *AIMS Instructional Leadership Program*   ____ Hosting information for *A Day with AIMS®* workshops
____ *AIMS One-Week Perspectives* workshops   ____ Hosting information for *A Week with AIMS®* workshops

Name _____ Phone _____

Address _____
          Street   City   State   Zip

We invite you to subscribe to AIMS
The Magazine

Each issue of the magazine contains a variety of material useful to educators at all grade levels. Feature articles of lasting value deal with topics such as mathematical or science concepts, curriculum, assessment, the teaching of process skills, and historical background. Several of the latest AIMS math/science investigations are always included, along with their reproducible activity sheets. As needs direct and space allows, various issues contain news of current developments, such as workshop schedules, activities of the AIMS Instructional Leadership Network, and announcements of upcoming publications. *AIMS the Magazine* is published monthly, August through May. Subscriptions are on an annual basis only. A subscription entered at any time will begin with the next issue, but will also include the previous issues of that volume. Readers have preferred this arrangement because articles and activities within an annual volume are often interrelated.

Please note that a subscription automatically includes duplication rights for one school site for all issues included in the subscription. Many schools build cost-effective library resources with their subscriptions.

YES! I am interested in subscribing to AIMS
The Magazine

Name _____   Home Phone _____

Address _____   City, State, Zip _____

Please send the following volumes (subject to availability):

_____	Volume	IX	(1994-95)	$10.00	_____	Volume	XIV (1999-00)	$35.00
_____	Volume	X	(1995-96)	$10.00	_____	Volume	XV (2000-01)	$35.00
_____	Volume	XI	(1996-97)	$10.00	_____	Volume	XVI (2001-02)	$35.00
_____	Volume	XII	(1997-98)	$10.00	_____	Volume	XVII (2002-03)	$35.00
_____	Volume	XIII	(1998-99)	$35.00	_____	Volume	XVIII (2003-04)	$35.00

_____**Limited offer: Volumes XVIII & XIX (2003-2005) $60.00**
(Note: Prices may change without notice)

Check your method of payment:

☐ Check enclosed in the amount of $_____

☐ Purchase order attached (Please include the P.O.#, the authorizing signature, and position of the authorizing person.)

☐ Credit Card   ☐ Visa   ☐ MasterCard   Amount $ _____

Card # _____   Expiration Date _____

Signature_____   Today's Date _____

Make checks payable to **AIMS Education Foundation.**
Mail to AIMS Magazine, P.O. Box 8120, Fresno, CA 93747-8120.
Phone (559) 255-4094 or (888) 733-2467 FAX (559) 255-6396
AIMS Homepage: http://www.aimsedu.org/

AIMS Program Publications

Actions with Fractions 4-9
Awesome Addition and Super Subtraction 2-3
Bats Incredible! 2-4
Brick Layers 4-9
Brick Layers II 4-9
Chemistry Matters 4-7
Counting on Coins K-2
Cycles of Knowing and Growing 1-3
Crazy about Cotton Book 3-7
Critters K-6
Down to Earth 5-9
Electrical Connections 4-9
Exploring Environments Book K-6
Fabulous Fractions 3-6
Fall into Math and Science K-1
Field Detectives 3-6
Finding Your Bearings 4-9
Floaters and Sinkers 5-9
From Head to Toe 5-9
Fun with Foods 5-9
Glide into Winter with Math & Science K-1
Gravity Rules! Activity Book 5-12
Hardhatting in a Geo-World 3-5
It's About Time K-2
Jaw Breakers and Heart Thumpers 3-5
Just for the Fun of It! 4-9
Looking at Geometry 6-9
Looking at Lines 6-9
Machine Shop 5-9
Magnificent Microworld Adventures 5-9
Marvelous Multiplication and Dazzling Division 4-5
Math + Science, A Solution 5-9
Mostly Magnets 2-8
Movie Math Mania 6-9
Multiplication the Algebra Way 4-8
Off The Wall Science 3-9
Our Wonderful World 5-9
Out of This World 4-8
Overhead and Underfoot 3-5
Paper Square Geometry:
    The Mathematics of Origami
Puzzle Play: 4-8
Pieces and Patterns 5-9
Popping With Power 3-5

Primarily Bears K-6
Primarily Earth K-3
Primarily Physics K-3
Primarily Plants K-3
Proportional Reasoning 6-9
Ray's Reflections 4-8
Sense-Able Science K-1
Soap Films and Bubbles 4-9
Spatial Visualization 4-9
Spills and Ripples 5-12
Spring into Math and Science K-1
The Amazing Circle 4-9
The Budding Botanist 3-6
The Sky's the Limit 5-9
Through the Eyes of the Explorers 5-9
Under Construction K-2
Water Precious Water 2-6
Weather Sense:
    Temperature, Air Pressure, and Wind 4-5
Weather Sense: Moisture 4-5
Winter Wonders K-2

Spanish/English Editions*
Brinca de alegria hacia la Primavera con las
    Matemáticas y Ciencias K-1
Cáete de gusto hacia el Otoño con las
    Matemáticas y Ciencias K-1
Conexiones Eléctricas 4-9
El Botanista Principiante 3-6
Los Cinco Sentidos K-1
Ositos Nada Más K-6
Patine al Invierno con Matemáticas y Ciencias K-1
Piezas y Diseños 5-9
Primariamente Física K-3
Primariamente Plantas K-3
Principalmente Imanes 2-8

*   All Spanish/English Editions include student pages in Spanish and
    teacher and student pages in English.

Spanish Edition
Constructores II: Ingeniería Creativa Con Construcciones LEGO® (4-9)
    The entire book is written in Spanish. English pages not included.

Other Science and Math Publications
Historical Connections in Mathematics, Vol. I 5-9
Historical Connections in Mathematics, Vol. II 5-9
Historical Connections in Mathematics, Vol. III 5-9
Mathematicians are People, Too
Mathematicians are People, Too, Vol. II
Teaching Science with Everyday Things
What's Next, Volume 1, 4-12
What's Next, Volume 2, 4-12
What's Next, Volume 3, 4-12

For further information write to:
AIMS Education Foundation • P.O. Box 8120 • Fresno, California 93747-8120
www.aimsedu.org/ • Fax 559•255•6396